FRAGILE

Stella O'Malley is a psychotherapist, writer, bestselling author, public speaker and a parent with many years' experience working as a mental health professional. Stella writes extensively about mental health issues for newspapers such as the *Irish Independent*, the *Sunday Independent*, *The Irish Times*, *The Sunday Times* and the *Irish Examiner*. She also frequently appears on national and local media such as RTÉ Radio 1, RTÉ television, Virgin One, Newstalk, and Today FM. She is one of the leading voices on what's influencing young people's behaviour in Ireland today.

FRAGILE

WHY WE FEEL MORE ANXIOUS, STRESSED
AND OVERWHELMED THAN EVER
(AND WHAT WE CAN DO ABOUT IT)

Stella O'Malley

Gill Books

Gill Books
Hume Avenue
Park West
Dublin 12
www.gillbooks.ie

Gill Books is an imprint of M.H. Gill and Co.

978 07171 8322 7

Design and print origination by O'K Graphic Design, Dublin
Edited by Susan McKeever
Proofread by Jane Rogers
Printed by CPI Group (UK), Croydon, CR0 4YY

This book is typeset in 11.5/17 pt Bembo with headings in Myriad Pro Condensed.

The paper used in this book comes from the wood pulp of managed forests. For every tree felled, at least one tree is planted, thereby renewing natural resources.

Poem on page 253 from THERE'S A HOLE IN MY SIDEWALK: THE ROMANCE OF SELF-DISCOVERY by Portia Nelson. Copyright © 1993 by Portia Nelson. Reprinted with the permission of Beyond Words/Atria 80011.s, a division of Simon & Schuster, Inc. All rights reserved.

A CIP catalogue record for this book is available from the British Library.

5 4 3 2 1

Information given in this book is not intended to be taken as a replacement for medical advice. Any person with a condition requiring medical attention should consult a qualified medical practitioner or therapist.

In the interests of confidentiality, names and identifying details have been changed throughout this book.

For my mam, Kathleen O'Malley

CONTENTS

INTRODUCTION

The extraordinary rise in the number of people experiencing anxiety has coincided with the growth of irrational, inappropriate and just plain wrong approaches to deal with it. I have written this book to highlight the most effective approach to combat anxiety and stress and also to stress how the media, society and the world in general are misguidedly promoting the worst possible strategies for managing anxiety. In this book readers will learn why, when it comes to handling anxiety, avoidance strategies don't help – in fact, they usually make your anxiety far, far worse.

It is not psychology but marketing forces, political spin and media scare stories that have created a world that leads ordinary people to fall down a rabbit hole where feeling tense, anxious and overwhelmed is more common than the reverse.

This book explores the way that we are weakening ourselves by using exactly the wrong techniques to deal with our anxiety. Not only that, but policies such as no-platforming, trigger warnings and safe spaces are leading people to the incorrect notion that we should avoid everything that makes us feel unsafe or uncomfortable. This has led to a situation where a lot of mental health messages, initiatives and projects are now being dumbed down and administered incorrectly.

Granted, certain avoidance strategies might feel good in the short term, but in the long term they can be like heroin to an addict –

providing some short-term relief in exchange for long-term pain. Most avoidance strategies only serve to worsen anxiety and train the brain to avoid helpful behaviour that could actually help reduce anxiety. Far better to learn to grasp control of your life and your mind than to live with this constant feeling of underlying tension and nerves.

This book aims to consign short-term dysfunctional techniques to the dustbin. We all need short-term strategies to get us through the day, but we cannot rely on these techniques in the long term. They are often debilitating and they dangerously collude with the flawed thought processes that lead us to fear our anxiety, encouraging us to believe that we can't cope with any uncomfortable feelings.

But with the right support and understanding, we can!

If you are to create a happier and healthier life it is necessary to identify the long-term therapeutic approaches that, with some work and commitment, have been actually proven to help you overcome your anxiety. This more comprehensive approach will lead you to an in-depth understanding of yourself and how you need to live your life so that you can be free to live without anxiety, stress or tension continuously hovering around the edges, always ready to attack and reduce you.

The first part of the book describes exactly how the anxious mind works and demonstrates how to get out of the common traps we fall into when we're anxious.

The second part focuses on how most of us are weakening ourselves by doing too much, trying too hard and consuming too much. We know it. We know we should calm down and just enjoy our lives but we can't seem to get off the relentless treadmill of being foolishly busy.

The last part of the book identifies different approaches that will enable readers to live a different, calmer, more satisfying life. Through strategies, tips and case studies, readers will learn how to withstand feelings of worry and panic and feeling overwhelmed. They will then be free to enjoy the relative wealth and stability that the developed world already offers without getting caught up in the constant search for more.

As the psychologist Oliver James warns us, 'Beware of authors bearing gifts of happiness. It is psychological snake oil.'[1] I'm hoping this book will be better than that. My aim is to make you feel empowered enough to find some meaning and purpose in the life *that you already have*, without feeling overwhelmed by gnawing anxiety and debilitating tension chipping away at you. You don't need to feel fragile any more; you can instead tap into the strength in your belly and go forth with your head up, your shoulders back, with confidence and positivity about your ability to live a life that is both satisfying and pleasant.

PART 1

HOW ANXIETY IMPACTS YOU

CHAPTER 1

How anxiety works

'The mind is its own place and in itself
Can make a Heaven of Hell, a Hell of Heaven.'

JOHN MILTON

Anxiety has been described as an over-estimation of danger combined with an under-estimation of our ability to cope. *Usually* the danger isn't so threatening and *usually* we will cope better than we imagine, but that's not how anxious minds work. Over-thinking, over-feeling and over-reacting are daily challenges for too many people because anxiety takes over and leads us to dismiss logical thinking and run with our emotional minds. Anxiety leads us to feel overwhelmed, it tramples on our wellbeing and consumes our minds with obsessive thoughts that we just can't close down.

But most people who crack up do it silently; most of their struggle is internal and most of their pain is turned inwards, which is why most people blame themselves instead of today's anxiety-inducing lifestyles. The problem is that we don't know when our friends and neighbours are cracking up, so everyone tends to think that their tension is a personal failing instead of a destructive trend in our society. I know that feeling anxious and stressed is an increasingly common complaint because as a psychotherapist I meet the clients who blame themselves instead of blaming the toxic level of pressure that is foisted upon them. It's clear to anyone who is working as a mental health professional that it is our toxic society rather than the individual that is causing most of the strain; *we* – the mental health professionals – all witness the destruction that society is wreaking on our mental wellbeing. But most people don't work in the mental health industry, so most people don't have the information to hand to see that stress, anxiety and feeling overwhelmed has become part of an enormously growing pattern that is happening to *everyone*.

Whether you have been diagnosed with anxiety or even if you just know you are feeling more anxious and overwhelmed than you'd like to be, this book should bring about more self-awareness so you can learn to spot what works best for you and what makes everything worse. If you are to free yourself from feeling tense and fearful, you will need to unpick the source of your tension so that you can counteract the underlying sense of anxiety and unease that is slowly growing within you and steadily becoming more unmanageable.

The challenge for people who experience anxiety is that they need to learn to live with it. Alcoholics can give up alcohol and cigarette smokers can give up tobacco but people with anxiety can't give up anxiety; just like the anorexic who has to learn to eat again, the anxious person needs to learn to live with anxiety. You can, however, *reduce the intensity, the timespan and the impact* of your anxiety. If these three elements can be significantly reduced, then it is usually enough for the anxious person to live a free and easy life unrestrained by the terrible gnawing anxiety that was previously making them miserable.

ARE WE ALL 'FEELING ANXIOUS'?

According to the latest research, we in the West are living through an unprecedented epidemic of anxiety with up to 33.7 per cent of the population affected by an anxiety disorder at some stage during the course of their lives.[2] The familiar tightness, tension and fear that grips us is being experienced by so many people that we are starting to believe that we should be accustomed to living with a chronically constricted spirit.

As we will see in Chapters 4, 5 and 6, the main reason for all this anxiety and stress is that our lifestyles are too demanding and our coping mechanisms are often deeply flawed. Society is going too fast; we're doing too much, consuming too much and asking too much of our minds and bodies. When we do too much we weaken and become too tired and anxious to feel satisfied so we search for the nearest short-term strategy that is close to hand – perhaps we drink too much wine in an effort to relax but then have to suffer the consequences of that particular short-term strategy. Or perhaps we avoid the source of our anxiety and by doing that, as we will soon see, we make the anxiety worse.

Anxiety makes you feel as if your brain is on fire, acid is burning in your stomach and you become completely consumed with obsessive thoughts that you just can't close down. The only truly helpful approach is to learn about the patterns of your anxiety, so that you can understand clearly what works best for you and what doesn't work and, ultimately, you learn to live a more satisfying and less stress-inducing lifestyle.

THE ANXIETY CHECKLIST

Read the following checklist[3] and answer whether you experience these sensations or thoughts.

DO YOU:

- ... feel jumpy or jittery?
- ... have trembling or shaky hands or limbs?
- ... feel like a tight band is tied around your forehead?
- ... have a tightness in your chest or in the pit of your stomach?
- ... feel sweaty or clammy? Or have tingly, cold or clammy hands or fingers?
- ... have a dry mouth?
- ... have difficulties with your breathing?
- ... have difficulties talking? Or have an unsteady voice?
- ... have a racing heart or a sensation of your heart pounding or skipping a beat?
- ... experience difficulty swallowing or feel like you have a lump in your throat?
- ... feel like you're choking or smothering?
- ... have digestive problems such an upset stomach, nausea or diarrhoea?
- ... need to pee more frequently than usual?
- ... cling to others for security?
- ... use alcohol or medication to calm down?
- ... avoid particular situations because they fill you with dread?
- ... become agitated for no apparent reason?

DO YOU:

- ... worry too much?
- ... think you're about to lose control?

... feel filled with a sense of dread that something terrible is going to happen?

... feel intensely impatient, intolerant or irritable?

... lack patience?

... procrastinate endlessly?

... need endless reassurance?

... become preoccupied with what's happening to your body?

... feel overwhelmed and unable to cope?

... feel like everything is going too fast?

... feel like the world is caving in on you? Or feel like the walls are closing in on you?

... become obsessed with tiny little details?

... have difficulty shaking off nagging, intrusive thoughts that don't seem to leave you alone?

... think you are seriously ill but know that the doctors disagree with you?

... have difficulty concentrating or maintaining your attention?

... worry that you are going to be all alone?

The more you can identify with the above feelings and behaviour, the more likely you are to be experiencing anxiety. Anxiety disorder is a serious ailment and it is essential for every person who believes they are suffering from this to go to their doctor first to ensure they receive proper medical treatment. Although more and more people are feeling stressed and anxious these days, some types of personalities are more prone to feeling anxious than others, but, as we will see in the next chapter, just because you are more sensitive and highly reactive than others doesn't mean you are condemned to a lifetime filled with stress and anxiety.

HOW ANXIETY IS TRIGGERED

The science of the brain is terrifyingly complex and, on the assumption that most readers aren't neuroscientists, I have simplified the descriptions in this book to make it more relatable and readable.

The amygdalae are two almond-shaped groups of nuclei which are located deep within the limbic system in our brain. The limbic system is often referred to as our 'emotional brain' and research shows that the amygdala performs a crucial role in processing our emotional responses.[4]

Another part of our brain, the cortex, is often described as the thinking, wiser brain as it is designed for higher thought processes. The amygdala keeps us alive in an emergency, while the cortex makes life interesting. Our wise brain is slow-moving, reflective, unsure, intelligent and wise. By contrast, our emotional brain is fast, furious, dramatic, not so wise and often a little bit thick.

When a person's brain gets a signal of danger, the amygdala within the emotional brain is triggered. This trigger, also known as the fight-or-flight response, is necessary because we need to be able to react to danger immediately and powerfully. (Some people believe that 'flight, fight, freeze or appease' is a more accurate description of this response.) However, we humans have evolved from a very different world from the one we inhabit today. When the world was full of predators, our main job was to get enough to eat without being eaten. The amygdala governed our survival instinct and it served as an emergency alert system to keep alert to the danger of passing lions and tigers and bears.

The psychologist Daniel Goleman coined the phrase 'amygdala hijack' in his 1996 book *Emotional Intelligence: Why it can matter more than IQ* to describe the immediate and overwhelming power of the amygdala when it has been triggered. When it is triggered, the amygdala turns into an emergency first responder and shuts down the more rational parts of the brain. With that, any hope of reason or logic flies out of the window. The amygdala works quickly – because speed is of the essence in an emergency; and it has no conscious awareness – because this is exactly when you have no time to think. The amygdala is also very powerful because we need to act with full commitment when we are faced with danger. Many people feel as if they are out of control when they are experiencing 'amygdala hijack', even though they are in fact being controlled by this tiny part of the brain. It is only in hindsight that we can see the impact of the amygdala on our decision-making – for instance, when we quickly pull a child back from walking in front of an oncoming car, it is the amygdala that totally controls the situation and propels us to action.

The problem with the amygdala is that it doesn't care how many times it makes an error. The amygdala doesn't care if you over-reacted and in actual fact the child was perfectly safe on the footpath while the car was way up the road, cruising along at a slow speed. When a person makes a decision based upon a false anticipation of danger it is known as a 'false positive'. The result of a false positive is that no one gets hurt – however, no one was likely to get hurt in any case, and being highly over-reactive is tedious both for yourself and for everyone around you.

A 'false negative' has the opposite effect, where the person decides that there is no danger from the oncoming car but it then hits the child. In this scenario, the person didn't get anxious, didn't react and then the child got hit.

The amygdala is constantly working away in the background, always asking the question, 'Am I safe?' It is madly concerned with avoiding false negatives and couldn't care less about false positives. The amygdala doesn't care about how anxious and unhappy you are – it only cares about keeping you alive by reacting to what it perceives as oncoming danger. Nor does the amygdala care if you are constantly over-reacting to random and highly unlikely dangers, nor that you are becoming a drain on yourself and on your loved ones. But you *should* care about false positives as they can mean the difference between living a pleasant life and living a wretched life. And, thankfully, the rest of your brain *does* care about your sense of wellbeing and about your relationships. It is intolerable living under irresolvable tension and crippling anxiety as a result of a trigger-happy amygdala, and it is your wise brain that might urge you to pick up a self-help book in a bid to quell your fiery emotional brain.

THE TAKEAWAY

We need to retrain the amygdala to calm down so we can get our act together and use other, better, parts of our brain to work out any forthcoming problems. If our rational brain is allowed space to think we will soon work out that we aren't living in a war zone and that really, if we look around us, life is mostly quite safe and with a bit of care and attention, we could live reasonably happy lives.

UNDERSTANDING YOUR AMYGDALA

Your amygdala is always on, always in the background watching out for danger. It acts like an emergency responder, and its motto is 'better safe than sorry!' When it perceives any danger, whether it is true or false danger, POW, it presses the big red button in your head – the fight-or-flight button – and fills you with fear and adrenaline so that you are suddenly ready for extreme action. The problem is that we live in AD 2019, not 2019 BC, and the amygdala, which is really quite prehistoric in its assessment of danger, often makes the mistake of seeing danger when there is none. The truth is that today we have never been safer than in any moment since the history of time – we live longer, we suffer fewer premature deaths – indeed we have less chance of dying a violent death today than at any other time in history. In the last one hundred years, the number of deaths from natural disasters has halved and, in the last 20 years, the proportion of the world living in extreme poverty has also halved.[5] The world is much safer and the world is getting much, much better. If we could just train our emotional and dramatic brains to appreciate just how safe we are, then we would automatically be freed from unnecessary worrying and tension.

The amygdala learns by association, not by reason or logic.[6] And so when you run away from danger the amygdala calms down from being on red alert and goes back to waiting in the wings. If your amygdala urged you to run away from a mugger or a rapist, then that is a good thing but if it urged you to run away from a social gathering that you were looking forward to, that is not so good. You might feel temporarily better, but you have also missed out on a party and you have created a destructive link in your brain. By running away and thereby calming down, you will have further cemented in your amygdala the idea that social gatherings are inherently dangerous. It has no reason to believe otherwise.

A key aspect of the amygdala is that *it isn't influenced by conscious thought and instead learns by conditioning and association.* This means that when you run away from the social gathering you will have inadvertently taught your amygdala to fly to your rescue in future situations like these and from this point on, it will urge you to run like the wind the next time you are confronted with a similar situation. No amount of consciously telling your amygdala that social gatherings aren't dangerous will get through the red alert wall. Reason, discussion or rationality don't work with the amygdala; what works is conditioning and association. This means that if you ignore your amygdala screaming RED ALERT and you go ahead, despite the crazy messages telling you to flee, and walk into the social gathering (to find you don't get eaten by a passing tiger), then the amygdala will *begin* to recondition your response to view social gatherings as safe places.

The amygdala decides what memories are stored and where they are stored.[7] Because of the way the amygdala learns, we need to make sure our associations are appropriate. For example, if a mother tells her young child that dogs are dangerous, the child's amygdala could become triggered by a dog, making the child very scared whenever they see one. If this fear isn't ever confronted and overturned through association, it can become an everlasting, irrational fear of dogs.

FIVE FACTS ABOUT THE AMYGDALA

1. The amygdala is triggered in less than a fraction of a second. This means that you 'feel' fear before you can understand what it is that you fear – for instance, you are scared by a 'snake' that turns out to be a rope.

2. Roughly 20 per cent of people are considered to have a more sensitive amygdala than others but not everyone with a sensitive amygdala goes on to develop anxiety.[8] Such people might be nervy and more reactive than others, but with the right coping mechanisms this can be managed perfectly well.

3. When the amygdala is triggered it releases stress hormones to put the body on alert. The metabolism speeds up, the heart beats faster, breathing increases and we literally get pumped up as our blood starts to pump directly to the muscles in the

body. The point of all this is to prime the body to be ready for a fight or to run away quickly; this is why so many people have physical responses to stress and anxiety.

4. The amygdala learns by association and conditioning; it is only by prolonged exposure to the triggering event that it can learn to associate safety with the event.

5. The amygdala can be retrained only by facing down the fear *in the moment*, i.e. when it has been triggered. If you wait until you have fled the scene before you try to tell your brain that there was nothing to fear, you have lost a golden teachable moment.

ARE YOU THINKING FAST OR SLOW?

Ever since the discovery that different parts of our brain rule different parts of our thinking habits, psychologists have been falling over themselves trying to come up with the best metaphor to explain how our brains function. While Daniel Goleman coined the evocative phrase 'amygdala hijack' (p. 8), the psychologist Daniel Kahneman, in his book *Thinking Fast and Slow*, described our brain functioning with the phrases 'system one' and 'system two' thinking.

System one thinking is centred on the quick and impulsive part of our brain. This helps us make snap decisions, particularly those focused on food, sex and immediate danger. System one thinking is fast, powerful and not very wise, and it is the direct opposite to system two thinking, which uses a slower, less certain, more considered and wiser part of our brain. System two recognises that what you see isn't always the full picture and that more analysis is often required.[9]

The psychologist Steve Peters, author of *The Chimp Paradox*, probably provided the easiest metaphor for all this when he called our emotional brain our 'inner chimp'.[10] Our inner chimp is fast and furious; powerful, exciting and a bit foolish. Market forces appeal to our inner chimp. 'Buy one get one free' appeals to our inner chimp; so does paying with a card instead of with cash. It could be argued that the majority of the internet appeals to our inner chimp – Twitter is made for the chimp; as are Snapchat, Instagram, Facebook and any media driven by clickbait; phrases such as 'make America great again' and other catchy, sloganistic politics are also perfect for our inner chimp.[11]

Indeed all slogans suit our inner chimp, so 'talk to someone', 'listen to your gut', 'focus on your feelings' and hundreds of other slogans (see Chapter 5) are a perfect fit. The basic premise of Peters' book is that we don't have to be at the mercy of our impulsive and reactive emotions and we can instead learn to organise and have command over our behaviour by appealing to the more rational part of the brain.[12]

Thankfully, we don't only have an inner chimp in our brain; we also have, according to Peters, 'the computer' and 'the human'. The human is a much wiser wizard, and, although either the chimp or the human can take control of our brain, they can also work together. According to Peters, 'the computer' is spread throughout the brain and stores programmed thoughts and behaviours. And so Peters suggests that we don't have to be ruled by our gut instinct, we can instead learn to wait and give some time for other parts of our brain to catch up: and if we wish to make wiser and more considered decisions we need to allow some time for other thought processes to overtake our inner chimp.[13] Our inner chimp leads us to avoid anxiety while the computer in our brain might do a cost-benefit analysis and understand that our initial anxiety will soon give way to more pleasurable feelings, and the human will help us to face down our initial anxiety.

HOW TO RETRAIN THE AMYGDALA

Because the amygdala only learns when you are afraid, you need to address your fears *in the moment* when it is triggered by a potential 'threat'. The rest of the time, when you are calm, the amygdala is on autopilot and isn't really listening to you. It lolls around at the back of the class playing hangman and not listening to your wiser brain. This is why you can end up like a prisoner to your old fears because your amygdala just doesn't pay attention to your wise brain and only learns when it is activated. The only way to get at the amygdala is in the middle of heightened emotion when the amygdala is fully on, and the only way to recondition the amygdala is to demonstrate to it, *in the moment*, that this isn't a dangerous situation; that RED ALERT isn't necessary and that it needs to chill. And as the amygdala learns from experience, if you can confront your fear *in the moment*, it will eventually get with the programme.

Here's one way to teach your amygdala a good response to perceived danger:

1. Activate the amygdala by exposing yourself to what you perceive as a mildly anxiety-inducing situation.

2. When the amygdala is activated, grit your teeth and behave appropriately, without running for the hills. This gives your amygdala the chance to learn by association that it got all worked up for nothing.

3. We learn to swim in shallow water. Begin with a relatively easy task. Don't choose a highly stressful situation as it might not work and you will then have further cemented inappropriate responses in the amygdala.

In this new scenario – and I'm not saying that this is easy – it isn't, it's incredibly hard – the amygdala learns that social gatherings hold no threats; that dogs won't necessarily kill you and that oncoming cars won't necessarily kill everyone in sight. The amygdala will then begin to recondition itself to view social gatherings, dogs, cars or whatever the fear *du jour* happens to be, as non-threats. With repetition, the amygdala will develop a new memory and will stop disrupting your life with inappropriate RED ALERT signals.

This doesn't need to be done radically or quickly; it can be done in your own time and at your own pace. The grand plan is to *make sure the fear leaves your brain before you leave the scene* as this is the way you will recondition your amygdala. Some people choose to use certain coping strategies such as deep breathing or distraction techniques to help them stay in situ while others just 'float', as the psychologist Claire Weekes called it, and stoically wait for the fear to subside. According to Weekes, floating is 'masterly inactivity' where you accept your panic and concentrate on mindfully being. All self-analysis about why you are afraid and why you shouldn't be afraid will cease when you 'float' and your struggle against anxiety then ceases. Weekes suggests that when you feel you are about to fall apart you don't try to 'hold yourself together' – instead, just allow yourself to be.

THE LIES WE TELL OURSELVES

Sadly, it is not just the amygdala we have to contend with when dealing with anxiety. There is also the rest of our emotional brain and the tendency most of have to tell ourselves lies because we don't want to face the truth. If we are to truly overcome our anxiety, we need to identify and address the lies we tell ourselves whenever our emotions are heightened.

Our emotional brain tends to reframe our perception of the world so we can continue to cope with life as we know it – and this can often involve avoiding the bitter truth. Deirdre, a mother of three boys, became convinced that the zipline in the local playground was unsafe when her eight-year-old fell off it. She wrote to the local county council to get it removed and put up a notice on the zipline to tell other parents that it wasn't safe. She also spoke to other parents at every opportunity to tell them about this dangerous hazard. Anxious people tend to inadvertently spread anxiety all around them, not realising the damage they do when they become desperate to infect everyone else with this dis-ease.

The county council were comprehensive in their defence of the zipline and backed it up with technical information from the professionals who had designed and built the equipment. Deirdre dismissed this as 'brown envelope politics' and preferred to believe that the designers were in cahoots with the county council over their shoddy equipment. She was willing to fight to the death to show that it wasn't she who was in the wrong. Deirdre's emotional brain was filled with anxious conviction and she felt compelled to tell everyone that she had exposed corruption in the town council. Her emotions were too highly charged for any level of critical thinking to emerge and so she lost her grip on rational thought processes as a consequence of her understandable anxiety over her child.

COGNITIVE DISTORTIONS

If you truly want to overcome your anxiety, you need to confront head-on the cognitive distortions – lies – that urge you to make the wrong decisions about how to manage your anxiety. It was the psychiatrist Aaron Beck, one of the pioneers of cognitive behavioural therapy (CBT), who first identified different cognitive distortions as common but defective ways of thinking. Cognitive distortions are inaccurate thoughts, ranging from 'subtle inaccuracies' to 'grotesque misinterpretations and delusions', that reinforce thought patterns or emotions and convince us of a reality that is simply not true.[14]

Our cognitive distortions make us feel better in the short term but in the long term lead to more complicated problems. If we don't know our cognitive distortions then we won't know when our amygdala is right or wrong. So we first need to identify our distortions, then commit to making a huge effort to challenge them, and finally we need to replace our distorted cognitions with healthier and more helpful cognitions. The process is long but the benefits are everlasting.

The following is a list of common cognitive distortions that could help you identify your own common pitfalls and also build your self-awareness. You might only identify with one or two of the following list, or you might find that you use them all a little bit; it doesn't really matter. The main thing is to identify some of the distortions that you use and then, with some effort and commitment, you can begin to retrain your emotional brain by consigning your distortions to the bin.

MAGICAL THINKING

From Santa Claus to belief in the power of prayer, it could be argued that magical thinking is used everywhere as a coping mechanism to keep us vaguely sane in an incomprehensible world. Magical thinking is defined as believing that one event happens as a result of another without a plausible link of causation.[15] For example, when Jane put a statue of Buddha in her garden, she hoped it would bestow great abundance to her home. Then when she received a gift or unexpected largesse she happily believed it was the Buddha working its magic charms. It's comforting to believe that there is some unknown magic working away in the background for our benefit and so almost all of us engage, on some level, in a bit of magical thinking to make us feel better. It is only when the magical thinking prevents us addressing serious issues in our lives that we need to knock it on the head and tackle the reality of life's challenges. This means that if Jane really needed more money, she probably needed to do a lot more than put a Buddha in the garden.

Fortune-telling and rituals

Just like magical thinking, fortune-telling is when a person 'just knows' a certain disaster is going to happen. When it doesn't happen, they tend to dismiss it as if their actions have prevented certain fallout and when it does happen, as a stopped clock is right twice a day, they use this as fuel to convince themselves they have some sort of second sight about impending disaster. They don't, though, and they are probably missing out on a shedload of happiness as they focus on future disasters. The expression 'Don't meet the devil halfway' comes to mind for this person as they need to practise some discipline in not allowing themselves to waste their life imagining future disasters and doing pointless tasks in a misguided bid to avert these disasters.

CASE STUDY: SALLY, 19

When Sally was a little girl she couldn't face the reality of her beloved father's alcoholism so she used cognitive distortions to deny the reality of her sadness and hurt. She believed she was casting a type of spell where everything would be okay if she tapped certain objects in a certain way. So whenever Sally felt overwhelmed by worry about her daddy and her parents' unravelling marriage, she would soothe herself by tapping her fingers along different surfaces. As life came to feel more and more uncertain and her father's drinking continued to disturb the family's equilibrium, Sally developed certain 'symmetry rituals' whereby she would turn her head first to the right and then to the left. She believed that if she engaged in her tapping and turning exercises, her father would stop getting drunk.

Of course, this didn't work and Sally felt even more anxious when her mother noticed her elaborate rituals and tried to make her stop them. Sally's response was to internalise her rituals – she began to silently count things and also to spell words backwards. Sally's mind became filled with elaborate rituals, chants and prayers that all served to distract her from her complex feelings about her father – she loved him and she hated him – and also served as a pretence that her rituals were keeping everything in control.

Eventually Sally was brought to counselling and the therapist used exposure response prevention (ERP, see Chapter 3), to help Sally move beyond her obsessive-compulsive behaviour. The therapist supported Sally by ever so slowly exposing her to reducing her rituals and confronting the source of her true anxiety. It took some time but eventually Sally's desperate need to engage in magical thinking to calm her frantic mind ebbed away and was replaced with a more helpful and self-aware understanding of her sensitive nature.

Religion, superstition and heaven's reward fallacy

The idea of organised religion is appealing to the type of person who likes to believe that everything is under control and that everything will make sense in the end. Religious people can feel comforted that every grain of sand is counted and all that seems uncertain and meaningless is really part of God's mysterious plan. The concept that we might be random accidents of cells with very little idea of where we have come from or where we are going makes many people feel anxious.

In many ways, the rise of tension and anxiety in the Western world correlates with the sharp fall in religiosity. It could easily be argued that a vacuum has appeared that was once filled with ideas of a benevolent God looking after everything. This has created intense feelings of anxiety for some people as they now feel that everything is out of control and no one has any idea what's going on.

Some religious people fall into a cognitive distortion called 'heaven's reward fallacy' where they cling to the belief that sacrifice or self-denial will pay off in the future. Some call this karma, and believe that karma will one day reward us for our good deeds. Of course, this can result in feelings of bitterness and resentment, especially when they see a particularly nasty person winning the lottery of life – it's then that they suddenly suspect that perhaps it's not all planned out so well and maybe, just maybe, they won't actually receive their just reward when they die.

In a similar way to religion, superstitious people can feel immediate relief when they cross their fingers or throw salt over their shoulder or perform any other random act that serves to let them believe there is a secret plan to everything in the universe. Yet again, this is underpinned by a need to believe that somebody, somewhere, is in control of the universe. Indeed, obsessive-compulsive disorder could be construed as an extreme form of superstition whereby, for example, the person needs to touch the handle three times on the way out if they are to have a good day and if they step on the cracks in the path they will have a bad day.

Shoulds, musts and the fallacy of fairness

It was the German psychoanalyst Karen Horney (1885–1952) who coined the phrase 'the tyranny of the should' as she believed that 'shoulds' divide a personality into an 'ideal self' and a 'real self' and the conflict between the two is a measure of the dysfunction of the person. When a person becomes ruled by what they 'should' or 'must' do, they soon lose a sense of life's pleasures and this joylessness can lead them towards anxiety and depression. If life has become a series of duties to perform then it can be helpful to draw up a list of the attributes of your 'ideal self' and your 'real self'. So your 'ideal self' might be easy-going, cheerful and flexible while your 'real self' could be anxious, moody and neurotic. The sooner you acknowledge the reality of who you really are, the sooner you can free yourself from inner conflict and come to a place of self-acceptance. Try listing below a few attributes that correspond to your two 'selves':

Ideal self: _____

_____

_____

Real self: _____

_____

_____

In a similar way, the American psychologist, Albert Ellis, a pioneering figure of CBT, wrote about how 'musts' create demands on ourselves and others and usually only result in anxiety and distress. We become angry, anxious and resentful when we 'musterbate' and become difficult people to be around. If we can eliminate 'shoulds' and 'musts' from our vocabulary, we can free ourselves from a shedload of mental distress.

'Shoulds' and 'musts' represent a sort of bargain that people make with the world – if we do X then we can expect Y – but this 'fallacy of fairness', just like karma and religion, has often been shown to be a sham. This belief that if we do what we 'should' do then life will go more smoothly isn't necessarily based on truth. It's usually based on magical thinking that you've created just to make you feel better about the uncertainty of this world.

A strategy for magical thinking

The sooner you accept that magical thinking gives your power away, the sooner you will feel more in control and empowered as you come to realise that you have power within you and you can make a huge difference to your lot in life. You will need to build your feelings of self-efficacy for this so that one day you can come to the conclusion that you have enormous potential to change your life just as soon as you stop giving your power away to others.

EMOTIONAL REASONING

This cognitive distortion involves thinking that if we feel a certain way, it must be true. People with this distortion tend to live in the emotional brain and assume that their unhealthy emotions reflect the way things really are – 'I feel it, therefore it must be true' is the modus operandi. Of course our emotions are not always indicative of the objective truth, but it can be difficult to look past how we feel. The guiding star for this type of thinking must be an unrelenting bid for accuracy.

Mental filtering/arbitrary inference/jumping to conclusions

Many anxious people tend to use a mental filter to filter out all positive aspects of a situation and instead focus exclusively on one single, unpleasant detail. This can make their vision of reality darkened and distorted and it is also false because this 'arbitrary inference' involves faulty reasoning in how we make conclusions. So they might say to themselves, 'I went wrong in question 8 so I've probably failed the exam. That's it! I'm a failure!'

When our emotional brains put the whole situation into a negative context with arbitrary inference, we start to believe that we 'know' things when we are in truth only guessing. You may be convinced that someone dislikes you with only the flimsiest of proof, or you may be convinced that your worst fears will come true before you have a chance to find out. This often means you will under-perform as, when confronted with a problem, you fly to the first conclusion and stubbornly remain there. You are being driven by your emotional brain and motivated by an inordinate fear of uncertainty rather than realising that your beliefs are influencing your brain.

Dichotomous thinking

This polarised 'black and white' thinking is a delusion that leads stressed people to believe that there are no shades of grey. Everything becomes all or nothing, with no room for complexity or nuance. If you don't perform perfectly in some area, then you see yourself as a total failure instead of simply unskilled in one particular task. This way of thinking is a pretty foolish method of analysis because it is too generalised and it lacks subtlety.

Whenever Joanne became anxious she tended to wildly over-generalise and so she would take one statement that her boyfriend said, such as, 'I feel we're going too fast in this relationship,' and she would jump to the nearest certain conclusion, 'He clearly wants out of this relationship. This always happens to me. I'll never get it right, I just can't keep a steady relationship!' Viewing a single event as part of an endless pattern of bad luck and making sweeping generalisations are seldom accurate or helpful. A good method to overcome this tendency is to move beyond your emotional brain by pushing yourself to think about the nuance involved in this situation – can you dig a bit deeper? Can you probe for a more accurate analysis? If you can't see anything positive then what are you missing?

Polarised thinking also occurs when you magnify the bad things in life and minimise the good things. Although it might seem like a common trait, it can be quite damaging if this is ongoing and it can have a significant impact on your wellbeing. Studies show again and again that having a negative perception of events makes your life harder.[16] It's probably unhelpful for pessimistic people to be told to be optimistic but being *realistic* and accurate is the best place for an anxious person to be – the dreaded situation, whatever it is, probably won't be quite as awful as you think and you will probably be able to cope better than you think you will.

Catastrophising and discounting the positives

This thought distortion involves expecting that the worst will happen or has happened, often based on a slight incident that is nowhere near the tragedy that you're making it out to be. For example, you might make a small mistake at work and then become convinced that it will ruin the project you are working on, your boss will be furious, and you will lose your job. The mishap moves seamlessly from a minor problem to a catastrophe.

If you tend towards catastrophising then, yet again, accuracy is the key. You need to do an accurate analysis of what the true outcomes of any given event are likely to be and call out your outlandish, catastrophic imagining for what it is.

A strategy for emotional reasoning

If you can learn to take a few deep breaths and have the patience to listen to the slow-thinking but wiser and more rational part of your brain, then you will soon see the difference in the quality of your responses. This will create a positive cycle of change where you will recognise the value of slowing down to wait for more considered thinking and that will further encourage you to be more probing with your thoughts.

CONTROL FALLACIES

Dermot became increasingly anxious about his thriving new business, to the extent that he began working every day around the clock; he just couldn't accept that, whenever he took some time off, his employees could survive without him. When we are anxious we can become obsessed with control and might falsely believe that we are in complete control. But this is seldom true and when Dermot, through tiredness and overwork, accidentally left a tap running overnight which flooded his whole premises, he realised that his need to control had gone out of control. Dermot didn't have to work all his waking hours and he needed to accept that he just couldn't cover all the bases. He needed to let go of his control fallacies and learn to live with a bit of uncertainty and imperfection.

Control fallacies involve feeling that everything that happens to you is only a result of external forces or entirely due to your own actions. The truth is, as always, somewhere in the middle ground; it's seldom completely all your responsibility, neither is it likely totally in the hands of someone else. Likewise, some people who are given to control fallacies tend to believe that they must control the actions of the people around them – the worry is that if other people are out of their control then the whole stack of cards will fall down. This is clearly a damaging way to think, since nothing is certain and very little is under control in life.

Personalisation

This is a thought distortion where you tend to believe that everything you do has an impact on external events or other people, no matter how irrational the link. The person suffering from this distortion will feel that they have an important role in the bad things that happen around them. For instance, Rosie came to me when she was feeling overwhelmed with anxiety about her boyfriend. She and Joe had been together for two years and Rosie was disappointed that they hadn't moved in together and there was no talk of the future. Rosie took this rejection very hard and began to put a lot more effort into her looks and her diet. She lost a lot of weight and spent a lot of her money on personal grooming and cosmetic procedures, all for Joe's pleasure. When this didn't work and there was still no sign of commitment, Rosie upped the ante again and became sexually outrageous in a bid to further attract Joe's attentions. The truth was that Joe's parents had gone through a very nasty divorce and Joe had personal issues with commitment. Joe's reluctance to commit had nothing to do with Rosie and everything to do with Joe's family of origin. It took some time before Rosie realised that her every move didn't directly reflect on Joe's actions. Sadly, Rosie only realised this when she met Joe some years after they split up and he still hadn't settled down. 'When I think about all the hoops I jumped through trying to get Joe to commit, jumping from the chandeliers, dressing for his pleasure, catering to his every whim; I just couldn't see that it wasn't all about me,' she reflected later.

Some people are almost the opposite of Rosie as they become consumed by the need to change another person – they think that once this person changes, their anxiety will leave them, but this is false. Either the other person never changes and so the anxiety continues on its way or else the other person changes and the anxious person becomes anxious about someone or something else.

A strategy for control fallacies

If this controlling behaviour sounds like you, it might be beneficial to undergo a course of counselling and psychotherapy to figure out when your anxiety is triggered and how you can slowly reduce your need to control.

PROJECTION

Many of us deny the existence of impulses or qualities in ourselves and instead project them on to others. For instance, we might tell our children that they look anxious and need to leave a noisy play venue somewhere, when in fact it is ourselves who feel uncomfortable and want to leave. Blaming is a common way to project your faults on others, but this is actually giving your power away as no one has more power to release you from anxiety than your good self. It can be quite comforting to tell others 'now you're making me feel bad' as then you don't have any work to do in fixing the situation. However, just because it's comforting doesn't mean it's either right or helpful – you are probably better off taking control of your life and refusing to lay the blame on others. This can be very hard to do because often our loved ones cause us profound pain, but in the long run it's always better for you to be part of the solution instead of playing the blame game.

A strategy for projection

If you tend to project your worries onto other people you would benefit by taking some time to begin to build some insight into yourself so that you can learn to have a more accurate understanding of your mind and your motivations.

UNDER THE INFLUENCE OF ANXIETY

If you wish to make an important decision while anxious keep in mind that this is akin to making a decision when you are drunk or on drugs. The decision-making process is impaired by fear and anxiety – the amygdala is too reactionary. Wait until your amygdala has retreated and you are in a calm state of mind before you decide on a course of action. You might choose to use slow breathing techniques or choose to exercise or talk your way out of the anxiety – whatever it takes to move beyond the chimp brain and towards your wiser, rational brain. It is only then, when you are calm, that you are in a fit state to make a considered judgement.

CONCLUSION: OUR BRAINS PLAY TRICKS ON US

Anxiety can cause people to have a gut-wrenching fear of *things going wrong*. The bad news is that things often go wrong. The good news is that, with some help and support, you can learn to live with this fact and still push your anxiety away to a distant shore. Information is power and the more knowledgeable you are about how your anxious mind plays tricks on you, the better you can become more truthfully self-aware. This will connect you more with your authentic self and you will be less likely to try to convince yourself and everyone else that there is danger everywhere. There isn't; this world has never been safer. The more you can acknowledge your strengths and weaknesses, identify your distorted thought patterns and figure out the accurate and rational account of events, the more you can practise acting and feeling stronger, more resilient and better able to cope with your world.

CHAPTER 2

'The anxious type'

'Truth is confirmed by inspection and delay; falsehood by haste and uncertainty.'

TACITUS

A re you 'the anxious type'? See how many of the following traits you can relate to. Are you … ?

❖ Self-doubting/self-critical
❖ Conscientious/overworking
❖ Obsessive/perfectionistic
❖ Avoidant
❖ Phobic/fearful/worrisome
❖ An insomniac
❖ Prone to panicking
❖ Highly reactive
❖ Sensitive/self-conscious
❖ Prone to physical ailments
❖ Imaginative
❖ Resistant to change
❖ Empathic
❖ Irritable/intolerant

Although everyone feels anxious from time to time, some personalities are just more prone to feeling stressed and anxious. The more you identify with the above traits, the more likely you are to become anxious. The most helpful element of this book will be to help you get to know yourself better – know when you are over-reacting, know when you are lying to yourself, know when you are falling into your old traps – and identify new, more helpful approaches to manage tension and anxiety.

With this in mind, have a read of the following descriptions of the different personalities of anxious types to see if you identify with any particular one. You might find that you're a hotchpotch of a few types, but this really doesn't matter; what matters is that you build a strong self-awareness of your weaknesses and strengths so that you can be more perceptive about whether your worried mind is driving you up the wall or whether it is a realistic fear that could propel you to action. Knowledge is power, so learning to recognise what parts of your personality contribute to high levels of stress in your life is your first step.

ANXIOUS PERSON #1: HIGHLY SENSITIVE AND HIGHLY REACTIVE

High sensitivity and high reactivity can be very good traits to have. This means you are much more likely to be empathic, understanding, kind and tolerant; you might be a high achiever and you can certainly make a very real contribution to the world. The downside of these traits is that life can be very dramatic and you can presume you 'know' stuff without any evidence because you are used to relying on your sensitivity. Not only that but you could be inclined to suffer extreme mood swings as a result of these traits and this can be tiring for everyone around you.

… If you are this type it is important that you own your personality and acknowledge the good and bad in you so that you can learn to be humorous about your tendency to over-react to every little event.

Another type of highly sensitive and highly reactive person can be completely oblivious to a tendency to always take the limelight. Sometimes this person is filled with self-righteous indignation and can become obsessive about the *terrible wrongs committed by other people.* Family and friends can feel quite disconnected from a person who is continually distracted by their latest source of crazed indignation as this person can prefer to stay in a position where no one can get close to them and thereby make them feel vulnerable. What can be perceived as self-absorption and a lack of empathy or sensitivity to others stems from a desire to avoid complicated feelings of intense vulnerability or hurt. The horror of being completely expendable and pointless might feel too much for you to bear and so you might prefer to big yourself up by focusing on other people's flaws. The problem is that all this anxious rage creates feelings of despair and overwhelm deep inside.

… If you are this type you might charge anxiously from one self-righteous fury to another without taking a breath and letting in some self-reflection. If you did engage in self-reflection you might become more compassionate and tolerant – to yourself and to others. Coming round to full self-acceptance with the help of art, music, literature and a good therapist can be very helpful.

Some people who are highly reactive or highly sensitive live in an almost perpetual state of offence. Do you feel offended often? Is your glass half empty? When you are sensitive it can be all too easy to become consumed by your own problems – you might be quick to feel slighted, and you could be quick to feel excluded. You often presume yourself to be the most sensitive person in the room and yet you might stand accused as being unintentionally insensitive to other people's feelings.

> ... *If you can begin to take responsibility for your own happiness and inner power and tap into your ability to change the way people see you, repeated claims that you have no luck and everything bad happens to you will diminish. The more you can take the focus off your own worries and instead become absorbed by other people's concerns, the more likely that you will free yourself from feeling consumed by despair and anxiety.*

Some highly sensitive people are incredibly empathic to the extent that they lack certain boundaries, especially around those less lucky than themselves. They sometimes use other people's problems as a way to avoid focusing on their own life and self-development by placing the focus on other people's self-development. These people, and I count myself among them, are probably motivated by a genuine wish to make the world a better place but often take on a caretaker role too much and too intensely. If a desire to do good sometimes arises from a desire to prevent you feeling powerless then you might be prone to a God complex. Women seem to be especially given to sacrificing their lives to tending to the needs of others. The true question to ask yourself if you are a saviour type is, 'Are you good or just afraid?' Extraordinary selflessness is often motivated by a fear of taking responsibility for your own life. Your dread of taking responsibility for your own happiness would be submerged deep inside and instead of worrying about your own life you prefer to worry about other people's lives.

> ... *To come out of over-caring for other people to your own detriment, you need to make yourself consider your own emotions whenever you feel*

compelled to save someone else. Are you feeling powerless or worthless? Can you force yourself to do some self-care before you jump into your natural role of caring for others?

ANXIOUS PERSON #2: THE DRAMA LLAMA

Do you find that drama and stress follow you wherever you go? Do you respond to most situations with extreme emotions so that you are almost constantly on an emotional rollercoaster? Perhaps other people view you as seeking the centre of attention while you feel bored or empty inside when there is nothing exciting going on? The drama llama and the highly sensitive and highly reactive person have a lot of traits in common – the main difference could be between the way both types communicate and interpret their emotions. Drama llamas are often addicted to the adrenaline rush of drama even though they know that the great stress and anxiety that comes with this drama can be very debilitating. If you need to feel hyped-up then you might unconsciously create conflict so that you can avoid feeling empty inside. Not only does this frustrate your family and friends but it is also emotionally exhausting for you.

There are many different ways to be addicted to drama; some people lurch from crisis to crisis while others get their rush of adrenaline through extraordinary achievements or through intense relationships. If you find you are permanently in a state of crisis or trauma, you might often fall in with a saviour or caretaker type who is willing to spend a huge amount of time rescuing you from yourself. Beware of this dynamic, though, because if you take up with another drama addict the initial passion can often give way to constant drama and arguments. The addictive highs and lows of the next crisis means that you tend to avoid facing your deeper problems.

Many 'drama llamas' are dismissed as attention-seekers, but this is usually a manifestation of mental distress. Nancy Tucker discusses attention-seeking in her acclaimed book, *That Was When People Started to Worry*:

> It is my belief that those suffering from mental illness are not attention-seeking, but attention-needing: their behaviour comes from a place of crazed, desperate determination to communicate internal distress. People who starve or slice or scald themselves do not want to be 'made a fuss of': they need to be seen and heard. In the moment, with emotions running high, the two motives can look similar, but they are worlds apart.[17]

If you need reassurance, attention and deeper connection it is no good denying these needs and it is much more conducive to your mental health if you can acknowledge them and go about meeting them.

> ... *If you identify with this type, addiction is often a danger as you operate from a place of self-sabotage, self-abandonment and an inner belief that you are basically flawed and not as good as anyone else. You may seek escape from yourself and you will do almost anything to avoid self-reflection. Although you are probably a colourful, vibrant person and very interesting company, your intensity can be off-putting and tiresome. You might benefit from a course of counselling where you can begin to reject your constant need for adrenaline and instead learn to fill your 'hole in the soul' with a sense of calm and acceptance.*

Another type of drama llama is the person who enjoys being centre stage and will do whatever it takes to keep the limelight on them.

When Ella first came to me for counselling she explained that she was highly energetic and 'always on'. I pointed out that she could easily end up feeling restless and anxious as a result of her endless effort to perform but Ella explained that she needed to feel special, 'otherwise what is the point of me?' she wondered. One day, Ella spoke sadly about how irritated she was when her best friend almost stole her limelight when they were out dancing in a nightclub the night before and so Ella, in a crazed bid to get more attention, took her top off. As we spoke we realised together that Ella's sense of insecurity and her rejection of her deepest self was becoming self-destructive. It was time for Ella to make friends with herself. She also decided to reduce her self-absorption by trying to focus on other people's needs and encouraging others to take the limelight. This led Ella to being a more self-compassionate and gentle person who was able to laugh at her OTT need to be the centre of attention.

... If you identify with this type you need to figure out how your behaviour and speech are creating tension and anxiety. Become vigilant about how you respond when you feel bored, listless or frustrated, because it is then that you will be most likely to create unnecessary drama. Devote a notebook or a file in your phone or laptop to record your latest dramas or projects and become more vigilant about whether the drama is necessary or unnecessary.

ANXIOUS PERSONALITY #3: THE PERFECTIONIST

The perfectionist's favourite word is 'should'. Driven by an inner slave-driver who insists they keep moving and keep achieving despite risks to their mental and physical health, the perfectionist doesn't recognise signs to slow down or relax. Indeed, anxiety and mental torment are often viewed as a badge of honour and an attribute of their hard work.

Perfectionism is often viewed as a strength masquerading as a weakness – just like the anorexic who is secretly quite proud of her extraordinary levels of self-control, the perfectionist might decry their perfectionism and yet secretly be very satisfied with it. However, although perfectionism might produce great results initially, these results are seldom sustained and any joy gets sucked out of life. The hard facts are that perfectionism is a crippling weakness, it's a source of intense despair, it creates unattainable standards and more often than not it sets people up for failure. Chronic procrastination is often a trait of perfectionists as they prefer not to do anything as they feel paralysed by their fear of getting something wrong.

Multidimensional perfectionism is the current buzzword to describe how many people feel pressure to meet increasingly high standards that are measured by a continuously widening collection of metrics. The millennial generation in particular has been shaped to seek out metrics. Everything that can be measured is now being measured – even our popularity. Of course social media is a favourite source of comparison for perfectionists, but even Justin Rosenstein, inventor of the iconic 'like' button on Facebook, is dubious about its pleasures: he has since likened Snapchat to heroin and now rations his use of Facebook.[18]

When Barbara first came to me for therapy she was proud of her ability to be flawless. She had impossibly high standards and was harshly critical of both herself and everyone else in her world. Barbara was hard work, she knew, and she didn't have many friends. Although Barbara was proud of her perfectionism, she soon realised, in the counselling context, that all this emphasis on winning was misguided and leading her to burnout, failed relationships and a myriad of health problems rather than unrivalled success. Barbara soon came to believe that she would be much happier being 'perfectly imperfect'.

In Japan, kintsugi is the art of repairing broken pottery with gold, silver or platinum lacquer so as to highlight the flaws as a unique piece of the object's history; embracing our flawed humanity is the most life-embracing way to handle our perfectionism.

There are a number of well-devised scales that can be found online to ascertain whether perfectionism is impacting you, but if you really want to get a grip on your life, the question is not whether you are a perfectionist, but are your perfectionist tendencies having a positive or negative impact on your life? If happiness and healthy relationships are important to you then perhaps you should attempt to take the monkey off your shoulder. If, however, you have a special talent and you are determined to fulfil your potential, then your perfectionism will probably help you achieve great things.

Howard Gardner's fascinating book *Creating Minds* examined the personalities of seven creative geniuses: Freud, Picasso, Einstein, Gandhi, Stravinsky, TS Eliot and Martha Graham.[19] These geniuses all shared common traits such as being intensely dedicated to their work, prepared to work long hours until they achieved their desired results and frequently neglecting other aspects of their lives and families.[20] From reading Gardner's work it soon becomes apparent that a certain degree of perfectionism is probably necessary if you want to achieve greatness — what also becomes apparent is that greatness comes at a high price and a sense of wellbeing and healthy relationships get in the way of extraordinary achievement.

It is difficult to be in love or to be friends with a perfectionist. Although, as a perfectionist, you might have lofty ideals about your work, your love life or your friendships, the high expectations and outrageous demands of the perfectionist can make it very hard to connect on a deeper level with you. Reasons are dismissed as excuses and mistakes are seen as inexcusable. The self-worth of the perfectionist is usually dependent on their latest achievements, so you might go from crowing about your success to intense feelings of self-loathing, depending on external achievements. Burnout, physical collapse and stress-related ailments are always a risk for the perfectionist because you probably haven't yet learned to heed mental or physical warnings to either slow down or adjust your expectations. The feelings of failure and despair that hit when things go wrong are almost overwhelming and it is usually only at this point that the perfectionist realises they need some support to live a kinder, more compassionate life.

> ... *If you are this type of personality, your main goal should be to be to understand that striving to be perfect is in itself an imperfection as every single person — even you — is inherently imperfect. You need to assimilate mistakes into your life as evidence of your imperfect perfection. You also need to learn how to listen to your body and your mind — when you feel tired you need to learn how to relax. You could do with attending a counsellor to help you adjust your high expectations so that you don't suffer the seventh circle of hell when you are disappointed.*

If you are concerned with how your perfectionism is impacting your happiness, the first thing you can focus on is getting your priorities straight. Consider the following strategies to help you to begin the recovery process:

* Change your focus to the 'process' rather than the 'outcome': This means that you should try to stay focused on what you're doing right now instead of what you might eventually achieve in the future. Disciplines such as mindfulness, meditation, yoga and tai chi can help a person to focus on the present and let go of judgement. Judgement all too often leads to unhelpful feelings of self-loathing, guilt and regret, so it needs to be viewed warily.

❖ Flexible thinking is the hallmark of a healthy mind. Whenever you start thinking in terms of black and white, all or nothing, do or die, stop; reach for a pen and paper and write down three additional ways to describe the person or outcome that you're thinking about, or three different ways to achieve the goal you wish to reach. Use words such as 'alternatives', 'possibilities', 'sometimes', 'occasionally' and 'compromise'. This exercise will expand your mind far beyond the narrow-minded outlook of black and white thinking.

❖ Avoid the tyranny of the 'shoulds': When you think of how you 'should' do something, take note; 'should' implies obligation. 'Should' suggests that you are trying to please someone else, or trying to live up to someone else's standards. Change your 'shoulds' into 'coulds' and you will free your mind to choose to live a life in keeping with your own values and desires. So 'I should call my mother' can be changed in to 'I could call my mother but I'm feeling fragile right now and we'll likely have a fight so I'll put that off until another day.'

❖ Become vigilant about the way you think and speak to yourself and to others. Imagine your thoughts as being leaves passing down a turbulent river − they come and they go. Whenever possible, try to use kind words to yourself and others; the words we use have a powerful impact on our feelings and our self-worth. The psychologist Carl Rogers advises us to practise self-acceptance and other-acceptance. If we can learn to be kinder to ourselves and kinder to others we can begin to lift ourselves out of a negative cycle of harsh criticism and self-loathing.

CASE STUDY: SARAH, 23

Sarah came to me for counselling when she was 23 years old. A classic over-achiever, Sarah had left the school system armed with a bagful of As and a bellyful of hope for a sunny future. However, college became increasingly difficult for Sarah because she didn't really enjoy the course she had chosen. She hadn't given much thought to her chosen course; she had picked it because it was considered a demanding course and so she thought it would be impressive if she studied it.

Sarah had been praised since she was a little girl for her brains, and her identity had become reliant upon impressing people with her abilities. This had influenced her personality to the extent that many of her peers found her cold and over-competitive. And so Sarah didn't have many close friends.

Sarah's parents were quite hung up on prestige and status and this is why they were so excited by Sarah's achievements. She learned the alphabet before she was two, and her auntie, who was a teacher of gifted children, declared that Sarah was clearly gifted. They became understandably committed to supporting their clever child.

Sarah's primary school was thrilled to have such a dedicated student but Sarah soon began to resent the easy lives of her peers compared to the relentless effort and achievement in her own. When she was eight, Sarah began to show signs of anxiety – she wet the bed and had nightmares. Her parents took her to a play therapist who recommended that less emphasis be placed on Sarah's ability and more focus put upon pleasure and freedom.

Sarah continued to achieve in secondary school and excelled in her Leaving Cert. The strategies from the play therapy had worked between the ages of 8 and 12, but her anxiety had returned and been quietly growing since she was 12, managed with an elaborate system of coping mechanisms such as tapping every door handle five times, repeating certain mantras one after the other and eating certain foods in a certain order. Sarah's psyche was shattered. She had no real friends; her parents were obsessed with her abilities and Sarah herself felt tired of proving herself to the world. She also felt very anxious that she would be 'exposed' as not being as brilliant as everyone believed.

College didn't prove to be the relief Sarah hoped it would be. Her attempts at making friends in college were clumsy and intense and she found her course – medicine – boring. She had only chosen it because it was a course that clever people did. The fallout was severe; over the first two years of her college course Sarah developed panic disorder, succumbing to frequent full-blown panic attacks.

By the time Sarah came to me for counselling she was in the middle of taking a 'year out' to get her head together. But her head wasn't coming together at all. She dreaded going back to college but couldn't face leaving her college course. Insidious thoughts of suicide had begun to grow in Sarah's head. During the course of counselling, Sarah and I began to deconstruct her life and she soon realised that she was so hung up on her performance, she had little focus on her sense of wellbeing. We concluded that she'd be more suited to studying the arts or humanities; third-level courses she had previously rejected as being 'the refuge of flakes'. We considered the many geniuses who worked in the humanities and the wonderful lives they lived. We also penetrated into Sarah's deep need to impress and whether there was more to Sarah than a clever brain. The panic attacks soon subsided when Sarah began to broaden her horizons and figure out that there was more than one way to be a success in life – and anyway, your life was hardly a roaring success if you were secretly miserable all the time.

Happiness and calmness became Sarah's new measurement for success. She eventually changed college course, found a few friends and even fell in love. Her panic and anxiety fell away when she connected with her true self instead of living a fake life, clinging to fake values.

ANXIOUS PERSONALITY #4: THE WORRYWART

Of course, everyone who experiences anxiety is a worrier, but the worrywart has taken worrying to an almost professional level. The extreme imagination of the worrywart means that their ability to imagine outlandish, worst-case scenarios is almost enthralling. 'What if?' is the favourite phrase of the worrywart; they eye everything with extreme caution and presume that doom and catastrophe are looming around every corner. If someone is late they imagine catastrophic car crashes, if a rash appears on the skin, they are off to Dr Google to find the imminent life-threatening disease. The worrywart tends not to focus only on themselves but on the safety and welfare of others (gee, thanks) and they are willing to expend incredible amounts of energy devoted to keeping their friends and family 'safe'.

All this worrying means that their emotional brain (see page 18) is always on red alert and so their rational brain isn't operating properly – rather it is focused on a more basic survival instinct that dulls creativity or intelligent problem-solving. Excessive worrying is likely to induce physical symptoms of fear and anxiety and so worrywarts are more at risk than others of panic attacks and physical ailments such as breathing problems, digestive ailments or chronic back pain. Their over-protectiveness to themselves, others and especially to children in their care stifles growth, hinders everyone's ability to assess risk and is an obstacle to self-development and healthy independence.

We all need to worry a little bit: worry is a form of problem-solving; it helps us anticipate problems and act in a way that will prevent regret; it also helps us adequately prepare for future events. The main problem with worrying is that, for some of us, it tips into over-worrying and over-worrying is bad for you, on every single level. The difference between worrying and over-worrying is that worrying is specific and necessary – perhaps you are late getting to the airport and worried that you may miss your flight – while over-worrying is often just a generalised sense of panic about anything and everything. Do you fall into over-worrying when you feel weak or tired? Most of us will vociferously deny that we are over-worrying as we feel too panicked to admit that it is needless. You may need to begin to differentiate the two types of worrying and put them into separate boxes in your mind.

Worry	Overworry

Exaggerating both the likelihood and the intensity of threat and danger is a common habit of the worrywart – when you are feeling anxious you may find you mindlessly blow everything out of proportion and focus on the worst-case scenario with an unending series of 'what ifs'.

If you tend to exaggerate danger:

* Become more self-aware so that you know and accept that your thinking is distorted.
* Learn to become vigilant to the patterns so that you are more prepared for when your worrying might explode into over-worrying. Be committed to moving out of the anxious thoughts with distraction, humour, mindfulness, conversation, exercise or whatever other strategy that has been previously pinpointed as effective in these situations.

… If you are this type of personality you need to understand that there are aspects of life that are beyond your control, no matter how hard

you try. Repeating a mantra, such as 'I am powerful and the world is improving every day', can be helpful for you to regain power over your mind. You might also benefit from a course of CBT where you examine your belief system that falsely informs you that tragedy and disaster are waiting around every corner.

ANXIOUS PERSONALITY #5: THE AVOIDER

The avoidant personality can manifest in a thousand ways – some people avoid anxiety through the use of drugs or alcohol, while others are busy all the time or project their feelings on other people. Still others avoid their anxiety by indulging in excessive food, shopping, working, social media or other forms of distraction. The list is long and it is endless. The busy bee avoider motors ahead, leaving dust in their wake. For this person relaxation is a dirty word unless it is a powerful and energetic type of 'relaxation'.

Áine's constant multi-tasking, impressive goals and complaining about being busy were the order of her day. Áine's avoidance was complicated to decipher because her busyness was her avoidance as well as the source of her anxiety; it was all a mind-numbing coping mechanism to dodge troublesome aspects of her unsatisfying job and her deeper, more troubling thoughts about her very existence.

Relentless movement creates tension and anxious people are often troubled with random physical ailments as the body attempts to communicate the 'dis-ease' within. Áine's irritable bowel syndrome was a direct result of her stress and anxiety, but it also created a vicious circle because her digestive system was causing her even more anxiety. Thankfully, when Áine took part in a mindfulness course she learned the art of being mindful and this encouraged her to face her inner demons.

Another type of avoider is the person with the naive persona who avoids any conflict or difficult feelings. Perhaps you shun the news and turn away from anything negative? Although your fixation on positivity is laudable, beneath your serene smile might be a black hole of fear and anxiety that is terrified to confront the reality of this beautiful yet horrifying world. The determination to deny ugly emotions or unpleasant reality means that it is more difficult for you to form deep connections with others – and vice versa – so you often feel lonely, disconnected, alienated and isolated from your loved ones.

Some people are avoidant by playing it too safe or by procrastinating endlessly. The obvious example is the person with social anxiety deciding to avoid all social situations at the expense of their personal and professional life. The problem with this is that the more you avoid, the less likely you are to learn to deal with the situation and so the more likely you will avoid the next obstacle (see Chapter 1). The solution, of course, is to begin to face down anxiety and triggers from anxiety. This needs to be done with support and compassion. It's a long road and it will take some time, but the more you learn to feel the fear and do it anyway, the easier you will find the next task. If you set a couple of achievable goals then, once you have achieved them, you will begin what is known in psychology as a 'positive cycle of change'. One successful task opens you up to the possibility that you may achieve other tasks, thus broadening your life experience.

> … If you identify with the avoidant personality, it's important to turn and face these dragons as it will make you much more able to connect with your loved ones. This in turn will give you some meaning in your life. You might also find it helpful to take a course in mindfulness or yoga. The discipline required to remain still and focus on being instead of doing will be difficult for you but it will release you from terrible feelings of tension and anxiety.

WHEN ANXIETY COMES IN PAIRS

Anxiety can be quite contagious because when you are anxious about something your primary goal is to convince whoever is nearest to you to become anxious about it too. You think, 'Either I'm a fool for being anxious or you're a fool for not being anxious.' The two people can't really authentically co-exist without some way to figure out which is the correct reading of the situation.

This is why, if you are naturally anxious, you need to become aware of the impact that other people have on your anxiety levels – some people make you feel more anxious and others make you feel calmer and vice versa. Try to identify who's who in your circle now, so that when you are feeling fragile, you learn to avoid certain people and gravitate to others. This might seem obvious, but it is usually when we are at our lowest ebb that we do *exactly* the wrong thing and make the anxiety worse.

Over the years in my work as a psychotherapist, I have seen many cases of anxiety manifesting in twos. This usually presents with mother and daughter, a relationship between lovers or two best friends, but can also be evident among siblings and friendship groups. When two people with anxiety meet they can collude with each other that the world is a dangerous place and that they need to take extreme measures to keep their anxiety in check. When you have a partner in crime agreeing with you and even adding extra layers to your anxiety it can be strangely enthralling. The brain seeks problems to solve and so it doesn't take long for you to see yet another threat and to voice your concern. On and on it goes, seeing danger everywhere, stealing joy from your life.

CASE STUDY: SANDRA, 39

Sandra came to me for counselling hoping to reduce her anxiety. She spent the first few sessions talking all about her daughter Katy, who seemed to be similarly anxious but was also reasonably happy. Sandra recounted how when Katy was younger she had resisted going to playschool because she wanted to stay with her mum. Sandra had got over this by staying with Katy in the classroom until she calmed down – this could last up to an hour in a three-hour session. Sandra explained how the first few years of primary school were also difficult for Katy as she became very anxious when confronted with change or new events.

Sandra was highly reactive (see page 31), particularly about her daughter's anxiety, and it's very likely this rubbed off on Katy. So a negative pattern formed where Katy became anxious about a small matter and, instead of calming Katy down, Sandra would act quickly to remove the object of fear. This meant that Sandra was a constant fixture in the school, asking teachers for all kinds of dispensations for her daughter, inadvertently heightening Katy's anxiety and leading her young daughter to believe that she couldn't cope.

Sandra's skewed, anxiety-driven vision compelled her to remove distress from Katy's life and, as a direct result of this, Katy had little or no experience of handling distress. She had been given the very clear message that she wasn't competent or able to handle fear.

Katy left primary school thinking of herself as an unusually anxious person – which she may well have been – but she also viewed herself as someone who couldn't bear much pressure, who couldn't – and shouldn't – handle any distress. Katy was brought up to believe that she needed the adults to step in to save her, and perhaps most damaging of all, that she needed special treatment if she was to survive in this world.

When I asked Sandra how she would describe both herself and Katy, she said that while she was anxious, Katy was much more anxious. I wondered aloud whether this was simply a consequence of the way that Katy's anxiety had been handled, but Sandra disagreed. I then explained how children need to learn how to handle distress from a safe perch. They need the opportunity to experience fear when they have loving parents or guardians ready to help them, so they can get ready to face the world with added understanding and depth. But at the first sign of fear, Katy's mother would immediately work tirelessly to remove the object causing that fear.

As Katy grew up, Sandra's power to shield her from pain reduced and so, when Katy found it difficult to make friends in secondary school, Sandra became highly anxious. There was little Sandra could do to alleviate Katy's distress and this caused Sandra intense pain and anxiety. It also brought about a rage in Katy that Sandra wasn't doing her job properly – the job of making Katy's life easier.

I explained to Sandra that she and Katy were behaving like two anxiety addicts. They colluded with each other in the belief that removing the fear was the only solution; that Katy couldn't withstand any distress and that the rest of the world just didn't understand how difficult life was for them.

Over time Sandra and I worked together, exploring how the world is made of positive and negative, and how best to fix the anxious pair. After a few sessions Sandra started to realise that Katy's world was narrowing all the time and if she wasn't careful Katy would soon be afraid of everything. She resolved to teach Katy how to confront her fears and to do this she needed to learn how to confront her own fears. Finally, the real therapy could begin.

If you find that you have fallen into an anxious twosome the first thing you need to do is declare it and bring some self-awareness to the situation. If your 'anxiety partner' isn't interested in getting better then you will need to go it alone until you have reached a steadier place in your mind. It can be very attractive for two people to address their emotional problems together but it is fraught with difficulties because if one falls off the wagon they almost encourage the other to fall off too so that they can get back on together. If it is at all possible, each person should find their own, separate path to recovery.

COMMON HABITS OF ANXIOUS TYPES

There are certain mental habits that anxious people will recognise and, in order to address them, it is important that you identify your own most common – and most destructive – habits.

The most abiding habit, if you are anxious, is worrying – worrying about today, tomorrow and yesterday. But in the vast majority of circumstances, worrying is never a form of problem-solving – it's just a repeated thought being unpacked, unpicked and analysed over and over again. As the saying goes, 'You can build evidence for ever' so if your thoughts aren't propelling you to do things to reduce your anxiety there is little point in you thinking yourself sick. On the other hand, to go a bit deeper, if you tend to become anxious about one thing, then, once you solve it, you immediately move on to the next piece of future terror, you might find that you need to learn to gain more control over your mind as you are in danger of becoming a serial worrier.

In his study of the science of the brain the neuropsychologist Donald Hebb coined the phrase 'neurons that fire together wire together' as a way to explain that the more we do something, the easier it is to do it because it is the same neurons that get triggered each time. This means that we need to become aware of the habits of our mind if we are to properly address our anxiety. If we aren't careful habitual anxiety can expand to become something that looks very like an addiction to anxiety.

The psychiatrist Harris Strayner from Mount Sinai School of Medicine pointed out:

> There are people who have extreme agitation, but they can't understand why. They therefore latch on to any cause to explain what they're feeling. That rationalisation doubles back and exacerbates the anxiety. Some people get addicted to feeling anxious because that's the state that they've always known. If they feel a sense of calm, they get bored; they feel empty inside. They want to feel anxious.[21]

This habit of anxiety can become very debilitating both for you and for your loved ones. Lurching from crisis to crisis, you might feel that you can't rest easy unless there's a crisis and then, when there is a crisis, you feel that you have a licence to allow your fears to run roughshod over everything.

It can be helpful, if you have become habituated to anxiety, to begin to notice the patterns of your thoughts so that you can predict when your mind might lose perspective and begin to pre-empt and divert it towards healthier thought patterns. Take a moment to ask yourself the following questions. It will help you to build self-awareness around your anxiety and you will begin to be more accurate at identifying the circumstances when you are more prone to anxiety.

1. Do you worry more when you are alone or with certain people?
2. Do you worry more at certain times of the day? The week? The month?
3. Do you worry more at work? When you're overworked or when you're idle?

4. What is your worry pattern? Does one fear tend to lead into another and another until you feel overwhelmed? Or do you fixate on one worry and become obsessed?

5. Do certain events, situations or people bring on 'the fear'?

LIVING IN THE FUTURE

It is said that people who are depressed live in the past, people who are anxious live in the future and people who are happy live in the present. This could be considered annoyingly simplistic, yet there is some truth in it. If you persistently live in the future, then you are in danger of missing out on huge swathes of your life. Although everyone needs a bit of time to plan future events, none of us can forecast the future so we can waste a lot of time thinking about things that never actually happen. I could slip in the shower today and die. But I've had many showers and so far I haven't had any accidents and so, really, I shouldn't think about this as there are more realistic and pressing worries to think about. All we can do is follow the spirit of 'best practice' for any given event and operate a cost–benefit analysis on each situation. For example, if you are worrying about a sick child with cancer, then it's entirely understandable that you are consumed with anxiety about their future, but if you are worrying about your healthy child's birthday party going well, then 'best practice' would be to realise that there is little point in wasting your time on this event and there is a significant danger in creating a sense of joylessness around the event if you continue to worry.

INTOLERANCE OF UNCERTAINTY

How do you feel about uncertainty? If you are anxious you may find uncertainty unbearable and so, just like a crazed Othello in a fit of frenzied emotion, find yourself jumping to the nearest, wildest conclusion in a bid to eliminate it. Shifting mindlessly from one worry to another, always seeking certainty in an uncertain world, is simply a self-inflicted form of torture.

The not-so-palatable truth is that to learn how to handle uncertainty, you need to practise experiencing it. This means that when a friend is vague about plans, instead of insisting on a time, date and venue, you could force yourself to experience the irritating feeling of not being sure when or where you are meeting until your friend decides to let you know. If you are used to being quite controlling and insisting on plans being fixed, it is actually quite good for you to go through this. Welcome the sense of unease that you feel with this uncertainty as it stems from your brain trying to learn new habits and this will feel uncomfortable until the healthy habits have taken root. Building a tolerance to uncertainty will take time and commitment, but if you achieve it, it will release you from this particular prison of anxiety and help you to build your ability to enjoy your life in so many ways.

'BLACK-WASHING'

When you feel highly anxious you might find that you habitually 'black-wash' events; this means that you throw a figurative tin of black paint over everything, making most ambiguous events appear negative, dark or threatening. This filtering process leads you to ignore all the positive and good things in your day to focus solely on the negative. Dwelling on the negative, even when surrounded by an abundance of good things, can then become a bad habit. For example, a socially anxious person will tend to interpret many comments as negative; 'That's an interesting T-shirt' can be interpreted as, 'What a ridiculous T-shirt'. This can be stressful for you and tedious for the people around you as they have to continuously reassure you that every given situation isn't necessarily negative.

Alternatively, you might find that you minimise or dismiss the importance of positive things, such as an accomplishment at work or a desirable personal characteristic, as your brain automatically dismisses the positive.

This bad habit of negativity might be deeply ingrained so it can take some time to instil more positive habits. When researchers examined the habits of 96 people over a 12-week period they found that it takes on average 66 days for a new behaviour to become automatic.[22] So if you can commit to 'white-washing' your interpretation of events every time you automatically 'black-wash' events, then after 66 days you will probably be up and running on the road to accuracy, realism and healthy functioning.

THINKING YOU'RE ALWAYS RIGHT AND DEFENSIVENESS

When you are filled with anxiety you can tend to think that you are right and that no one else understands the inherent 'dangers'. Yet it is foolish to presume that you always know better than others – especially when you have worked out that you are often anxious. When you feel anxious you might need to accept, in the moment, that your anxiety might make you *feel* right and might make you *feel* panicked that everyone else is too easy-going, but you also need to accept that *most anxious people are wrong more often than they are right.*

It can be helpful for someone recovering from anxiety to make a commitment to begin to listen to other people's points of view without becoming defensive. Some anxious people partner up with easy-going people – this pairing fits because the anxious person can do the worrying for everyone and the easy-going partner can provide the light relief. If you want to overcome your anxiety you could ask your partner to shoulder some of the worrying as you try to free yourself from always being in the responsible position.

SELF-ABSORPTION

Just like any profound pain, anxiety consumes your mind. When we feel anxious we may become too focused on 'does she like me?' or 'am I boring?' instead of actually listening to our friends and family. But as Nietzsche tells us, 'Whoever fights monsters should see to it that in the process he does not become a monster. And if you gaze long enough into an abyss, the abyss will gaze back into you.' The self-absorption that is often associated with anxiety is usually a result of great mental anguish – it is very hard to be considerate of other people's feelings when you are preoccupied with inner mental torture. Self-absorption is one of the many traits common to the mentally ill that is quite difficult to deal with. Sadly, what can often begin as a mild and understandable absorption can soon, in certain environments, lead to total self-absorption and even narcissism. That is not to say that everyone who is anxious is hopelessly self-absorbed, but anxious people need to be vigilant that their mental torment doesn't lead them to become over-absorbed in their feelings.

The good news is that if you can become more absorbed by other people, events and situations, you will automatically become less anxious. For this reason it might be beneficial for you to watch a gripping movie or read a thriller when you feel that you are in the very early stages of over-worrying. It is key that you try to distract yourself before you are gripped by total anxiety – because when you are in the grips of anxiety there is very little you can do but wait until the storm passes (see Chapter 8).

CONSTANTLY NEEDING REASSURANCE

The heightened search for clear answers might lead you to seek relief by trying to elicit reassurances from others than everything will be all right, making you highly reliant on loved ones to provide you with this reassurance. This can not only damage relationships, it is also psychologically ineffective as it is cementing the feeling that the solution is external rather than internal.

Initiate an open (and possibly difficult) discussion with your loved ones on this cycle, explaining that constant reassurance is akin to giving drugs (reassurance) to the drug addict (you), so you will all be better off if you could be weaned off these drugs or even try to go cold turkey (perhaps with the understanding that we all fall off the wagon sometimes).

AN EXTERNAL LOCUS OF CONTROL

A locus of control refers to the belief system of an individual regarding their control of any given situation. A person with an 'internal locus of control' believes they have some control over their success or failure in any given situation. This person believes that they are in charge of their life and that any success or failure they experience is mostly down to them and that, with some effort and commitment, they can usually improve their situation. For example, when receiving exam results, people with an internal locus of control tend to hold themselves responsible for their results while people with an external locus of control tend to place the blame or praise on external factors such as the teacher or the exam process.[23]

Someone with an internal locus of control will keep themselves motivated with self-talk such as, 'If it's to be, it's up to me' or 'I'll have to upskill if I want to get on'. In sharp contrast, a person with an 'external locus of control' believes that someone or something else is controlling any given situation. This something else might be the government, their parents, fate or the gods; it really doesn't matter who is in charge, but the person with an external locus of control's strong belief is that their fate is not in their hands so they look to the outer world for relief from anxiety. Although both internal and external loci of control confer advantages and disadvantages, an internal locus of control is associated with less stress, more psychological resilience and better health, and an external locus of control has been shown to be correlated with anxiety.[24]

An interesting study that followed more than 7,500 British people from birth onwards showed that those who had an internal locus of control by the age of ten were less likely to be overweight at age 30, less likely to describe their health as poor and less likely to show high levels of psychological stress.[25] The research concluded that children with an internal locus of control behaved more healthily as adults because they had more confidence in their ability to shape their life and influence the outcomes in their life through their own behaviour.[26]

If you can begin to cultivate an internal locus of control, you will soon feel that, although you might not be able to control everything, nevertheless, your actions can certainly have a big impact on your life.

FEELING UNABLE TO COPE

When a person feels anxious, they habitually tend to perceive themselves as weak and unable to handle things – don't forget that anxiety involves overestimating the danger while underestimating our ability to cope. The more a person doubts their level of competence the more they worry about the impact of a negative outcome. For example, Jamie came to me for therapy because he was overcome with anxiety about failing his exams. His overly high levels of arousal were automatically making him under-perform and so I introduced him to some deep breathing exercises to bring his levels of cortisol down a few notches. From this, Jamie needed to assume a greater sense of personal control about the exams and so he needed to build his internal locus of control: he needed to learn to think logically and accurately about his exams and he needed to study more so that he could believe that he would do well.

Competence instils confidence and many people can only adopt a confident attitude when they feel well-rehearsed and competent. If you feel unable to cope, try breathing exercises and more active problem-solving strategies.

CHOKING UNDER PRESSURE

Many of us who have tried to give a speech or sing a song in company know full well the devastating impact of performance anxiety. We may have practised the piece a thousand times but then, when all eyes are upon us, we end up sounding high-pitched and strangled. The combination of too much attention and excessive arousal worsen our performance. If our levels of arousal are too low we will be both bored and boring, distracted, unfocused and we will under-perform. Likewise, if our levels of arousal are too high, our focus of attention becomes too narrow and we can lose sight of important information. Hyper-focus can mean, for example, that we go down the rabbit hole of over-answering one question in an exam to the detriment of the rest.

For situations where we need to perform, we need the Goldilocks level of arousal; neither too high nor too low, but just right. A good trick is to reframe your nerves as excitement. Whenever you feel the anxiety rising within you, tell yourself, 'I am excited by this.' It is right and proper to be excited by important events and it is appropriate for your levels of cortisol to be raised but not heightened at these times.

Practise handling your excitement with easy tasks initially – start at the shallow end before negotiating the deeper waters. For instance, you might pick an easier event and notice your excitement as you approach your local café or a group of good friends. As you notice your arousal growing you could tell yourself, 'I'm becoming excited and this will be fun.' As time goes on you will retrain your emotional brain to become more accustomed to feeling excited and you will learn to cope with growing arousal. If you can successfully manage to direct your nerves towards excitement with the easy events, then, over time, the habit of welcoming appropriate excitement will extend to the more challenging events.

DISTORTED INTERNAL BELIEF SYSTEMS

A major task in any bid to help a person to manage their anxiety is to teach them to become more aware of the falseness of their emotionally driven beliefs and to learn to think more accurately and more logically.

Emma came to me for counselling as she was highly anxious. Over time we worked on her distorted thought patterns and we eventually identified the belief that 'everyone will do you down' was a negative belief that Emma had learned from her mother. Emma's mother was a bitter woman whose life was filled with regret and Emma was horrified when she realised that she had internalised this belief from her mother. She replaced this belief with a more helpful one: 'Some people will help you and some people won't but that's okay.' Emma decided to repeat this as a mantra three times, three times a day, as a way of reinforcing her new belief and getting rid of her old belief.

The thing to remember about our internal belief systems is that they are often just a mental habit that hasn't been discarded. So you might have a few bad and a few good habits from childhood – these habits are often mindless and no longer fit for purpose; for example, my husband went to boarding school and he neatly and, in his world,

59

obediently, puts his knife and fork together after every meal, waiting no doubt for some servant type to come and collect the dirty dishes. (They never come).

It is worthwhile to write down some old beliefs that you may have internalised from your childhood and replace them with more appropriate beliefs that you have gathered from your own wisdom and experiences so they are there, ready to counteract the old ones. See below for some examples:

Old, internal beliefs	New, improved beliefs
◆ The devil makes work for idle hands	◆ It's healthy to relax
◆ Boys don't cry	◆ Sometimes crying is good for you
◆ Good girls don't get angry	◆ Everyone gets angry
◆ Don't air your dirty laundry	◆ It can be helpful to confide in friends
◆ Never trust a man	◆ Some people are trustworthy

CONCLUSION: LIVING WITH UNCERTAINTY

Some anxious people find it can be helpful to spend their time making sure that they are a force for good rather than trying to wrench control and certainty out of life. We won't find certainty in this life beyond death and taxes and so we would be better off trying to find some purpose or meaning. Rather than stressing ourselves out in a futile bid to control things and stamp out uncertainty, we could instead acknowledge that uncertainty will always be with us. The challenge is to live a meaningful and satisfying life in the face of this uncertainty – we need to become more comfortable with uncertainty as uncertainty is one of the few things we can rely on in this world.

CHAPTER 3

What are you *really* avoiding?

'If anxiety is our chief malady, avoidance is its coddling nurse.'

LISA MARCHIANO

Avoidance is a perfectly natural defence mechanism that we use to cope with many kinds of pain and trauma. When a person is fearful of something, their immediate instinct is to avoid it. Anxious people are often masters of avoidance, but in the long run, avoidance makes anxiety worse. It works beautifully in the short term but unless used wisely, offers long-term psychic pain. It's like heroin to the heroin addict – the addict wants it, they crave it, they'll convince everyone around them that they need it – but it *only* provides short-term relief and, unless managed carefully, *always* leads to long-term pain.

The temporary relief that avoidance provides can be very exciting and relieving but then the sufferer can become fixated that this strategy is the solution and so become determined to keep trying to push the idea that they must keep using avoidance tactics to avoid the distress inside themselves instead of taking a more proactive attitude

61

and actively seeking a satisfying life that counteracts the short-term feelings of distress. The problem with many avoidance strategies is that they don't confront the basic problem that underlies the anxiety; these tactics are successful at the time but their efficacy just doesn't last.

The permutations that an anxious person will go through to avoid an anxiety-inducing situation are truly magnificent – and also very self-destructive. Exposure is the enemy of avoidance as it asks the anxious person to face their worst fears. It works properly if the person is in a safe and trusted environment and feels in control of the situation. This therapy takes the form of a plan that slowly but surely helps the person to confront their fears and decrease their patterns of avoidance. Unless your anxiety stems from a medical condition such as hyperthyroidism or psychosis, learning to confront and handle your anxiety is the most effective treatment to combat pervasive anxiety and structured exposure is the treatment of choice for just about all the wide range of anxiety disorders highlighted in the DSM-5.[27]

Are you avoidant? Ask yourself the following questions to find out:

- ❖ Do you avoid speaking when you've something to say?
- ❖ Do you avoid events that you know will be good because you can't face the stress of it all?
- ❖ Do you use technology to avoid speaking directly with people?
- ❖ Do you seek reassurance from people that a situation is unbearable when you know you're exaggerating so you can get permission to avoid?
- ❖ Do you work yourself up into a fever until you feel there is no option but to avoid?
- ❖ Do you cancel events and dates with people because you just can't face them?

❖ Do you tend to make your anxiety worse, not better?

❖ Does your behaviour reinforce the idea that you can't cope?

❖ Do you seek short-term relief at the cost of long-term gain?

❖ Are you unsure about how to tackle your anxiety?

❖ Do you tend to dodge the real problem and focus on the surface problem?

❖ Do you find yourself easily distracted from the real issues?

❖ Do you sometimes make inaccurate associations as a result of your fear and anxiety?

❖ Do you often focus on the wrong goals?

Does avoidance cost you:

… your fun?

… your friends?

… your relationships?

… your career?

… your sense of self?

… your dignity?

… your peace of mind?

… your freedom?

THE PENDULUM EFFECT

Galileo Galilei, a medical student in the Italian city of Pisa, was 17 years old and at Sunday service in the cathedral when he idly observed a chandelier swinging to and fro. There were no watches at the time but Galileo used his pulse to confirm his suspicion that the chandelier was keeping a steady beat; no matter how wide or narrow the swing, it always corresponded perfectly on the other side. Filled with excitement, Galileo raced home straight after mass and recreated a similar pendulum by suspending a weight from a long string so that he could properly examine this phenomenon. From this experiment Galileo developed his theory of the 'pendulum effect': that movement in one direction causes equal movement in another direction.

When Galileo first identified the natural law of the 'pendulum effect' he perhaps had no idea that it would be applied to psychology, but psychological research into the 'pendulum effect' suggests that, in many aspects of life, the further we swing one way, the further we swing the opposite direction; the greater the boom, the greater the bust. For example, diets can create a feeling of lack and make a person obsess about food and, ultimately, many people put on weight after a diet. Similarly, attempting to avoid or suppress our thoughts usually results in a higher frequency of the thoughts and tends to increase our preoccupation with these distorted thoughts. So the stronger the attempt to avoid or suppress anxiety-triggering situations, the stronger our anxiety may be in the long term.

THE WALKING WOUNDED AND THE WORRIED WELL

Anxiety can occur in many forms including panic attacks, social anxiety, phobias, anxiety attacks and plain generalised anxiety. The fully diagnosable anxiety disorders that are described below are not as common as the low-lying anxiety that many people feel; however, many readers might relate to one disorder more than others and find that they can address their issues within the parameters of this description. These 'walking wounded' – those who suffer intensely but haven't been diagnosed – often receive less attention and less concern than sufferers who have a fully acknowledged and diagnosed disorder but that's neither right nor fair. If you are suffering from low-lying anxiety, please don't suffer in silence – get the help you need. Whether or not you have been diagnosed the importance of getting professional help at the earliest opportunity cannot be overstated.

The 'worried well' is the term used for those of us who visit our doctors seeking reassurance when we are worried about something. The worried well don't usually need medical treatment – they need something deeper than that; they need something that will calm the distress in their deepest selves. But too many of us are joining the ranks of the worried well as we are becoming anxious as a direct consequence of living in an anxiety-inducing culture. Sometimes amateur psychologists dismiss the worried well as 'over-sensitive attention-seekers', 'drama queens', or something equally barbed. But beware. What can look like dramatic or attention-seeking behaviour often comes from a place of deep-rooted need for recognition of pain.

If you worry that your behaviour is 'attention-seeking', then perhaps you really need some attention. Maybe you need to feel truly seen or heard, or perhaps have a deep need to be listened to or understood? If this is so, then you will have to authentically reveal yourself. Many of us remain in a more superficial level in our relationships because we are uncomfortable with the feelings of vulnerability that are needed to be authentic. Brené Brown tells us, 'Staying vulnerable is a risk we have to take if we want to experience connection.' If you feel lost or lonely then more authentic connection will lead you to feeling more settled in yourself and more connected with others. Although it may take more than a few attempts – because many people feel too busy and stressed these days to have time for friendships – it is worth trying to rekindle old friendships as well as finding new ones, because once the light is flickering, it will be easier to keep it aflame.

GENERALISED ANXIETY DISORDER

Generalised anxiety disorder (GAD) is characterised by excessive, uncontrollable and often irrational worrying.[28] This worry can become an obstacle to daily functioning as you become over-concerned with everyday challenges such as problems related to family and friends, work, money, death and health. For a formal diagnosis of GAD, symptoms of anxiety such as those described below must be consistent and ongoing, and persisting for at least six months.

Physical symptoms of GAD:[29]

* Fatigue
* Fidgeting
* Itchiness and rashes
* Headaches
* Numb hands or feet
* Muscle tension
* Difficulty swallowing, upset stomach, vomiting, diarrhoea
* Breathing difficulty
* Difficulty concentrating
* Trembling
* Irritability
* Sweating
* Restlessness
* Sleeping difficulties
* Hot flushes
* Inability to fully control the anxiety

Even if you aren't diagnosed with GAD but you relate to many of the symptoms above, try to address the underlying cause of all this anxiety. It can be all too easy to charge down the rabbit hole of your latest anxiety but it is much more helpful to step away from this latest source of tension and give yourself some room to reflect upon the themes that might be a common denominator for all your worries.

Treating GAD

Exposure-based therapy is psychological treatments that have been developed to help people combat their fears and this type of approach has been shown to be the most effective treatment for people with GAD.[30] Exposure involves confronting your fears instead of avoiding them, no matter whether it is actual (in vivo) or imaginal (visualised) treatment and most therapists use variations of exposure therapy in the belief that this will help clients combat their anxiety.[31] Indeed, exposure-based therapies have been shown to be effective treatment for people with anxiety disorders such as phobias, panic disorder, social anxiety disorder, post-traumatic stress disorder and generalised anxiety disorder.[32]

This is not to say that exposure-based therapy always works – there is, unfortunately, no silver bullet in this world. But it is considered the most common and the most successful therapeutic approach that is currently used to combat anxiety.[33] It is incredibly important that readers who suffer from an anxiety disorder don't randomly decide to undergo a DIY form of exposure therapy – this will just set you up for failure and could leave you feeling in the depths of despair. Instead ask your therapist – and if you don't have one, get one – to engage in some exposure therapy to aid your recovery.

It can be helpful to think of your anxiety as a 'psychological allergy'. People who suffer from normal allergies are overly sensitive to, say, nuts or pollen (triggers known as allergens). So the person suffering with a pollen allergy can have a dramatic reaction to what others would find a mildly irritating level of pollen in the air. Likewise, a person who is highly sensitive to triggers in their psyche can have a dramatic reaction to what others would consider a mildly worrying event.

Some allergy sufferers can desensitise themselves by being exposed to tiny and gradually increasing doses of the allergen and, in a similar way, so can people who suffer from what is akin to a psychological allergy.[34] Managed carefully, and in a controlled situation, the anxious person can teach their nervous system to tone down their over-reactive response to perceived danger. Over time, the anxious person can be desensitised to the triggers and eventually stop over-reacting to them.

There are many variations of exposure therapy:

* **Graded exposure** occurs when a therapist works with a client to construct a hierarchy where the feared objects, situations or activities are ranked according to difficulty. The client begins with mildly difficult exposures, then, over time, progresses to harder challenges. This client might use imaginal exposure – purposely imagining the feared object, situation or activity – or they might go straight for a small dose of physical reality to confront the fear. This could be something like committing to attend a function they had previously avoided, feel the uncomfortable anxiety for five minutes and then leave, with a commitment to returning to this again and again over a number of months.

* **Systematic desensitisation** is when the exposure is combined with relaxation exercises such as deep breathing or progressive muscle relaxation in order to make the tasks more manageable and to begin to associate the feared objects, activities or situations with relaxation, safety and control (see Chapter 8).

* **Interoceptive exposure** involves deliberately bringing on physical sensations that are harmless but feared. When Jenny came to me first her life was severely curtailed as a result of her

fear of having panic attacks. As the weeks in therapy progressed and Jenny and I discussed the worst-case scenario in detail, Jenny acquiesced to 'bringing on' the feelings of a panic attack by running on the spot in my office. People who are given to panic associate a speeding heart with panic and so deliberately speeding up the heart, with the support of a therapist in a safe environment, can challenge assumptions that calamity will ensue if your heartbeat increases. As Jenny became more used to the feelings associated with rapid heartbeat and shortness of breath, she soon learned to view her fear of panic attacks as more debilitating than the actual panic attacks.

❖ **In vivo exposure/flooding** is the opposite of graded exposure as it involves the sufferer jumping in at the deep end and facing the most difficult challenge first. The grand plan is that once the most horrible task is completed then all other challenges feel easier. It might sound counter-intuitive, but I have seen this approach work very well with some people. For example, someone with social anxiety might be instructed to join Toastmasters and give a speech in front of an audience. This full-on confrontational approach might not be some people's bag, but others are attracted to the clarity of the challenge.

❖ **Virtual reality exposure** is often used when in vivo exposure is not practical – it might not be realistic to expose a person to their fear of flying and so the person might instead take a virtual flight, using equipment that provides the sights, sounds and smells of the aeroplane.

Clients are often relieved to hear that exposure can be paced at different levels depending on the person. But fast or slow, it doesn't really matter so long as the anxious person feels in control of events and realises they can back out whenever they wish. Ultimately, though, if a person persistently backs out of the task with little interest in truly exposing themselves then this avoidance would eventually be challenged by the therapist.

PANIC DISORDER

Panic disorder is characterised by unexpected and repeated episodes of intense fear accompanied by physical symptoms that may include heart palpitations, chest pain, shortness of breath, dizziness and/or abdominal distress. Many sufferers tend to avoid going to places where they have previously suffered a panic attack as they fear another episode will be triggered, but it is far better to confront the episodes and address the underlying issues that could be at the heart of your distress. All too often, when clients come to me suffering from panic attacks, they have been feeling anxious for a very long time. Here are some tools to introduce when panic attacks:

- ❖ Recognise that you are having a panic attack; remind yourself that it will be very uncomfortable but it will pass.
- ❖ Find somewhere safe.
- ❖ Know your personal symptoms.
- ❖ Pay attention to your breath; inhale counting three and exhale counting three. Slow your breathing down. Count your breaths. Breathe in through the nose and out through the mouth. If you're unable to slow your breathing, visualise yourself doing it instead.
- ❖ Acknowledge and accept your anxiety by repeating your personal mantra – it could be something like, 'This too shall pass' or 'I can do this' or 'I have inner strength and reserves.'
- ❖ Label your emotions. Allow the attack to happen.
- ❖ Sit with the fear and let it pass.

❖ Count five things you can see, four you can touch, three you can hear, two you can smell and one you can taste.

❖ Write down your thoughts and emotions on your phone or on a piece of paper.

❖ Fiddle with a toy that engages your senses.

❖ Try to sing all the words of your favourite song.

❖ Practise positive self-talk. Talk yourself through it, out loud.

❖ Cuddle a pet; give someone a hug.

❖ Play with worry beads, a ring or whatever piece of jewellery you keep to hand for these difficult times.

❖ Give your panic attack a name, a character and speak to this character as if you are talking to your annoying younger sibling who won't stop pestering you.

❖ Go outside and take some deep breaths of cold air.

❖ Drink some cold water.

❖ Say the alphabet backwards. Count backwards in sevens from a hundred. Multiply 27 by 8. Distract your mind with whatever works for you.

Once the panic attacks have subsided it is essential first of all that you treat yourself with gentle self-compassion so that you can recover from the trauma, and second of all, that you refocus your efforts to figuring out what is causing your anxiety. It might be your environment (see Chapter 4) or a more specific problem – it doesn't really matter; if you don't resolve your feelings of anxiety then your life will be shaped by fear of prospective panic attacks.

So what should you do to recover right after a panic attack?

❖ Treat yourself tenderly, as you would if you had woken from a particularly horrible nightmare.

❖ Call someone you know and love who will give you the support you need.

❖ Write down what you think triggered your panic attack, what made things worse during the build-up and what you could have done differently.

❖ Consider what happened in the attack and if you could have done anything differently.

❖ Schedule an appointment with your therapist.

❖ Be kind, be kind, be kind. Practise self-compassion and self-acceptance.

Anyone who knows anything about anxiety will know that anxiety has little respect for success and there is a very long and illustrious list of famous people who have suffered from panic attacks, such as Lena Dunham, Ellie Goulding, Oprah Winfrey and Emma Stone. Sometimes, it is precisely when we have no time to pause because we're too busy winning all around us, that anxiety decides to rear its ugly head. Other times, it is when we feel calm, sitting watching TV in our sitting room, without a care in the world, that our brain decides to have a mental explosion.

Stefanie Preissner, author of the hit TV show *Can't Cope Won't Cope*, fell into the former camp. In February 2014 she was sitting in her dressing room after a performance in Australia when she had her first panic attack:

I don't think I was any more stressed than I usually was, I hadn't had any major problem or grief or trauma in the days or hours leading up to the event. I was missing home a little, concerned about the reviews and the reception of the show, I guess. One review had called me 'a very large girl' and maybe I was more affected by that than my water-off-a-duck's-back response had let on. But to this day, I do not blame any one thing for the panic attack. I'm still baffled about how it happened and often wonder if I'll be somewhere one day and be caught off-guard again.[35]

It isn't unusual that Preissner doesn't attribute anything in particular to her panic attack as this is often the most unnerving aspect of panic attacks. Indeed most people who have suffered panic attacks are baffled by the ordinary day preceding the most frightening moments of their lives. The 25-year-old writer had already scored a hit with her one-woman show *Solpadeine is my Boyfriend* and she was on tour in Australia, getting rave reviews along the way. Life was good for this rising star, although perhaps a bit full-on. Preissner was advised by the doctors to take it easy, and so, following doctor's orders, she decided to err on the side of caution, cut short her Australian show and go home to Ireland. Perhaps because she was embarrassed, Preissner took the fateful decision to hide the fact that she was returning to Ireland.

Up until then Preissner's social media was filled with the usual gushing remarks from her friends and acquaintances such as *'OMG it looks so fab, you're having a ball'*. Preissner decided to continue to fill her social media with fictionalised accounts of her fabulous tour – all while she was cowering in her bed in Dublin ravaged with anxiety and distress. Had Preissner chosen to tell the truth at this crucial moment she could have struck a blow against our performing-monkey culture but instead, almost like poacher turned gamekeeper, this astute observer of modern life fell into a very modern pretence. Just before her flight home from Brisbane airport, Preissner ran to the airport shop, took some photos of typical tourist destinations and saved them on her phone. She told her first lie on the stopover in Singapore as she uploaded a picture of Ayer's Rock and tagged herself on social media. Instant gratification and reassurance from anyone who will provide it is always welcome for the anxious individual. And so Preissner immediately felt much better the very instant that the first comment appeared: *'That looks like magic. You're so lucky. #jealous.'*

> By the time I got to my house in Dublin, I had virtually visited the Great Barrier Reef, Sydney Harbour Bridge and some island that I can't guarantee isn't New Zealand … The reality was that I was in bed, in Dublin, with no prospect of any visitors because for me to call for company and support would uncover the lie and ruin the illusion.

Thankfully, in a searing account of why she felt the need to pretend she was living the dream, Preissner did eventually come clean about this pretend trip and, in so doing, she undoubtedly helped a lot of people suffering with anxiety. Yet despite her many successes, Preissner still feels pressure to succeed and gets up at 4.30 a.m. to write as it's the only time she has to spare in her day: 'If I didn't do all of the things that I am afraid to do I would never do anything. I stand in vulnerability every day and I operate from that place despite all the Instagram posts telling me to be "fierce".'[36]

If you suffer from panic attacks then you must first attend your doctor to make sure you are receiving the best possible care. After that it is often helpful to see your panic attacks as a symptom of your anxiety instead of the essence of it. If you can learn to reduce your anxiety and if you get the right professional support to tackle your panic attacks, then you will find that your compulsive episodes will significantly reduce. You might retain a residue of these episodes, but the very fact that you know you can handle them leaves you feeling stronger and more able than before.

SOCIAL ANXIETY DISORDER

Social anxiety disorder (also known as 'social phobia') is the third–largest mental health care problem in the Western world today.[37] It is characterised by extreme anxiety surrounding social situations, especially those that involve interaction with other people, and it usually stems from the fear of being negatively judged and evaluated by other people. If you suffer from social anxiety you would probably benefit from addressing your old internal beliefs (see Chapter 7) as you need to free yourself from allowing others to have such power over your mental health.

Dr Harry Barry has written extensively about mental health and in his books he often makes reference to his 'Raggy Doll Club'. According to Dr Barry, there are many members of this club the world over, and the only requisite to entry is that we don't allow other people to judge us, neither do we judge ourselves. If we can overcome our judgemental mindset we have a much better chance of staying well. This, of course is easier said than done, but I have found that repeating the mantra, 'Don't be so hard on yourself and don't be so hard on others' can be helpful. The impact of cultivating compassion in your life can be everlasting so it is well worth making the effort to bring this into your life.

CASE STUDY: MARTIN, 24

Martin came to me because he felt consumed by his fear of attending social functions. He had been diagnosed with social anxiety and he was prescribed anti-anxiety medication by his doctor but his anxiety was steadily growing worse.

The first part of therapy involves establishing a good therapeutic alliance between the therapist and the client and this part was easy for Martin and myself. Martin was a very funny and personable person who had no difficulty at all in outlining his fears and the many ways they were causing him difficulty. 'I'd love to socialise and find some friends in real life – and even a girlfriend – but I just can't face going out and meeting random strangers. I don't even know how to get off the starting blocks; I can't do small talk, it just crucifies me.'

Martin was 24 years old and spent most of his waking hours gaming. He still lived with his parents and worked from home in a tech job. By the time he came to see me most of his contact with people was online. Although he spoke to plenty of people online, beyond the virtual world, he didn't meet anyone other than his family. Martin loved his work but in many ways it had exacerbated his social anxiety as he didn't have to meet people any more.

As counselling progressed, I began to give Martin some small tasks to complete during the week. The first task was to go into the small shop near my clinic and buy a bar of chocolate. Martin avoided it the first couple of weeks but then I offered to go in with him and this offer galvanised him on some level – he suddenly thought he could do it. In he went without further ado and came back jubilantly with the chocolate held high. From then on we worked together to figure out appropriate challenges that Martin should face. Most of these tasks involved Martin entering anonymous places where no one knew him as he wasn't up to meeting anyone he knew just yet.

Over time, Martin became accustomed to facing his fears. With that he decided it was time to terminate therapy. I wondered aloud if this was another avoidance strategy as he still hadn't managed to socialise or make any friends in real life yet – neither had he rekindled past friendships, even though he had spoken about his wish to do this.

Martin assured me that this wasn't avoidance at all and that he knew what he was doing. My professional training and my own gut instinct reminded me that ultimately the client knows best and so I wished Martin well.

The months rolled by and then I received an email from Martin outlining how he hadn't moved forward at all. When he came back to therapy for a second time he was very different. This time he knew that a certain level of active participation would be required from him and he also knew that, no matter how he avoided doing these tasks, as his therapist, I was never really going to let it go. This time round Martin didn't bother using avoidance-coping strategies or excuses to tell me why he hadn't performed any agreed task – he either did it or he didn't. And if he didn't he had gained enough self-compassion to say, 'I was just too nervous.'

Consequently the therapy moved along much more quickly and Martin became willing to try more difficult tasks such as attending a local football match where there were bound to be people he knew and lots of small talk. Martin joined his local gym and started attending regularly, and it was a small start. He also joined a film club and began going to films every Tuesday night and from this he was invited to become part of the local film festival. As Martin's social life slowly but surely began to widen, we both happily came to the conclusion that he no longer needed therapy.

OBSESSIVE-COMPULSIVE DISORDER (OCD)

OCD occurs when a person gets caught in a cycle of obsessions and compulsions. Unwanted, intrusive thoughts, images or urges that trigger intensely distressing feelings characterise this disorder and it can have very severe ramifications for the sufferer and their loved ones and friends. The author Bryony Gordon eloquently described how she had suffered from anxiety and OCD since she was 12 years old and the extraordinary impact that this had on her life in her book *Mad Girl: A Happy Life with a Mixed-up Mind*. OCD can play tricks on your mind and can lead people to behave in a manner that is very hard to understand. Gordon herself describes how she used to take her iron to work with her every day so that she didn't have to suffer intrusive thoughts that she had left the iron on at home. 'And not just a normal iron – a steam iron,' she said. 'You know those big steam irons that go in a dock and look as if they're going to go into space? Which was ridiculous, because I didn't even iron.'[38]

OCD can wreak havoc on a person's life and often their loved ones feel condemned to helplessly watch the horror unfold as the sufferer becomes ever more determined to engage in this ritualistic behaviour in the hope that it brings a sense of calm. But these rituals seldom bring calm – just as the chronic alcoholic says 'I'm never drunk but I'm seldom sober', the OCD sufferer will argue that the rituals might not bring calm but they stave off terror.

When the travel writer Laurie Gough's father died in 2012, her soccer-loving ten-year-old, Quinn, was suddenly transformed into a 'near-stranger dominated by bizarre rules of magical thinking all designed to bring his grandpa back to life'. Laurie read everything she could about OCD and figured out that her son's anxiety stemmed from his unwillingness to grasp the finality of his grandpa's death. In an elaborate bid to avoid dealing with his grandpa's death, 'the OCD Monster' was his way of feeling in control in the world. Quinn engaged in tapping behaviour, counting and other ritualistic behaviours 'making things even' (also known as symmetry rituals). Laurie gives a powerful account of her son's OCD in her book *Stolen Child* and on the website www.theocdstories.com.[39] She describes how she became intrigued by the writings of the cognitive scientist

Jim Davies as he explained that being able to detect patterns in the world has been crucial to our survival; how, in the wild, being alert to patterns can be the difference between living and dying.

> The more I read the more puzzled I became by the compulsive behaviours themselves. Where did they come from? A new behaviour I'd noticed was that Quinn had to leave a room by the exact route he'd used to enter it, sometimes even walking backwards, retracing his steps. This in itself wasn't any more unusual than his other baffling behaviours, but what I found intriguing was that this one, like making things even, seemed so common for people with OCD. Quinn called it erasing. According to the OCD Foundation, erasing, cancelling, and undoing are all common OCD compulsions.

The science writer Michael Shermer also interested Gough as he explored how we're descended from hominids who were the most successful at detecting patterns. According to Shermer, the ability to detect patterns helped our species to survive and perhaps people with OCD are detecting patterns in some sort of atavistic primal instinct to survive.

Many rituals, be they religious rituals, spells, curses or witchcraft, form the basis for superstition and magical thinking and Shermer also posited that many OCD rituals are reminiscent of these rituals. As Gough wrote:

> I was reminded of this every time Quinn placed his hand on his heart, looked up at the sky and started chanting: 'Please come back, please come back, I love you, please come back,' over and over. Where did he get this hand-on-heart, heaven-gazing chant behaviour? Certainly not from his nonreligious upbringing. It

made me think of Catholics making the sign of the cross on their hearts and saying Hail Marys while counting rosary beads, all in the hopes of making something happen, or warding evil away. Other religious rituals that curiously resemble OCD rituals include numerology and counting, repetition of mantras, hours of body cleansing, and rules on how to enter and leave holy places. Not performing these rituals leaves the religious participant and the OCD sufferer with a sense of dread. Where do these religious rituals originate and why do people with OCD – even little kids who know nothing of religion – also perform them? Nobody seems to know.

Weighed down in sorrow by her son's distress, a glimmer of hope was lit one day when her husband Rob bounced into the room with news about a therapeutic approach called exposure and response prevention (ERP) that could help their boy. ERP is a programme of exposure therapy that is used specifically for OCD. This is a variation of exposure therapy where the solution lies in refraining from using your avoidance tactics to escape from distressing thoughts, feelings or behaviours. Not only are you exposed to the feared stimulus but you refrain from using any avoidance strategies within the therapy sessions and in between sessions too.

The American Psychiatric Association recommends ERP for the treatment of OCD as it offers the best results.[40] Although this therapy can seem brutal and very cruel in the short term, just like chemotherapy or other equally brutalising but effective treatments, the long-term reduction in obsessive and compulsive symptoms make the treatment worthwhile.[41] It wasn't all plain sailing – the improvements were gradual and sometimes the therapy didn't progress at all and Laurie wondered whether she would ever see her giggly, fun-loving boy again. Rob and Laurie became like ghosts, so traumatised were they by the 'OCD Monster' but then Laurie made the decision to reach out to her friends and neighbours describing how their little boy was in trouble and they needed help. The community in their little Quebec village rallied round and this also made a huge difference to the Gough family.

And then, one day, Laurie couldn't find Quinn in the house and she went outside and came across her boy singing at the very top of a tree in their garden. When she asked him what he had been doing, he explained to his mummy in a strong calm voice that he sang 'Somewhere Over the Rainbow' to his grandpa and then he 'let him go'.

> I'd realise later that letting his grandpa go up in the tree that day healed something that was broken in his heart. The OCD Monster was still quietly slithering in the pathways of his brain, but the fight was now on. What came next would be a final battle bordering on the miraculous … It has been three years and the OCD Monster has never made a comeback.[42]

Although OCD can be all-consuming, for some sufferers it vanishes and never returns.

HEALTH ANXIETY

People who are affected by health anxiety become obsessively preoccupied with the idea that they are suffering from a physical illness. Dr Google is the worst enemy of a person with health anxiety as it's so easy to look up symptoms, then find obscure results that fit your current anxiety. Just as there are pro-anorexia sites, there are many forums available where other sufferers of health anxiety will confirm your greatest fears and agree with you that the doctors know nothing and are useless. This, of course, triggers your emotional brain, confirms your cognitive distortions and is *very bad* for your anxiety. If you have health anxiety you will need to put some serious controls on your use of media and tech – it is no accident that the growth in the number of people suffering from health anxiety has coincided with the growth of the internet.[43] Imagine if you had to seek illnesses to match your complaints from a big, heavy, wordy encyclopaedia instead of a forum filled with people convincing you that your worst fears are probably right and that your doctor knows nothing. Your health anxiety probably wouldn't be quite as active.

The following questions are a good checklist for anyone wondering whether they are experiencing health anxiety:[44]

* Do you spend a lot of time thinking about your health?
* Do you think there is something seriously wrong with your body despite evidence to the contrary?
* Is it difficult for you to focus on anything other than your health?
* Do you get annoyed if someone tells you that you look well when you feel ill?
* Do you find that you are ultra-sensitive to your bodily functions?
* Do you get the impression that your loved ones and the professionals aren't taking your illnesses seriously enough?
* Do you feel irritated when your doctor tells you that there is nothing wrong with you?
* Do you spend a lot of time thinking that you are over-anxious but could still be right about this illness?

If you have health anxiety and you wake in the morning with a numb hand, you don't consider that you might have slept on it; you immediately rush into worrying about multiple sclerosis and motor neurone disease.

An interesting intervention for a person with health anxiety is to focus for five minutes on one part of your body such as your left hand or right foot; after five minutes you will notice a tingling sensation in that part of the body. This illustrates how, with enough focus, our minds can create worrying symptoms.

Rather than speaking about symptoms, which generally only makes you feel more anxious, going to therapy and talking around your greatest fears about the symptom is a good way to overcome health anxiety – this gives you the opportunity to give voice to your innermost fears and learn what is driving you and what is underpinning your anxiety.

What are you avoiding when you have health anxiety?

Usually a person with health anxiety is projecting their fears onto whatever illness they have fixated upon. Perhaps a sister has died from cancer and so you become obsessed with cancer; perhaps you were in a car crash and have become consumed with thoughts of random and frightening accidents. If you can speak with an understanding counsellor about the underlying concerns that drive you to worry about health issues, you will soon find that your obsession with symptoms subsides.

POST–TRAUMATIC STRESS DISORDER

Post-traumatic stress disorder (PTSD) is triggered as a result of experiencing or witnessing a terrifying event. There are many symptoms that characterise PTSD, including:

- ❖ Flashbacks
- ❖ Nightmares

❖ Panic attacks

❖ Invasive memories of the event

❖ Extreme physical reactions to reminders of the event

❖ Loss of interest in daily life

❖ Feeling numb and detached

❖ Amnesia

With a condition as serious as PTSD, it is essential to go to therapy to help manage these difficult issues. Graded exposure often works with PTSD, for example, the therapist might ask the sufferer to recall the traumatic experience in a bid to reduce the fearful feelings. With some time and effort the person begins to get a grip on their anxiety and establishes in their brain that the fear is worse than the reality.

Some psychologists and mental health professionals advise clients to write down carefully and completely any memories that cause them extreme emotion. With enough attention to detail and repetitive analysis, these memories might stop having such an effect on them. This exercise can be difficult and make the trauma sufferer very anxious, but with the right support, it is highly unlikely that anything deeper than nasty feelings will come of it.[45] The aim is that emotional maturity arises from the process as the person learns to confront their more difficult emotions.

Eye movement desensitisation and reprocessing (EMDR) is a therapeutic approach that asks the sufferer to recall distressing images while generating a type of bilateral sensory input, such as side-to-side eye movements or hand tapping. This approach is designed to reduce negative feelings relating to the traumatic event by using rapid rhythmic eye movements. It should only be utilised under the care of an experienced therapist.

People with PTSD often try to avoid cues that remind them of their trauma but although they might avoid triggering their memory by, for instance, avoiding watching a violent film, it is often quite difficult to predict what will end up being a trigger. For example, a sufferer could be triggered by some random sight, sound or smell around them.

PHOBIAS

Phobias are an excessive fear reaction characterised by a deep sense of dread or panic about something quite specific. The impact of a phobia can range from irritating to severely disabling. Quite often, a sufferer can easily avoid the source of their phobia without it seriously interfering with their lives. Irrational phobias such as consecotaleophobia (a fear of chopsticks) and triskaidekaphobia (fear of the number 13) are probably easy enough to avoid and so there is, perhaps, a valid argument for not bothering to do the work required to confront and overcome these phobias.

I had a phobia of mice that didn't impact my life at all until I moved to the country. For a period of time I needed to learn to move my irrational, extreme reaction to mice to a more rational place of reasonable distaste. I still don't like mice, but with a bit of effort I've changed the irrational, screaming phobia to a more rational aversion that I can handle. We have now moved back to urban living so seldom come across mice but I've taught my kids to dispose of any dead mice our cat brings in. This is a situation I can live with so I don't have to bother trying to conquer this milder phobia. And so, if the avoidance doesn't interfere with your day-to-day life and/or is fairly rational (such as a fear of snakes), it is unlikely to significantly impact your wellbeing in the long term – as with everything in life, moderation and balance are crucial.

It is when your phobia interferes with your daily functioning or when your avoidance strategies are irrational, impair functioning or hinder progress towards long-term goals that you should probably be encouraged to expose yourself to the feared object or situation. This exposure can be a structured and therapeutic approach or it can be a commitment from the anxious individual to slowly challenge their fears.

What avoidance-coping strategies work for phobias?

The phobic person tends to believe something truly dreadful will happen if they cannot avoid the feared object or situation, for instance, getting in a lift or walking through an open field. Finding a counsellor to guide you through a slow process of exposure will demonstrate that this avoidance is a falsehood that mostly serves to make you feel worse in the long term.

THE PLEASURE PRINCIPLE

Sigmund Freud described the 'pleasure principle' as the way we instinctively seek pleasure and avoid pain in a bid to satisfy our biological and psychological needs. According to Freud, we only achieve maturity when we learn to endure the pain of *deferred* gratification. When we consider anxiety, it is quite clear how we are motivated to quell our anxiety through the pleasure principle and how it could be beneficial to learn how to defer gratifying our instinct to avoid the pain of our anxiety.

In July 2018, Dr Harry Barry and the CBT therapist Enda Murphy spoke on RTÉ Radio One about Freud's pleasure principle in relation to feelings of anxiety and frustration.[46] Dr Barry highlighted the way anxiety comes about when a person is seeking certainty in the world and they become frustrated when they can't change the world to suit them better. Barry identified three pertinent questions to ask ourselves that will teach us how to adapt in a positive way to emotional upheaval:

1. What is my long-term goal here? What do I want to achieve?
2. What is my short-term discomfort? What short-term discomfort am I trying to avoid?
3. What changes in my thinking and behaviour do I need to change to achieve my objective?

Essentially, this means that we need to choose our poison: we can avoid the anxiety until we are ready to begin the process of recovery or, alternatively, we can go through a certain level of specific short-term pain and confront this pain. The way we do this is by exposing ourselves, in a therapeutic context, to a situation that may cause discomfort but will ultimately bring about longer-lasting beneficial changes in our psyche.

USING DISTRACTION AS A SHORT-TERM STRATEGY

Sometimes there comes a time when we know all about our inner demons, thank you very much, but we still need the sticking plaster on the wound just to get us through this specific day. At times like this, distraction is a helpful way to interrupt our anxious thoughts and symptoms and this can prevent the snowflake forming a snowball or an avalanche of anxiety.

When people are beginning to recover from anxiety, they sometimes use a million different strategies that keep them from avoiding the source of the fear, and this is perfectly fine. For example, you might stay where you are and restrain yourself from running away – but to ensure you don't explode in panic, you use *minor* avoidance strategies so you don't opt for the *major* avoidance strategy and just stay home.

For example, Annie used to avoid her work meetings because she couldn't face the anxiety she would feel. When she started therapy she used to force herself to attend these meetings, even for five minutes, as a way to break through this avoidance. To help her remain longer at the meeting, Annie would silently repeat an old poem that she had learned in school, just as a way of remaining in situ and not breaking for the border. She would also distract herself by counting patterns on the wall and counting people. Over time, with support from her therapist, Annie lost her reliance on short-term strategies and developed a new-found confidence from learning to stay longer and longer at these meetings. Whenever she felt completely overwhelmed Annie would excuse herself and go to the toilets where she would catch up on social media as a way to distract herself from her mental anguish. Finding a way to distract herself enough so that she could stop thinking about how everyone was judging her worked for Annie as she slowly but surely learned to confront her fears.

Dr Harry Barry recommends that some people who suffer from panic attacks should get out their phones and text their feelings to their therapist; other CBT therapists recommend that we should wear a rubber band on our wrists to flick every time we fall into our old destructive habits to remind us to think differently. Indeed, there are a million different ways to distract yourself – some people listen to music, count, sing to themselves or chatter away excitedly to whoever is near them as they enter a situation that is causing great anxiety. This can be a very effective way to make sure you enter the situation, training your brain gets you accustomed to the experience and so after some time you may not need to use these distraction tactics any more.

OVERCOMING 'AVOIDANCE COPING'

'Avoidance coping'[47] is the behaviour we choose when we try to escape from our anxious feelings. This can involve 'doing' – for example, someone who cleans excessively to escape fear of contamination – or 'not doing', for example avoiding someone because we can't face saying hello. The problem is that avoidance causes anxiety to snowball because the act of avoiding creates and reinforces the anxiety.

The following examples show the complicated ramifications of avoidance strategies:

* ❖ People who suffer from panic attacks engage in avoidance coping by avoiding certain places, but the more they try to avoid situations that trigger their panicky feelings, the more situations trigger their panicky feelings. It soon becomes a vicious, ever-decreasing circle.
* ❖ People who over-think are often engaging in avoidance coping when they become mentally obsessed with x as a means to avoid thinking about y. The y in this scenario is usually complex and distressing feelings of uncertainty. So when Lynn suspected her new husband of having an affair, she became obsessed with her looks as a way to avoid thinking about the destruction of her marriage.
* ❖ People with OCD avoid fear and uncertainty by channelling their fears into things like excessive cleaning or tapping or counting, but the more they do this, the more their lives become consumed by their behaviour and the less likely they are to understand or be aware of the underlying issues that prompt the anxious feelings in the first place.
* ❖ People who constantly ask for reassurance engage in avoidance coping by avoiding their own feelings and looking externally

– to other people – for reassurance instead of exploring deep inside. This can then create further distress as the other person becomes irritated by the constant need for reassurance. So when Sophie constantly asked her friends for reassurance, over time they became fed up with her neediness and began to belittle her as a result of feeling irritated and bored.

These three steps are an effective approach to recovering from avoidance coping:

1. Recognise that avoidance doesn't work.

Accept that you have used avoidance-coping strategies and recognise that this is your automatic go-to tool. Challenge yourself with the following questions: What are the feelings and thoughts that you are trying to avoid? Are you feeling afraid? Awkward? Anxious? Are you thinking that you're not good enough?

2. Recognise how much avoidance is costing you.

How much time and mental energy have you wasted using avoidance strategies? How has this impacted your wellbeing? Your relationships? Your sense of yourself as a competent human being?

3. Build your tolerance for distressing thoughts and feelings.

Building the ability to tolerate distress is a key step for everybody recovering from anxiety. If you can learn to endure uncomfortable feelings or thoughts then you will soon learn how these thoughts are temporary; they will pass and you will soon feel better. A good way to do this is by following these steps:

❖ Prepare yourself for the anxiety that will inevitably arrive at your door. This will automatically decrease your anxiety; if you kid yourself that your anxiety will never return, the deep disappointment that you experience when it does return can be devastating.

❖ Learn to soften rather than tense yourself in response to anything that triggers your anxiety – soften your body, jaw, belly and facial muscles and soften your thoughts and feelings.

❖ Learn some physiological self-soothing skills, such as these: slow breathing will slow your heart rate down; going outside into nature and noticing movement such as the trees swaying in the breeze or the clouds scudding through the sky will distract you; running one or two fingers over your lips will stimulate the parasympathetic nervous system. This is sometimes called the 'rest and digest system' as it slows the heart rate and helps the body to conserve energy. A technique called progressive muscle relaxation will also distract you by forcing you to focus on different muscles. Slow your thoughts from hot to cool; sit with yourself; slow your movements down. Be like water. (See Chapter 8 for more detailed descriptions.)

❖ Learn to recognise that your thoughts are often distorted by your emotional brain and so are unreliable. Regard your thoughts as a particularly verbose unreliable gossip who has an agenda. This chatterbox will succeed in making you feel awful but seldom has anything constructive to add to the conversation.

❖ Build your capacity to self-regulate – this is like going on a diet. You need to commit to talking yourself down from the ledge instead of talking yourself up onto the ledge and then hoping others will talk you down. Various techniques such as slow breathing, progressive muscle relaxation, self-talk or mindfulness will help with this (see Chapter 8).

❖ Use 'defusion skills' to 'stop, step back and observe'. These skills relate to the ability to distance yourself and disconnect; to see thoughts and feelings for what they are versus what you assume them to mean. For example, you may feel filled with dread if you have to eat or drink in front of people. If you can 'stop, step back and observe' you can notice what's happening to you: your thoughts are speeding up, you are physically tensing your body, your amygdala has been triggered and now you're in fight or flight mode. The combination of all this makes you think that you need to run for the hills. The more you can defuse your thoughts by noticing how you tend to catastrophise things, the easier you will find it to step away from the madness, soften your body and your thoughts, and step forward into any given situation.

WHEN EXPOSURE FAILS

Of course, when it comes to the human psyche, there is nothing that 'always' works and one size definitely doesn't fit all. Yet, in my work, I have noticed certain themes emerging for people who don't connect well with exposure therapy. The most common reason is that the anxious person tries too much too soon and then loses faith in the process when it doesn't work. Once a person loses faith in the process, it can be very difficult to start again and it is usually more effective to try another approach.

Another problem with exposure therapy is that in the early stages, you can feel worse before you feel better. Nancy Tucker is a young author who has experienced serious mental illness and her highly acclaimed book on this subject highlights this issue: 'During this phase, you can expect to feel perpetually uneasy – it's a great sign that the seeds are firmly embossed!'[48] It can make all the difference if the anxious person expects the cure to be difficult. Nobody likes feeling 'perpetually uneasy' and not many people enjoy the challenges that need to be experienced if a person is to recover from feeling anxious.

But sometimes we need to take the medicine, however brutal, if we are to recover and be freed from a lifetime of pain.

When Ally came to me for counselling to help her combat her performance anxiety, she decided, in the first session, to confront her fears head-on and attend a wedding that she had been dreading. I wondered if this baptism by fire would be too much, but Ally assured me that she simply had to go for it, that fear and anxiety had been ruining her life for too long. Jumping in the deep end didn't work for Ally and she suffered the first of many panic attacks at this wedding. For the next few months in therapy, there was little point in Ally continuing to face her fears as the panic attacks were coming fast and furious, so I tried a different tack and focused on guided meditation and cultivating more pleasurable activities in Ally's life.

A common reason why exposure to the fear ends up being ineffective or even damaging is when the person flees the scene before their anxiety levels drop. This means that the idea that this is a fearsome and dangerous situation becomes further entrenched in the amygdala because there has been no opportunity to teach the amygdala that it is tolerably awful. Some situations don't last long enough to have the opportunity to retrain the amygdala because the event is over in a matter of seconds. If you have difficulty finding opportunities to face prolonged exposure to the triggering situation then it can be useful if you contrive to find similar situations so that you get the chance to practise and retrain your emotional brain.

Equally, exposure therapy can be ineffectual when a person doesn't practise it enough for the amygdala to get the chance to retrain the brain to learn new associations for perceptions of the event. This was the case when Philip came to me for help with his panic attacks on special first dates. Philip was in search of love and was using online dating apps to find a partner. He was an extrovert type and he was perfectly confident when he didn't particularly fancy his date – it was only when he fancied his date that he would become anxious and sweaty, given to nervous laughter and generally nothing like the suave, sophisticated person he wanted to present. It is relatively difficult to give the amygdala the opportunity to retrain for such a specific occasion and so this was a challenge.

In a bid to help Philip process his fears, I told him the story of the world-renowned American psychologist Dr Albert Ellis, who over the course of one summer approached more than 100 women in the Bronx's Botanical Gardens and asked them for a date.

Dr Ellis had spent much time admiring good-looking females in the Botanical Gardens but, suffering from a severe form of social anxiety and a petrifying fear of rejection, he had never approached any of them. Ellis had read a lot of philosophy and psychology and was well versed in the benefits of exposing yourself to fear. And so, during the month of August 1932, when Ellis was 19 years old and in his senior year of college, he set himself the task of approaching more than 100 women over the course of a month. In the end he approached about 130 women and although about 30 women of these women walked away from Ellis, the remaining 100 spoke to him about various subjects and one woman agreed to go on a date. Sadly, this woman didn't actually turn up for the scheduled date.

The good news was that all that effort turned out to be enough to cure Ellis of his social anxiety. He went on to develop a highly successful form of therapy known as rational emotive behavioural therapy (REBT) and he became one of the most influential psychotherapists of the twentieth century. He wrote many critically acclaimed books, including *How to Control Your Anxiety Before it Controls You*, and is now considered one of the grandfathers of CBT.

My client Philip was intrigued by this story and began to read a lot about Albert Ellis and his work. He went on more dates. We soon figured out that it was a fear of rejection that was crippling Philip so we explored this fear while at the same time Philip purposely went on lots of dates, thus exposing himself to being rejected. Ellis's story gave Philip heart as he found he could cope better knowing it was a common and understandable fear. Although Philip will always be triggered when he is faced with rejection, he now knows enough about himself to book some counselling whenever he feels rejected: that is enough for him to stay on the tracks.

CONCLUSION: FACING THE DRAGONS

When we are faced with distress, it is much more helpful to turn and face the dragons, for if we don't give ourselves the opportunity to become dragon-slayers, we will never know how much power is available within us. The acclaimed writer Andrew Solomon explained this much more eloquently in his seminal book *Far from the Tree:*

> If you banish the dragons, you banish the heroes – and we become attached to the heroic strain in our personal history. We choose our own lives. It is not simply that we decide on the behaviours that construct our experience; when given our druthers, we elect to be ourselves. Most of us would like to be more successful or more beautiful or wealthier, and most people endure episodes of low self-esteem or even self-hatred. We despair a hundred times a day. But we retain the startling evolutionary imperative for the fact of ourselves, and with that splinter of grandiosity we redeem our flaws.[49]

PART 2

HOW THE WORLD IS MAKING US ANXIOUS

CHAPTER 4

Always on: The age of anxiety

'The shocking fact is that most ill health now comes from our lifestyle.'[50]

PROFESSOR DÓNAL O'SHEA

ave a look at the statistics in the list below.

- ☆ About one in five people experience a mental health issue in any given year.[51]
- ☆ Anxiety disorder is the most common mental illness in Ireland, Britain and the United States.[52]
- ☆ Roughly 40 million adults, 18.1 per cent of the population of the United States, have been diagnosed with an anxiety disorder.[53]
- ☆ With the exception of PTSD, women are twice as likely as men to suffer from anxiety disorders.[54]
- ☆ Anxiety disorders are highly treatable, yet only approximately 36.9 per cent of those suffering receive treatment.[55]
- ☆ Anxiety is the biggest issue facing young Irish adults today.[56]
- ☆ There has been a 1,200 per cent increase in diagnoses of anxiety since 1980.[57]

☆ More than one in ten people are likely to have a 'disabling anxiety disorder' at some stage in their lives.[58]

☆ At present 40 per cent of disability worldwide is due to depression and anxiety.[59]

Professor Jim Lucey of St Patrick's Hospital has said that we are 'living in an age of anxiety'.[60] Notwithstanding the fact that professionals have become better at diagnosing and that our normal and natural existential worries are now being clinically diagnosed as mental health disorders, the fact remains that higher numbers are experiencing anxiety. Although there are many and varied explanations, psychologists, psychiatrists and researchers broadly agree that it is mostly our toxic lifestyle that is making us sick.[61]

This is why, although it is undoubtedly important to ascertain *how* we are all more anxious, it is also important to explore *why* we are more anxious so that we can to reconfigure our stress–inducing lifestyles.[62]

WHO'S GETTING ANXIOUS?

Well, we're all getting more anxious, but some are getting more anxious than others. Anxiety is an affliction that is heavily influenced by gender, age and class. There has been a 70 per cent increase in depression and anxiety among teenagers over the past 25 years in the UK.[63] Record numbers of third–level students are seeking help for challenges to their mental health and, with 40 per cent of Irish students seeking counselling for anxiety, it is the single biggest issue of concern among the demographic.[64] Over the last decade there has been a 68 per cent rise in the number of girls hospitalised owing to anxiety and depression–related self–harm. A UK government report in 2016 suggested that more middle–class children were reporting anxiety than any other demographic.[65]

Research from the University of Cambridge shows that adults under 35 are more prone to experiencing anxiety attacks and women are almost twice as likely as men to be diagnosed with anxiety disorders.[66] The author of the study, Oliva Remes, suggested that women could be more anxious because of a spike in female progesterone and oestrogen levels, which influence our moods and create a heightened sense of responsibility. However, as the writer Megan Nolan – herself a sufferer – pointed out:

> From one perspective, it's unsurprising that women experience so much anxiety. We are socially encouraged to be fearful, to present ourselves as vulnerable, and are encouraged not to be strident and aggressive. Given the expectation that we act as emotional beings, it may be easier for us to confess to the fear and dread that characterise anxiety.[67]

Many, many factors play a part in the rising tide of people seeking support to help them deal with their anxiety – lack of resilience, problem-solving skills and coping mechanisms to handle normal life challenges are most often highlighted by mental health professionals as elements that contribute to the rise of anxiety among young people today. However, the most common reason offered is usually stress: our busy, perfectionistic and materialistic lifestyles are the key factor in all this emotional distress.

THE DISEASE OF BEING BUSY

I don't consider myself a naturally anxious person but it seems anxiety is touching almost everybody these days and, just like almost everyone else, I too have noticed that now, more than ever before, I find myself becoming overwhelmed by anxiety and panic about how much 'stuff' I have to do every day. And the latest research suggests that most of us are feeling as I do. When we look at the symptoms of anxiety – racing thoughts, panic, uneasiness, sleep problems, heart palpitations, shortness of breath and being unable to stay calm or still – we can see how our fast culture is feeding this disorder. Doing too much is a sure-fire path to anxiety; it overworks the brain and it makes it more likely that our emotional brain will be triggered. Too many people are trying – and failing – to do too much and the upshot of all this effort is an epidemic of stress and anxiety.

Omid Safi wrote about 'the disease of being busy':

> I saw a dear friend a few days ago. I stopped by to ask her how she was doing, how her family was. She looked up, voice lowered, and just whimpered: 'I'm so busy … I am so busy … have so much going on.' …
>
> And it's not just adults. When we moved to North Carolina we went to one of the friendly neighbors, asking if their daughter and our daughter could get together and play. The mother, a really lovely person, reached for her phone and pulled out the calendar function. She scrolled… and scrolled… and scrolled. She finally said: 'She has a 45-minute opening two and half weeks from now. The rest of the time it's gymnastics, piano, and voice lessons. She's just … so busy.'
>
> Horribly destructive habits start early, really early.
>
> How did we end up living like this? Why do we do this to ourselves? Why do we do this to our children? When did we forget that we are human beings, not human doings?[68]

LIVING IN A MATERIAL WORLD

According to the psychologist Oliver James, our continuous mission to have bigger and better is making us more stressed and anxious: 'Nearly all of us want bigger and better,' he says.

Houses, breast implants, penis extensions, televisions, cars. We define our lives through earnings, possessions, appearances, celebrity and it's making us more miserable than ever before. The bad news is that a quarter of British people have been mentally ill in the last 12 months and another quarter have been on the verge. The good news is that it doesn't have to be that way.[69]

Although mental illness averages at 23 per cent among Americans, Britons, Irish, Australians, New Zealanders and Canadians it is interesting that challenges to mental health average at a more respectable 11.5 per cent among Germans, Italians, French, Spaniards, Belgians and Dutch.[70] The difference that James identified is that the English-speaking nations place a higher value on money, possessions, appearance and fame than the non-English-speaking nations and this leads to greed, inequality, unrealistic aspirations and unfulfilled expectations which in turn lead directly to unhappiness.

We live in a society that promotes the notion that 'you're worth it' and if you want to feel good about yourself you should 'give yourself a treat' – i.e. you should buy something to make yourself feel better. The anxious feeling garnered from being too busy can often lead to depression, so in an attempt to stave off these overwhelming feelings, we book a hair appointment or we buy ourselves something that makes us feel special. This, of course, ensures that we continue to work too much and spend too much. All the while ignoring the fact that the passing thrill is just another way to avoid the reality that our lives are becoming unmanageable.

It is human nature to want something that we cannot have and the marketing world indicates that being busy and difficult to access is the way forward. The moment I became fully booked in my practice was also the moment my stock suddenly went up among potential clients as they preferred to remain on a waiting list than take my fervent recommendations to see another therapist.

TIME MANAGEMENT?

The general consensus seems to be that if we could manage our time effectively we would win the game. But the truth is that the game is unwinnable; there will always be more to do and although it's possible to stay on the treadmill and squash everything in, it is usually much more important to learn how to manage your life so that you don't become a victim of our busy culture.

Often difficulties with time management are rooted in a mismatch between what you expect of yourself and what you actually get done in the time allotted. Can you take the pressure off yourself by lowering your expectations? Can you begin to factor extra time into your day so that you aren't always feeling that you're behind schedule?

Paul Roberts pointed out in his polemical *The Impulse Society: What's Wrong with Getting What We Want?*, 'An economy reoriented to give us what we want, it turns out, isn't the best for delivering what we *need*. The more efficient we have got at gratifying individual desire, the worse we have become at satisfying other, longer-term *social* necessities.'[71]

If we look at how the interior architecture of our homes has changed in recent years we can see how our so-called needs have moved far beyond anything near a need and instead look very like the maddened whims of a crazed oligarch. In the 1980s most people would have been proud to own a house with a garden. The cladding, number of rooms and extra additions might have been a feather in your cap, but most ordinary people weren't prepared to kill themselves working for these extras. This attitude has changed, though, and over time it has now become all about the trimmings – the necessities are assumed and the extras are where it's at.

In the 1990s, conservatories became a desirable addition to our houses, so many people took out loans and worked harder in their bid to build one. We now know that they are often the most underused and difficult to heat room in the house. In the early noughties there was a marked trend for outside decking, patio heating and even outdoor jacuzzis. Now, in 2018, the new trophy home is all about bi-folding sliding French doors to create the 'inside outside' feel. Not only that, but random additions such as spacious walk-in wardrobes, overhead rainfall showers and handless push-and-glide drawers are suddenly considered key attractions among prospective house buyers. Kitchens are now so luxurious that we have moved far beyond the ubiquitous kitchen island to enjoy double ovens, steam ovens and warming drawers.

But we are paying for all this – and in more ways than one – because the net result of all this extra fabulousness is that many of us are becoming stressed and anxious by working too hard to fund a needlessly materialistic life.

CURING YOURSELF OF THE 'BUSY DISEASE'

Let's look at a few tweaks you can make to free yourself from the disease of being busy. Make a list of what you need to do less of and what you would like to do more of. Identify days of the week and times of the day that can be safeguarded for these activities.

Less ...

❖ Time on social media – limit to 6 a.m.–7 a.m. and 6 p.m.–7 p.m.

❖ Answering emails – limit to twice a day – once in the morning and once in the evening.

❖ Working – can you ask for reduced hours?

More ...

❖ Hanging out with friends – be proactive and ring-fence specific days to meet friends.

❖ Pottering in the house – ring-fence Sundays as a pyjama-and-potter day.

❖ Having baths – declare a weekly bath night, just for you.

TRYING TO CONTROL THE UNCONTROLLABLE

Permanent jobs are on the decline, mortgages and house ownership are beyond many people's reach and the net result is a feeling of impermanence and anxiety – nothing feels solid and everything is movable. This triggers our brains to seek some form of certainty in an increasingly uncertain world. This is why you might find yourself disregarding the impossible problem of buying your own home and instead suddenly fixate on some smaller problem that seems much more manageable, such as your personal grooming or your social media profile. Anything that will provide a quick hit of feeling on top of things can seem attractive and calming in comparison to the vast problem of managing a future career or buying your own home. But of course that's a lie – these are only distracting and shallow hits for our ego – the true pathway to calm is to learn to *live with uncertainty*.

Wait! Before you throw the book at the wall, I know exactly how infuriating it is to hear we must learn to live with uncertainty; I know how much more attractive it would be to be told 'Here's a strategy that will give you the keys to the kingdom and make you feel all calm and Zen inside' and yet, deep down, we all know that there is no strategy; that no one has really figured out the secret of life and only snake-oil salesmen are still peddling that particular dream.

All we can do is learn to stumble along in our bumbling way. The reality of life is quite pedestrian: if we can protect our wellbeing, learn to handle conflict and find some meaning in our lives, then we will find that we can enjoy our lives much more than when we mindlessly allowed stress and tension to take over. As Matt Haig says in *Reasons to Stay Alive*:

> The world is increasingly designed to depress us. Happiness isn't very good for the economy. If we were happy with what we had, why would we need more? How do you sell an anti-ageing moisturiser? You make someone worry about ageing … How do you get them to buy insurance? By making them worry about everything. How do you get them to have plastic surgery? By highlighting their physical flaws. How do you get them to watch a TV show? By making them worry about missing out … To be calm becomes a kind of revolutionary act. To be happy with your own non-upgraded existence. To be comfortable with our messy, human selves would not be good for business.

ARE WE MINDLESSLY WORKING TOO MUCH?

In 1930 the economist John Maynard Keynes famously predicted that technological advances would mean that by the year 2030, most people would work a 15-hour week and that our standards of living would rise significantly.[72] What Keynes missed in this prediction is that our levels of competitive consumption would rise so powerfully and so, today, the averagely ambitious young adult feels that they cannot afford to live a life where they are free to enjoy their friends and family instead of spending many years slaving away at the office at their job. Indeed, this life where we could expect to work fewer and fewer hours seems as far away as ever.

And yet we could have gone in that direction – the many technological innovations developed around Keynes's time sold us the promise of an easier life. And in the 1950s and 1960s well-off, middle-class people appeared to lead fairly easy lives – the age of convenience arrived and with that housewives were suddenly freed from the terrible drudgery of relentless housework. Daddy went to work, Mammy stayed at home and minded the children and the family could afford to live well on only one income.

Second-wave feminism beginning in the 1960s and lasting through to the 1980s, told women to join the workforce – and this made sense, because it was by joining the workforce that women became independent. It seems likely that a combination of a search for meaning and purpose and a desire for education and independence has supported the ever-growing rise of women joining the workforce. Yet, joining in on the pursuit of work and money hasn't provided women with much more freedom – it has merely swapped our chains from housework and drudgery to full-time work and scheduling household activities.

Today, the old model of one parent working and the other minding the children is simply not within the reach of most households. For many families, working two jobs is the only way to stay afloat and many parents work long hours and make use of their extended family and professional childcare so they can put a roof over their heads and food on the table.

The current structure of society is that a child is born and generally has the full-time care of a parent for approximately the next six months, then, usually for the next 12 years or so, the parents are under serious stress and pressure to juggle who is minding the children while they struggle to keep on top of work demands. Some lucky parents have enough money – or enough security, confidence and/ or foresight to live with less – to enable one parent to stay at home, but this parent needs to feel strong enough in themselves as society increasingly looks askance at anyone who chooses not to work for a long period of time.

Meanwhile families where both parents are working dearly hope the infants are happy in the crèche or with the child minder as they dash guiltily off to work. It is when the child becomes sick that the whole stack of cards fall and one parent – most often the mother – guiltily stays home with the baby while fretting about how their absence is perceived in their workplace, whether it will impact their career prospects and how they need to put in more hours to combat this. When the child reaches the teen years, the childcare issue may reduce but the heavy pressure is then ladled upon the kids to buckle down and work hard so that they do well in their exams, so that they can go to college, get a good career and repeat their parents' lifestyles. And so the circle continues...

CASE STUDY: ANNEMARIE, 42

'I love my work as a designer – I wouldn't be without it. But the hours are too long. I would love to be on a three-day week but my boss laughs whenever I try to bring it up. He's right of course, the company just isn't structured so that their key designer is unavailable two days a week – not only should I be there five days a week, but I am also expected to work in the evening. When I come home at 6 p.m., I collect the kids from the after-school facility and then we go home. It's always a fraught time because we have to fly through the homework – the homework club never really do it properly – then put on the dinner, eat the dinner and get the kids to bed. It's frantic and there are always fights. Then I collapse in front of the TV with my laptop open and tick away on the projects that I have to do. The weekends are spent catching up on the never-ending round of domestic stuff. It's all a bit relentless and joyless – the only time for fun seems to be the holidays, but that's not enough and, anyway, the holidays just remind me of how much I'm missing out. I don't think it's really a healthy lifestyle for my kids. I feel I'm missing out on their childhood. But what can I do?'

Late nights, conference calls, caffeine highs and sugar lows, full-time workers are accustomed to them all. Many people in full-time work are living for tomorrow and the grand plan is that one day all this hard work will pay off. Of course, work is fulfilling for some people – but it is few people who enjoy their work *and* enjoy their working hours – usually we can have one or the other but seldom enjoy both. Today, it is all too easy for our identity to be caught up in our work because this is exactly what society is telling us to do: the capitalist model tells us we need more stuff and more experiences, generating the need for people to work ever-longer hours in jobs they don't like. But too many people find their work meaningless and feel imprisoned in difficult lives. For the people who are lucky enough to work in meaningful jobs and who really enjoy the work, it is the long hours that intrude upon their wellbeing.

ARE YOU MINDLESSLY OVERWORKING?

The novelist Fay Weldon pointed out that, 'Most women don't have careers, they have jobs. They're told they have careers, because that suits the employers. "Career" is such an artificial concept. It's just people up there making money out of people down here, I'm afraid.' She's right, of course; the work many of us do really isn't that important. The world won't stop if I don't work any more – some of my clients will miss me and then find another psychotherapist; other people will write newspaper articles and books. We know it well: nobody is irreplaceable, but it suits the current employment structure for each employee to think they are vital links in the chain.

There are difficult questions to answer around this debate. If you quite like your work but the constant demands are killing you, perhaps you should move to a different job? Do you have to keep the nebulous dream of a 'satisfying career' alive? Should you perhaps look for work that suits your lifestyle instead of a vague notion of a 'successful career'?

For you, what does success look like? Is it a vaguely interesting career that is busy, busy, busy with little time off, is it lots of money or is it a satisfying and full life?

Many adults in their twenties and thirties are working longer hours and the lack of job security is causing huge levels of tension and anxiety. Zero-hour contracts and short-term contracts are creating such feelings of uncertainty that many people respond by making hay while the sun shines and so they work ever-longer hours for fear of having no work soon. How can people plan their lives or careers if they don't know whether they'll even have a job next month? As a result, the mantra has become: work, work, work, for who knows what will tomorrow bring?

David Graeber, a professor of anthropology at the London School of Economics, examined the rationale behind meaningless employment in his book *Bullshit Jobs: A Theory*.[73] Job titles such as HR consultant, communications co-ordinator, PR researcher, financial strategist and corporate lawyer are identified by Graeber as surplus to requirements: 'Technological unemployment, as [John Maynard Keynes] called it, did happen. People have been talking about the rise of robots, saying it's nonsense – people have been talking about that for years. But actually it did happen; it's just that we made up jobs for people to seem to be working.'[74] Now, according to Graeber, jobs are fetishised. If we look at the wailing and gnashing of teeth that happens around the gender pay gap we soon see how politicians, analysts and the media mindlessly presume that it is ultra-important for everyone to work very long hours. The evidence that many women don't actually want to work full-time is conveniently ignored as it is assumed that every woman between 18 and 65 (and soon it will be 70 as the age of retirement is continuously pushed back) wishes to work all the hours they possibly can.[75] The reality is that many working mothers would prefer to work three days a week. This is because when both parents work full-time, no matter how enjoyable their work is, something generally gives – and what usually gives is the mental wellbeing of the family.

Graeber's book highlights how society has arrived at a place where 'bullshit jobs' are ruling supreme while necessary jobs that contribute to society have little status; if every corporate lawyer in the world went on strike, there would be very little impact, but if every nurse in the world stopped working, the fallout would be catastrophic. So why do we pay corporate lawyers so much more than nurses? Of course, society is structured that way and it is very difficult to dismantle elaborate structures. But that doesn't mean that we, on an individual level, have to handcuff ourselves to meaningless work for the rest of our working lives.

IS WORK MAKING YOU ANXIOUS?

How can we continue to work in satisfying jobs but do shorter hours? That is the nub of the problem for many people – it seems to be easier to get a low-paid unsatisfying job in a large organisation that allows us to work fewer hours, but it is much harder to work fewer hours in a meaningful job. Meaningful jobs enrich people's lives while meaningless jobs diminish them. But meaningful jobs are so attractive to many people that the organisation behind the job can – and does – offer low pay while meaningless jobs often offer better pay. So we are caught in a trap and either condemned to work in secure jobs that have little meaning or purpose – and so make us feel stressed and discontent – or else we love our work but become anxious about how much of it there is and our lack of financial security.

As anyone who has suffered the prison of a mental health illness knows, without your mental health nothing else really matters, so we should always put our mental health first. In the same manner that passengers on a flight are advised to put on their own oxygen mask before they attend to their children's, it is not okay to put your career first and your mental health second. If you think you have to stay in a job that is causing you stress because you can't afford to survive without it, you need to think creatively about how to get out of this trap. But this needs time and space to think, and when you are working in a stressful job, time and space are usually the first casualties.

Of course, this might give some people the rage as they truly believe that there is nothing they can do and that it's easy for me to say that they have choices. Indeed, I often meet clients who tell me, 'I hate my job, I know it is making me stressed and anxious, but I can't leave it so how can I feel better and still stay in my job?' These people are usually already taking medication to combat the more severe elements of their anxiety but have found that, over time, their symptoms return. But of course they do.

However, if we allow our thought processes to open a bit wider, we will soon see that there are always other options. It's too easy to dismiss this, but all-or-nothing thinking is the royal route to mental ill health. Can you lower your standards? Perhaps you could get another job that is less stressful but pays less? Learn to spend less?

Sociologists and business analysts argue that it is an increase in consumerism and materialism, driven almost solely by capitalism, that has got in the way of a life that should have increased leisure and ease. Because working very long hours in meaningless employment doesn't only lead to stress and anxiety – it also leads to feelings of emptiness and pointlessness. We need meaning if we wish to live satisfying and purposeful lives. Way back in 1857, the writer Henry Thoreau identified this issue in his letter to Harvard alumnus Harrison Blake when he wrote: 'It is not enough to be industrious; so are the ants. What are you industrious about?'[76]

An inevitable result of all this impossible effort is anxiety in the face of overwhelming expectations and demands. Achievement is valued over wellbeing and this has created hordes of over-achievers who are ready and willing to destroy their mental health in the bid for outward success.

Unfortunately our 'winner takes all' culture creates an awful lot of disappointment as when we fail, we silently wonder what is wrong with us. But 'failure' is really quite common and the vast majority of us don't actually reach the dizzy heights that we see in the media all around us. The idea that anyone can be Bill Gates or Mark Zuckerberg is of course a fallacy that millions of people around the world currently wedded to their dreams don't recognise. And why would they? Many of the 'inspirational' messages we see on social media would lead anyone to believe that we only have to wish hard enough for something for it to happen.

For those of us who can remember the feeling of self-importance and earnest dedication that impelled us at different points to work too hard, the life and death of Pradnya Paramita, who went by the handle Mita Diran, is a cautionary tale. Paramita often tweeted about the long hours she worked in her job as a copywriter for the ad agency Y&R Group in Jakarta, Indonesia. She was a dedicated and hard-working employee who seemed to feel a mixture of pride and inevitability about her ridiculous working week. Mita clearly felt under pressure to perform – she was a very self-motivated young woman and wanted to 'take the next step' in her career. She kept her energy levels up by drinking vast quantities of Red Bull. Evidently a funny and driven young woman, she thought getting home before midnight was a victory. One of her tweets read, 'Home before midnight after three long, exhausting weeks. MISSION ACCOMPLISHED,' while another tweet read, 'Alright, one full week of going home past 2am from the office. Ladies and Gentlemen, I believe we just broke a record.' Soon after her last tweet, '30 hours of working and still going strooong', Mita Diran collapsed and died from a combination of overwork and too much Red Bull. Mita's mother, Yani Syahial, criticised the excessive work ethic that culminated in this tragedy and yet her stepfather appeared unbowed as he defended the advertising industry, saying that Mita knew what it took to succeed. Y&R Group, whose clients include Dell and Xerox, closed the office for one day to mourn the loss of their 24-year-old employee.

ALWAYS ON: HOW OUR TECH IS MAKING US ANXIOUS

Back in the day we used to have set times – nine to five, five days a week or whatever times we were offered – but now we are always semi-working and seldom properly 'off'. We now work in an infinite time-space continuum and it has created stress and pressure.[77] Work can call us anytime; we are literally never finished. No sooner do we clear out our inboxes but more messages arrive; no sooner do we read an interesting article on the internet, another five linking articles are recommended. The whole system is rigged so that we never actually feel 'done'. If you're good at your job, you'll find more work is passed your way. If you get on top of your email or social media, you'll almost immediately be sent more. It's relentless and it's bad for the psyche – the feeling of being 'done' is mentally good for us but these days it seems unattainable.

Many people may be officially working fewer hours and yet we feel much, much busier. Society, with its emphasis on expectation, appearance, materialism, branding and judgement, means that even when we are following more leisurely pursuits, we're finding them more stress-inducing.

We are digesting overwhelming amounts of information and, thanks to WiFi, we are always 'on', continuously interrupted by random pings from our tech to tell us that yet another message has come through. Advances in technology have resulted in information overload and blurred the boundaries between when we should or shouldn't contact people. Twenty years ago a phone call late at night or early in the morning constituted an emergency but nowadays we can send and receive messages any time of the day or night – and so we do.

TECH STRESS: REDUCING THE PINGS

The message from society is that being 'in demand' and busy is inherently a good thing has created a situation where most of us feel guilty if we have nothing to do. Busyness is wrongly associated with success and fulfilment and being idle is wrongly associated with dissipation and failure. Indeed, the only palatable way to be idle, according to society today, is to meditate or practise mindfulness –

something as simple and pleasant as just kicking back and spending the day pottering around the house is often frowned on these days.

All this effort creates a backlash in the body and so, as a direct result, we tend to 'relax' by vegging out in front of screens. Although it is often more accurate to call it 'collapsing'. And then the screens sell us pictures of perfect lives as we mindlessly scroll down and down in a never-ending loop of wired exhaustion. Social media is pitched perfectly at the tired and wired generation who haven't the mental brain space to engage with anything more challenging than clips of cute cats and funny memes. Of course, other sites are focused on style and beauty, which can feel like a visual holiday for our brains, but it is often hours later when we realise that we have wasted most of the evening and cut in on our much-needed hours of sleep, yet again. We then feel guilty about behaving like a slob, never mind that we've worked our heads off and this is more a state of mental collapse than slobbery. It's a vicious cycle and we need to be aware of it if we're to do anything about it.

Are you in charge of your phone or is your phone in charge of you? Take a moment to go into the settings on your phone and turn off the notifications. You don't need to know when your emails arrive; you don't need to know when someone has sent you a message on WhatsApp, LinkedIn, Facebook, Twitter, Snapchat, Instagram or anywhere else. You can check in once or twice a day or week, depending on your usage, to see if there are any messages you need to attend to and leave it at that. If the very idea of this makes you want to throw up, choose just one social media stream that notifies you and let that be your go-to – for instance, let your friends know that you are just communicating on WhatsApp and limit your messaging on the other platforms. If you are to save your mental health, you need to be willing to reduce the pings.

WHAT DOES TECH DO TO OUR BRAINS?

A fascinating study by the psychologist Dr Aoife McLoughlin showed us how using modern gadgets like smartphones can actually make time appear to go by faster.[78] McLoughlin's research looked at groups of people who are always connected to technology compared to people who rarely use technology and she found that those who were always on tech overestimated the amount of time that passed compared to the luddites. 'It's almost as though we're trying to emulate the technology and be speedier and more efficient,' McLoughlin told *Science Alert.* 'It seems like there's something about technology itself that primes us to increase that pacemaker inside of us that measures the passing of time.' Using fast technology makes us process information faster – we literally speed up. That might seem good on the face of it, and yet, if we are all becoming anxious wrecks as a result of all this speed maybe it's time we learned to slow down?

According to Dr McLoughlin, as our pace of life increases, our subjective feeling of our available time decreases and this creates that all-too-familiar feeling of time pressure within us. It's as though we're all living in one of those thriller-type movies that has a timer on how long we have left to live and we're constantly trying to fight against the clock. Dr McLoughlin explains how 'interacting with technology and technocentric societies has increased some type of pacemaker within us. While it might help us to work faster, it also makes us feel more pressured by time.' And so now the common advice to relax by switching off our mobiles and getting off the internet is completely backed by science. 'What I'm arguing is that there is a genuine quantifiable cognitive basis for this advice, rather than it simply being about taking a step back,' she said. 'It's a scientific reason to stop and smell the roses.'[79]

SOCIAL MEDIA'S ROLE IN THE RISE OF ANXIETY

Relentless discussion and analysis of everyone's actions contributes to our wildly rising levels of stress and anxiety – all the heightened emotion, constant judgement and continuous gauging of approval and disapproval from likes and shares on our social media is causing higher levels of anxiety and stress in the ordinary person. Never before did pictures of our every night out become the subject of approval and ratings from people we barely know; never before have regrettably drunken nights of 15-year-old kids 'gone viral' and become a global talking point; and never before did vague attempts to flirt with a guy on an aeroplane become exposed to millions of people for their judgement and analysis before the pair had even disembarked from the flight.

Rosey Blair and her boyfriend, Houston Hardaway, asked a woman whose name was later revealed as Helen, a fellow traveller on a flight from New York to Dallas, whether she would switch seats so they could sit together. Helen agreed; maybe, they joked, her new travel companion would end up being the love of Helen's life. From then on (unbeknownst to Helen) Blair and Hardaway took to Twitter and documented, with videos, pictures and words, the friendly, mildly flirtatious conversation that took place between Helen and her new seatmate – Euan – during this four-hour flight. We can only imagine Helen's horror when she realised that Blair was a 'social influencer', and more than 300,000 people retweeted this thread documenting the conversation between Helen and Euan. Nearly a million 'liked' it. The 'story' was taken up by *The Today Show* and by *Good Morning America*. Helen later revealed with a legal statement that didn't disclose her full name that she was a private person who had no knowledge of Blair's Twitter frenzy and, had she known about it, she would never have given permission for Blair to report and document her every move and utterance.

Of course, some people would like nothing more than to go viral – the Euan in this story was perfectly okay with his newfound fame. But the risk that we could end up 'going viral' or the various dramas of our life be turned into a 'funny' meme has created a continuous low-level anxiety and tension about our every embarrassing and humiliating encounter. For some people, especially for people like Helen who value their privacy, this is all very worrying and it creates feelings of needless stress and anxiety.

MIND YOUR MEDIA

Don't get me wrong – I love my social media and I don't propose we shut down all our accounts go back to using smoke signals and carrier pigeons to communicate. However if we are to make a serious commitment to reducing our stress levels, then we have to admit that our use of social media needs to be closely examined. Whether it's the need to keep up your streaks on Snapchat or the endless pings from messages on your WhatsApp, or your FOMO (fear of missing out) as you constantly check your Facebook page that's causing you stress, really doesn't matter. What matters is that you attend to the fact that it's causing you stress and you do something about it.

Try following at least some of this advice to relieve the stress caused by your social media:

- ❖ Turn off all (or a lot) of your notifications.
- ❖ Get into the habit of putting your phone on silent at least twice a day for set periods of time.
- ❖ Learn to turn off your phone once a day – this is a habit worth cultivating. It may make you nervous at first but it will lead to a calmer, more in-control you.
- ❖ Embrace your JOMO – joy of missing out – when you look at pictures of nights out, and remind yourself why you chose

to relax at home in your jammies – sometimes the simplest pleasures are the best.

❖ Decide how often you will check various social media platforms and stick to it.

❖ Give up entirely on checking your media first thing in the morning and last thing at night – in the morning it primes you to check in all day and it disturbs your sleep last thing at night.

❖ Make a set time to check in and make it a more elaborate event – just as you have a specific time for lunch and for work, make a set time for social media so that it is no longer a mindless, never-on-but-never-off scenario, e.g. Facebook and Twitter at about 11 a.m.; Snapchat and Instagram on the train on the way home from work.

❖ Become more cautious of your moods when you go on Instagram as it has been shown to be the social platform that is worst for your mental health.[80] Well, whaddayaknow – all that perfection just creates feelings of inadequacy and anxiety.

TEENAGERS AND THE INTERNET

The internet has created a whole plethora of ways for people to explore their dark side with a colluding community. This is very difficult for everyone but perhaps especially for parents of pre-teen and teenage girls as they can often be histrionic anyway so it can be almost impossible to try to decipher which episodes of emotion should be taken seriously and which shouldn't.

Nancy Tucker's incisive account of mental illness, *That Was When People Started to Worry*, gives a harrowing description of how three girls – Georgia, Maisie and Charley – descended into self-harming through a combination of anxiety, peer pressure and social media.

Searching 'self-harm' on Tumblr is like stepping into a world where all the colour has been drained away. The people in charge of the internet try to block it, but it's all still there if you know where to look. Before you're allowed to see the search results, a little message pops up asking if 'everything is OK' and giving you the number for the Samaritans. The first time we read that message we laughed and laughed, because of course everything wasn't OK; in fact everything was so not-OK we had lost track of what had even made everything not-OK in the first place.[81]

The internet is a wild and unfettered place where emotions are thrown about with wild abandon, and the darker the emotion online, the more attention you will receive. When your internet use goes awry, it can be very hard to get it back to a healthy place and this is why there is so much advice about tech addiction and unhealthy use of social media. The force of nature that characterises some pre-teen and teenage girls has to be experienced to be understood. When the psychotherapist Lisa Damour was in graduate school, the professor teaching the psychological testing course presented her with a pile of tests to score with the words, 'Double-check the age of the person whose test you are scoring. If it's a teenager, but you think it's a grown-up, you'll conclude that you have a psychotic adult. But that's just a normal teenager.'[82]

In my work as a psychotherapist, I heartily concur. Teenagers experience much more powerful emotions than the rest of us and they really are at the mercy of their emotional brain for these tumultuous years. As Damour says, 'Emotional input rings like a gong for teenagers and a chime for everyone else.' She advises parents to interpret their child's broadcast as reflective of how they are experiencing life at that moment; they really are that intense, so parents need to take their emotions seriously. This doesn't mean that we go down the rabbit hole with them but it does mean that we register just how difficult they are finding life. And it definitely means that the adult population should be wary of allowing teenagers unfettered access to the internet.

SO WHAT SHOULD WE DO?

We know that there is an unprecedented epidemic of anxiety happening all over the Western world and yet it still remains difficult to turn our back on the relentless pressure to succeed and to perform that seems to be trailing our every move. This is why we need to be protective about our mental health and why we need to learn balance in this complicated world.

If we can learn to live our life with more emphasis on 'being' instead of being swept along by the fashionable tide of doing, spending, working and consuming, we will become more satisfied with what we have instead of charging ahead, killing ourselves to achieve more and more.

BEING APPROPRIATELY BUSY

Most of us like being reasonably busy; indeed, the need to be busy is one of the traits that differentiate us from other animals. (Others are the need for purpose and meaning, but more on that in Chapter 9.) It is human nature to strive for better and to search for meaning, and being busy is one of the ways we improve our lives and assign meaning. Although being busy is an important tool in our arsenal for feeling content, the problem is that being 'foolishly busy' gives us a short-term feeling of satisfaction but more long-term feelings of discontent and anxiety. So long as we are appropriately busy instead of foolishly busy, we can free ourselves from the anxiety of being 'always on'.

The upshot is that although being busy can feel invigorating and energising, being *too* busy can feel stressful and anxiety-inducing. The key, as it always is, is balance. Charles Dickens's line in *David Copperfield* about debt can equally be applied to nearly all aspects of life: 'Annual income 20 pounds, annual expenditure nineteen six, result happiness. Annual income 20 pounds, annual expenditure 20 pound ought and six, result misery.' If you're giving out more than you're taking in, you'll end up miserable.

TOO MUCH IS TOO MUCH – CHOOSE YOUR POISON!

Most of us like the satisfaction of a job well done, we like using our brain for productive purposes and we like feeling that we matter and that what we do is important. Zookeepers apparently report the highest job satisfaction – even though they spend a large part of their working days shovelling shit.[83] The reason why they find their work satisfying is that they assign meaning to their work: they can see the benefits of keeping the animals' homes pleasant and so they don't resent the poo and pee.

For many people, work is okay, our friends are lovely and our jobs are reasonably interesting; the only problem is that we just have too much of everything going on. And too much is too much. We like being busy but would like to be less busy. We love our friends but we don't see them often enough – we're too busy, you see. We like our homes but we feel they should look better. We enjoy our work but there is too much of it.

The challenge is to free ourselves from needless stress and anxiety, by aligning our expectations with the level of energy we're willing to expend on any given situation. If you hate working but you love spending money then, right there, you have a conflict that will give rise to mental distress. If you hate grooming and beauty products and you don't have the time or money to go to salons on a regular basis then you might need to bring your expectations of your appearance down a couple of notches. You can't have it all – you can either have a perfectly groomed appearance and be irritable that you spend so much time on beauty care or you can have a messy appearance and be happier as you spend more time and money following your pleasures – you have to choose your poison.

GET YOURSELF CONNECTED

Just because someone throws us a ball it doesn't mean that we have to catch it, and just because society is throwing us stressful lives it doesn't mean we have to accept the stress. If you find that certain aspects of your life always make you stressed then right now, while you're in the middle of reading about how to handle your anxiety, is the time to address them.

Compiling a fairly simple chart that sorts out the stressful activities from the invigorating activities can lead us to becoming more self-aware and more likely to start addressing the problematic areas in our lives. See below for an example giving problems and solutions:

Stress-inducing activities	What to do about it
Spending too much time online	Commit to disciplining your tech behaviour. Turn off your tech once a day.
Working too much	Take steps to reduce your spending so that you can reduce your workload.
Making or receiving phone calls	Practise with easy, non-threatening friends or relatives.
Attending work functions	Attend for shorter periods of time.
Dealing with conflict	Learn some self-assertion; buy books, get counselling, etc.

Of course, it'll take more than limiting stress-inducing activities to make a person feel less anxious; however, the one thing that pretty much *always* makes a person feel better is feeling connected with people who understand and appreciate them. (This doesn't include connecting with people online!) When we are disconnected from ourselves and from others we create a deep hole within our souls. This hole is created by self-abandonment and other-abandonment and can feel like a vacuum which we are insatiably trying to fill. The only true way to fill this vacuum is to begin to accept ourselves, to reveal ourselves as we truly are and to meet other people who accept us fully.

It's all about the quality of our relationships

One of the world's longest studies of adults tracked the physical and emotional wellbeing of 268 Harvard sophomores and 456 working-class men from Boston's inner city over the course of 75 years and showed that the quality of our relationships is a powerful influence on our lives.[84] But tending to them is often hard and so many of us remain too busy in a bid to avoid the complications of human relationships. Because if you want to deeply connect with someone you must be willing to be revealing both to yourself and to others – otherwise the relationship will remain superficial.

People who feel connected within the community are far healthier than people who are isolated from the community. So to address your anxiety, you could try deepening your connections with the people you love and admire – for they are your tribe. This means that you might work fewer hours to make time to meet your good friends. It doesn't necessarily mean more nights out, though – we all need to eat, and you can have your friends over for dinner without it being a 'dinner party'. You can invite your friends to watch a movie in your house or you can go for a walk with a work colleague who seems to understand you. The main point is that you place more importance on your quality relationships and give them more priority and authenticity.

When 25-year old Gillian came to me about her anxiety it soon emerged that she had placed too much emphasis on appearance and not enough on authenticity, making her friendships quite shallow and competitive. Over the course of a few months, Gillian and I worked together to identify the true friendship among the cast of thousands who were her 'friends'. Gillian made more efforts to be her real, fallible, insecure self to these friends and from this deeper connections were formed. Friendships and relationships can be difficult and scary, yet when they go right, they are worth their weight in gold.

Authentic connection doesn't entail *'U ok hun?'* on social media; authentic connection means that we choose to open ourselves to rejection and misunderstanding. The author and researcher Brené Brown, an expert on social connection, conducted thousands of interviews to figure out what was the most important element of deep social connection: the results were that vulnerability is the key factor. Brown tells us that 'Rarely can a response make something better, what makes something better is connection. And that connection often requires mutual vulnerability.'[85] If we can gather our courage to be vulnerable enough to create deeper connections with our friends and family – so what if they see our messy homes or find out about our disastrous financial woes? – then we are much more likely to live a more satisfying life and feel less anxious and stressed.

HOW IS YOUR HAAL?

A lovely greeting common in many Muslim countries is the way they ask how someone is doing: in Arabic, '*Kayf haal-ik?*' or, in Persian, '*Haal-e shomaa chetoreh?*' This question, 'How is your haal?', seeks to find out how is the transient state of your heart; literally, how is your heart doing at this moment, at this very breath? Is your heart joyful? Is it aching? If you feel overwhelmed, stressed or achingly busy, take a moment to breathe. Breathe in through your nose and out through your mouth and ask yourself, 'How is my haal?'

CHAPTER 5

Is it always 'good to talk'? Misinterpreting mental health messages

'The greatest weapon against stress is our ability to choose one thought over another.'

WILLIAM JAMES

O ne of the best things about living in the twenty-first century is that there seems to be a genuine willingness for people to address challenges to their mental health. It's great that we've started the mental health conversation but now that it's up and running, perhaps it's time to hone this message with a little more accuracy and subtlety? Because if we look at the data, it soon becomes clear we need to up our game – our current lifestyle is contributing to our anxiety and if we continue to go the way we are going almost everyone will end up anxious and stressed.

The *Guardian* columnist Hannah Jane Parkinson wrote an insightful article about why she was 'done with the mental health conversation'.[86] Parkinson is 28 years old and an astute and critical observer about what can be a simplistic attitude to mental health.

She has experienced mental health problems since she was 13 and has been in the psychiatric system for the last ten years.

> In the last few years I have observed a transformation in the way we talk about mental health … It seems as though every week is now some kind of Mental Health Awareness Week … I have lost count of the times mental illness has been compared to a broken leg. Mental illness is nothing like a broken leg.
>
> In fairness, I have never broken my leg. Maybe having a broken leg does cause you to lash out at friends, undergo a sudden, terrifying shift in politics and personality, or lead to time slipping away like a Dali clock. Maybe a broken leg makes you doubt what you see in the mirror, or makes you high enough to mistake car bonnets for stepping stones (difficult, with a broken leg) and a thousand other things. …
>
> It isn't a bad thing that we are all talking more about mental health … But this does not mean it is not infuriating to come home from a secure hospital, suicidal, to a bunch of celebrity awareness-raising selfies and thousands of people saying that all you need to do is ask for help — when you've been asking for help and not getting it.[87]

She's right of course, getting help is often incredibly difficult and a lot more than the 'right help' is needed. Jaunty mental health slogans like 'Mental health can be complex — getting help doesn't have to be!' plastered on public walls are all good but I wish some of these slogans were a little bit more comprehensive. Because, paradoxically, some of these messages have resulted in many people feeling worse. Some of these messages appear to encourage people to place too much emphasis on their feelings and to disregard the hard, cold facts of any given situation. Others seem to disingenuously claim, as Hannah Jane Parkinson pointed out, that all a person has to do is 'ask for help' when the stark reality is that asking for help is often only one solitary step on a very long, difficult and lonely road.

Some mental health professionals believe that we are now perhaps in danger of over-selling the mental health services to the public as increasingly there seems to be an attitude that all we need to do is to find the right therapist or the right medication and there you go, the miracle cure has arrived. Sadly, it seldom works like that – even for people without mental health challenges, life is often very hard. It is much more common for people with challenges to their mental health to delay and procrastinate about getting help for as long as possible, and then, when they finally look for support, they suddenly realise that there is no magic solution; that the bulk of the work – and there is a lot of it – is done by the clients and that therapists tell us little that we couldn't read ourselves in a book or on the internet. This is not to undermine the power of a good connection between a client and therapist, but there is a danger that the message being communicated isn't exactly the message that is being received.

Probably the most insidious aspect of the proliferation of misinterpreted mental health slogans is that too many people use them naively and end up mindlessly travelling quite some way down the wrong road. We all know people who emphasise their feelings over facts and belligerently dismiss rationality by using catchphrases such as, 'If it doesn't feel right, then don't do it' and 'It's okay not to be okay' and 'You wouldn't tell someone with a broken leg to get up and walk so don't say such a thing to a person with mental illness.' Although these phrases mean well, they can often be misinterpreted as giving people permission or even encouragement to wallow in their negativity.

The 'illusory truth effect' phenomenon means that repetition has an extraordinary impact on our minds and the more we hear even the most outlandish claims, the more likely we will eventually believe they are true. You might *think* that the familiarity of the message has no effect on you, but science tell us otherwise. This is why it's important to be vigilant about these messages that are plastered all over social media and public walls – certain phrases impact our brains, even while we're rolling our eyes at their simplicity.

I've no doubt that since we were living in caves, hackneyed, simple-minded phrases have always been uttered as if they contain great depths: I can easily imagine the cave-mother comforting her heart-broken teenage daughter with 'What's for you won't pass you' as she proffered her a bone to chew. But now that mental health has become a mainstream political topic, we need to further develop the issue towards a deeper and more thoughtful place. And a good place to start is by sharpening up those glib mental health slogans that have been taken out of context, dumbed down beyond recognition, and assimilated as if they are universal truths when in reality they are anything but.

'TALK TO SOMEONE'

The basic point of the message 'Talk to someone' is perfect: we should all seek to talk to someone when we feel troubled because if the conversation goes as planned, we will feel much better. If you can speak to someone appropriate and if they respond with care, consideration and empathy, you *will* feel a million times better. But in our busy culture many people are quite impatient, have very little time to spare and feel so stressed themselves that they are pretty useless as listeners and so, with all those rubbish listeners out there, 'Talk to someone' can be a bit of a dangerous message.

If you're feeling anxious or depressed and decide to talk to someone in a bid to cheer yourself up then you are immediately in a very vulnerable position and it is incredibly important that you choose the right person to speak to. If the listener is dismissive or unkind or impatient the emotional person can feel a hundred times worse. And so perhaps this message should be tweaked to 'Talk to a good listener' or 'Talk to someone appropriate' or something similarly specific.

CASE STUDY: MAY, 22

May was 22 years old when she came to me for counselling as a last resort. May had been feeling lonely and suicidal for many years and she thought she'd try counselling as one last-ditch attempt to see if she could pull herself out of the hole.

'I try to tell my friends about my distress,' May told me in that first session. 'But they just dismiss me and tell me "God, you're such a snowflake" and this just makes me feel worthless.' It was only when May attempted suicide that her friends finally took her sadness seriously. But they took this opportunity, when May was at her most vulnerable, to preachily explain that she needed to 'pull herself together' and not to be 'so selfish'.

'When I came out of hospital,' May explained, I was feeling very low and I thought I'd reach out to them. My friends, Becky and Christine, are sisters and they've known me my entire life. I know their family and they know mine. So I visited them and told them how I was feeling. It was a disaster. Becky got up and started doing the dishes, putting away the cutlery, just foostering around hoping I would just shut up. While Christine kept on repeating these asinine phrases at me as if she thought she was on stage giving a motivational speech or something. I felt so lonely and misunderstood.'

May felt much worse after this disastrous conversation and she went home soon after. She took another overdose that very night but thankfully she fell asleep and vomited all over herself. By an extraordinary turn of circumstances, as May lay dazed in a pool of vomit on her bed, she heard a voice on the radio – one of those repeat shows that are broadcast in the middle of the night – where I was being interviewed about why people should try counselling if they feel like giving up. Something, somewhere rang a bell for her and the very next morning she gave me a call and we arranged an appointment. We established a strong connection right from the beginning and she no longer feels so overwhelmed and anxious. And she has found some better friends.

'IT'S GOOD TO TALK!'

Yes, yes, it *is* good to talk. I spend my days and nights communicating; it's my favourite pastime. But there is a kind of ghoulish intensity that seems to grip too many half-baked amateur psychologists who insist on making the people around them express their feelings even when it is abundantly clear that this isn't helpful for the person.

CASE STUDY: ALISON, 32

Alison, a mother of two in her early thirties, is an exuberant cheerful burst of energy. Alison's son and my son attend soccer together and when her little boy witnessed a horrible scene at a soccer match she went into full counsellor mode: 'You must TALK about what happened, Fiachra! It's the ONLY way you'll feel better!' Little Fiachra did his best to give an account of what was a harrowing incident for him. But Fiachra was only eight years old and he didn't really have the words to articulate his feelings. He stumbled and backtracked and got mixed up and became increasingly miserable. Alison bent down very low and spoke to him directly in his face. 'Fiachra, you don't understand – if you don't SPEAK about this and tell me everything you are feeling, this ATTACK will HAUNT you for the REST OF YOUR LIFE!' Fiachra looked suitably horrified and bravely tried to express his feelings.

Although it wasn't my place and I knew I would receive a sharp rap on the knuckles from Alison for it, I could bear it no longer and hopped into the conversation. 'Ah no, Fiachra, it won't necessarily work like that. You might process it in a different way.' He looked a bit shocked at my audacious interruption but also heartily relieved. 'Some people find it good to talk,' I said, ignoring Alison who was getting ready to throttle me, 'but other people find other ways of dealing with it. Or they might even talk about it in a few days when they have figured out their feelings. There isn't only one way to understand something upsetting.'

Fiachra looked questioningly up at his mammy and she nodded curtly. Later on I had a good chat with Alison and I pointed out that, although many people find it wonderfully cathartic to talk about distressing events, some people, especially perhaps small boys, haven't yet got the capacity to unpick their feelings with words. Love, warmth, cuddles and tenderness sometimes might be all that some little boys need after a traumatic event.

It brings to mind a well-known story about a highly respected child psychologist, who was speaking with two boys about a horrible incident that they had experienced. The psychologist went into glorious detail about how important it is to talk about your feelings; how this is the way to feel better and how unburdening yourself from all the complicated thoughts you might have inside you will set you free. The boys nodded sagely. The psychologist then asked the boys, 'So then, George and Sam, tell me how you feel?'

George replied that he felt tired. Then Sam said in a small voice, 'I feel hungry.'

End of conversation.

The thing is that, for some people, it's only good to talk if it's at the right time, with the right person, in the right way. A difficult conversation that goes nowhere and leaves the listener frustrated and the speaker feeling inadequate is a disaster. Mindless acceptance that it's good to talk needs to be challenged so that the listeners up their game and so the speakers can choose to refrain from talking to the wrong person at the wrong time.

'ASK FOR HELP'

The problem with this message is that it's based on the assumption 'Ask and you will receive', but most of us need to ask for help again and again and again. And we still can't be sure of getting the right help and so we might need to ask for some more help. Equally, if the right help is offered at any given time in your life, it has to be the *right* time – there is little point in someone receiving help when the person has no interest in being helped; try 'helping' the bipolar individual when they are on a manic high and you will soon see that timing is crucial. As Hannah Jane Parkinson wrote, the mental health process can be heart-wrenchingly difficult:

> It's the offer of a Valium in an inpatient ward to calm you down upon hearing that they don't have your regular medicine ... It's being told by doctors for more than a decade that this medication is imperative. And then being told by a doctor that that medication is wrong, and if he had his way there would be no medication for mental illness at all – and not recognising that this might be an alarming thing to hear.
>
> The waiting. The offers of therapies that aren't suitable because there is nothing else. The being matched with a therapist who, through no fault of her own, is unsuitable (you have friends in common) but who you don't ask to change because you know there isn't another. The 10-minute GP slots that take weeks to secure.

Even when everyone is doing their job well, and many do, the treatment of mental illness is a slog.

Recovery from mental illness requires a phenomenal level of effort and commitment from the sufferer. Although there is often a tokenistic reference to the fact that we have to do the work ourselves, for too many people the presumption is that with the 'right therapist' their recovery will be, if not easy, then certainly seamless. Some people believe that it is the 'wellness industry' that is at fault as the idea that we can be well and happy if we just try hard enough is promoted by people who have products to peddle. Sadly, recovery is seldom easy and 'being happy' is almost always a fleeting sense of satisfaction between the waves of life. More often than not, recovery is excruciatingly difficult and even after recovery, life itself is pretty difficult anyway.

Yes, we need to 'ask for help' when we are suffering but, sadly, we also need to put it out there that asking for help is often only the first step of a traumatically long process of recovery. Nancy Tucker, in her extraordinary book *The Time In Between: A Memoir of Hunger and Hope,* articulates perfectly the complex relationship between the client and the therapist and how, ultimately, the client has to do most of the work:

> The Right Therapist helped me because, after a certain point, she couldn't help me. She could support me; scaffold me; offer me succour — but she couldn't do it for me. She could hold my Empty Child when my arms were not yet strong enough, but she could not offer the self-care; self-acceptance; self-love it craved. She could be by my side as I struck the demons down, but it could not be her wielding the sword. The realisation that I had found the best ally I could hope for, and that the battle was still mine

and mine alone, somehow gave me permission to stop searching for a Magic Cure. It rid me of excuses; put the responsibility squarely back on my shoulders. It was uncomfortable. It was hard. But it was Right. After years of side-stepping, ducking and diving, I finally had to put my head down and make the change.[88]

FOCUS ON YOUR FEELINGS'

Although I'm a psychotherapist and I will always *include and respect* a person's feelings in any given situation, it just doesn't do to focus *only* on your gut feelings and ignore the facts. After many centuries of ignoring our deepest emotions and sweeping our feelings under the rug, there is now a strange and unhelpful tendency, especially among younger people, to focus intensely and solely upon their feelings.

Giving too much importance to our emotions has brought us to a very dysfunctional way of thinking where people are led to believe that their emotions are more important than anything else. But they aren't, and this deceptively persuasive idea isn't always the best way to approach mental distress.

This misguided idea that our emotions supersede all other cognitions has resulted in scores of anxious teenagers and young adults avoiding school or college or refusing to make a phone call or leaving work because they couldn't handle performing an uncomfortable task. Invariably, the reason they give is that it 'just didn't feel right'. This has led to many young people believing that their feelings override the facts of any given situation and so they understandably conclude that they should avoid everything that causes them distress – but if they never have the opportunity to learn how to experience distress then how will they ever learn to handle it?

Although I certainly don't propose to return to the bad old days where we buried mental illness, nor do I wish to prop up the current bad new days where many aspects of life are creating stress and adding to our anxiety.

As we learned in Chapter 1, our emotions are powerful, influential and unreliable and we need to use our slower, more rational brain if we are to become wise and purposeful human beings. Being led by our emotions was never for a moment considered a desirable way to live until relatively recently when suddenly pop psychology started to advise us to 'follow your feelings' as if our feelings would bring us to a higher level.

But they seldom do.

It is our feelings that encourage us to message an ex in a drastic, drunken late-night moment; it is our feelings that lead us to have an anxiety episode at an interview, the very moment when we wish to be on top of our game; it is our feelings that seduce us into thinking that volatile arguments with strangers on social media are an effective and satisfying way to spend an evening. Being led by your emotions, by your 'gut instinct' can feel very powerful and satisfying *in the moment*, but in the long term, we more often than not regret words and actions released in high emotion.

Perhaps the advice to 'focus on your feelings' should be replaced with the more unwieldy 'become aware of your feelings but don't get carried away by strong feelings'? Hmm, I'm not sure if it will fly.

CASE STUDY: JEANNE, 19

Jeanne came to me suffering from social anxiety. She was 19 years old and her life had been severely blighted by anxiety to the extent that she seldom left the house without her mother in tow. She hadn't attended college in months, although she was keeping up with her schoolwork by electronic means. Jeanne's mother Margery also suffered from anxiety and in many ways the mother and daughter colluded with each other and made each other's anxiety worse. (See page 47 for more on anxiety that comes in pairs.) So Jeanne might say that she would try to attend the morning classes in college the next day. Margery would be thrilled but immediately anxious that Jeanne might fail at this task. As the evening progressed the tension would rise as both mother and daughter would endlessly discuss how anxious Jeanne was feeling and how difficult it would be in the morning. Margery would do her utmost, killing herself with effort, to be empathetic with Jeanne and would try to draw out every last residue of anxiety in Jeanne. Jeanne would try to articulate how awful she was feeling and then inevitably would feel worse. Usually these kind and caring conversations disintegrated into a fight as emotions became progressively heightened.

The next morning Margery would feel like she could burst from trying to keep it all together. Jeanne tended to feel furious as a result of all the excessive emotion and the tense expectation. Jeanne would then pick a fight with her mother over breakfast and would usually, inevitably, storm to her room yelling that her mother had ruined everything. Jeanne would yet again avoid college and Margery would feel devastated.

Competence breeds confidence, competence comes about from practice and competence makes us safer. A person will only feel safe if they feel they can handle whatever they face and if a person has never had the chance to practise mastering their fear they will inevitably be incompetent at learning to manage it. Starting with the playground, children need to learn that sometimes they might feel uneasy high up in the air but then when they realise that the ground below them might hurt but won't kill them and there is a loving adult nearby ready to kiss them better after they fall, they realise that a fall isn't always catastrophic and they can quickly recover. This is how a child can practise facing their fears. As we mature and develop, we soon realise that certain experiences might initially make us feel anxious but then, if we can learn to face the fear and do it anyway, often the cost-benefit analysis shows us that the initial nerves are worth getting through.

We need to learn what it is to dig deep and unearth hidden strengths in our deepest reaches. We can do this more effectively if we live within the safety of a loving household or with the inherent safety of the support of good friends and family, but if our friends and family collude with the misguided notion that we should avoid ever feeling unsure, or that we should emphasise our feelings over logic and intelligence, then we weaken ourselves and our ability to recover.

'LISTEN TO YOUR GUT'

It's worth repeating; we need to ensure we use our wise brain when we are making important decisions because the part of the brain that is responsible for higher-order functions provides us with much more wisdom than our emotional brain. The 'emotional brain' is the part of the brain that inflames people with emotions such as red-hot anger or chilling fear. It is the most powerful, the fastest and the stupidest part of any person's brain. Do not, *please*, do not rely on your emotional brain to excessively influence your decisions – because if you do that you will be using the least intelligent part of your brain to dictate your behaviour.

We really should adjust this slogan from 'listen to your gut' to the less catchy but more accurate 'be aware of your gut feelings and make sure to take some time so that your wise brain can catch up and assess whether your gut feelings are right'. Another keeper!

'IF IT FEELS WRONG, DON'T DO IT'

One of the consequences of this emphasis on the superiority of our emotions is the ill-advised strategy that has grown wings in recent years where many people now believe that 'if it feels good, do it' and also that the reverse, 'If it feels wrong, then don't do it' is an appropriate way to live. But it isn't — sometimes we are better off if we suffer situations that don't feel good and oftentimes avoiding the source of the anxiety is inadvisable.

CASE STUDY: JOSH, 26

When Josh developed agoraphobia he was initially afraid of going into intensely crowded areas. And so he successfully avoided these areas. Once crowded areas had been successfully vetoed, then Josh became fearful of areas that had the possibility of becoming crowded. Over the course of a few years, and through a series of avoidance strategies, Josh eventually chose to avoid many social engagements for fear he would have a panic attack. As we saw in Chapter 1 and Chapter 3, avoidance tactics don't work and exposure therapy has a higher success rate than other strategies. Josh eventually arrived in my office after a series of cancellations and other avoidance tactics. It was Josh's girlfriend who insisted he get some treatment. It was a revelation to him when I explained that the treatment would involve a lot of very difficult feelings — almost like going through chemotherapy for cancer — but that, if he was willing to experience this discomfort, he could one day expect to see an improvement in his symptoms. 'I thought that I was supposed to avoid discomfort,' Josh later remarked. 'I had it the wrong way around.'

Josh was right, of course; avoiding the source of any distress is usually exactly the wrong way to approach mental distress. All too often people who suffer anxiety and distress are told by well-meaning friends that 'if it feels bad, don't do it', but as the controversial Canadian psychologist

Dr Jordan Peterson warns us, 'avoidance necessarily and inevitably poisons the future.'[89]

There is a whole plethora of reasons (see Chapter 6) why society has fallen into a negative pattern of belief that avoiding the source of distress is good for us, and this is why well-meaning friends advise us, 'If it doesn't feel right then don't do it' and other trite platitudes. Indeed, in my work as a psychotherapist many clients often tell me this is why they haven't done the tasks or experiments we have agreed on. But any therapist worth their salt knows well that removing the fearsome object does not remove the fear; it only gives the object more power and strength in the distressed person's mind. Worse than that, it often imbues the 'monster under the rug' with more power than it should. The fearful person needs to learn to handle their fear, not obliterate everything that makes them feel scared or anxious. Creighton Adams, the US general who commanded the military in the Vietnam War, advises us, 'When eating an elephant take one bite at a time' and that's exactly how we should confront anxiety. If we can confront the anxiety one bite at a time then we can learn, slowly but surely, how to handle the world.

'THINK POSITIVE THOUGHTS!'

One of the many issues involving 'positivity' is that qualities such as accuracy and flexibility have been shown to be healthier and more helpful than irrational and narrow-minded positivity. When writer and political activist Barbara Ehrenreich was diagnosed with breast cancer she found the continuous admonitions to think positively heavy-handed and also quite dismissive of the understandable trauma she was experiencing. In her book *Smile or Die: How Positive Thinking Fooled America and the World* she busted the myth that people really needed to think positive if they wanted to beat cancer.

By looking at the scientific data Ehrenreich demolished the simplistic idea that positive thinking is the answer to all our problems. It turns out that positive or negative thinking makes no difference whatsoever to a person's rate of recovery from cancer. Although positive thinking might make your journey more pleasant – thus reducing your anxiety – it actually has no bearing on the statistical rate of your healing. You can wallow in negativity or you can repeat positive affirmations all day, every day, but no data indicates either approach will impact your recovery rate from a serious illness.[90]

Added to this, excessively positive thinking can encourage some people to disengage from reality and imply that sufferers are somehow complicit in developing their illness. In Ehrenreich's book one researcher described the advice to think positively as 'an additional burden to an already devastated patient'. The words of one woman's entreaty to Deepak Chopra demonstrate the emotional anguish that can take place when a person feels chained to positive thoughts: 'Even though I follow the treatments, have come a long way in unburdening myself of toxic feelings, have forgiven everyone, changed my lifestyle to include meditation, prayer, proper diet, exercise and supplements, the cancer keeps coming back. Am I missing a lesson here that it keeps re-occurring? I am positive I am going to beat it, yet it does get harder with each diagnosis to keep a positive attitude.'[91]

It's often more helpful to feel our feelings as they come without always trying to polish and shape ourselves into a shinier, more cheerful model. If we can free ourselves from the need to think positively we are immediately freed to consider our emotions with compassion and authenticity. Although we can learn from some experiences, not every rejection or every failure has to be a golden teachable moment – some experiences are just sad, mad and bad.

But not only does cheery advice to 'think positive' disturb many people, some people can also feel alienated by the phrase 'positive mental health'. In his book about anxiety, *Me and My Mate Jeffrey*, Niall Breslin explains why he dislikes this phrase:

> I have a slight problem with the phrase 'positive mental health'. If someone is deeply depressed or experiencing constant panic attacks, the worst thing you can say is 'be positive!' or 'At least you are not living in a war-stricken country'. When you're down low, the ability to be positive is virtually impossible and in my case, I don't try to be. The time that I practise positivity is when I am not feeling really anxious or low, when there are breaks in the clouds and I am in a clearer state of mind, and this was becoming a more common occurrence. Wellness is like going to the gym for your brain because it is not about mental health, it's about mental fitness.[92]

'YOU CAN BE ANYTHING YOU WANT TO BE'

This sort of dangerous message can be found all over social media and, unfortunately, in schools. But no, actually, we can't be anything we want to be. And that's okay.

Granted, some people, with a lot of talent, a lot of hard work, a lot of luck and a lot of mental resilience, can manage to achieve their dreams; but a great many more with just the same strengths don't quite pull it off and it simply isn't fair to blame these people for failing to achieve their dreams. A more insidious aspect of the message that 'you can be anything you want to be' is that you *should* be whatever you want to be and, if you wish hard enough, almost like a character in a Disney film, then your wishes will come true. But it's not true and it leads to terrible disappointment and anger. A more realistic phrase might be something like, 'If you work very hard and are willing to forgo a lot of pleasure, you can probably become quite successful; but whether that success leads to happiness depends on your mindset.' Doesn't sound quite so catchy though.

'IF YOU LOOK GOOD, YOU FEEL GOOD'

This slogan seems to be accepted as a universal truth among the millennial generation. And yet it has created a mentality that can be shockingly harsh on the less good-looking among us. It's not so hard to look good when you are young but when you are old it's a different story – it's really quite difficult to look good and be old; likewise it is almost impossible to look good when you are sick or suffering. Lots of life's challenges make it harder for us to look good and, if we're at a low ebb, we don't need pressure to look good from outside sources. Of course, the grand plan behind this message is that if we make the effort to make ourselves look good then we will naturally feel better inside ourselves; and there's something in this, because it often works. But – and it's a big but – all this effort comes at a price and sometimes we just don't have it in us to try to look good. Other times, when we're feeling lousy inside, we don't want to be judged on our looks and we certainly don't want some *Strictly Come Dancing* glam type shrieking at us to put on our lippy because 'if you look good, you feel good!'

Perhaps more important, the pressure to look good has spawned a generation who are caught in a narcissistic bind where their looks are considered a representation of their deepest self. But they're not. Sometimes when I'm feeling good I look absolutely rubbish – there I am in my old trackies, greasy hair in a ponytail and having a laugh walking home from school with my kids when I meet someone and the look of horror on their face suggests that I'm clearly feeling downtrodden and wrecked. But just because I look awful doesn't mean I feel awful! We messy ones have to fight for the right to look awful.

The beautifully poised and polished teenagers who come into my office usually look great but their thin veneer of sophistication tends to hide a deep well of unhappiness. Looking good is deceptive and it often means very little. As the novelist Khaled Hosseini pointed out, 'Beauty is an enormous, unmerited gift given randomly, stupidly.'

Lizzie Velásquez, an inspiring motivational speaker, was born with a rare disease that didn't bestow her with the looks that most of us take for granted. One day Lizzie came across a post on social media where she was described as the 'ugliest person in the world'. She tearfully went through every single comment in that post. When you hear Lizzie speak you soon realise that her beautiful thoughts and insight far, far outweigh how she looks. Perhaps we need to bring back the phrase 'Beauty is only skin deep'? Or perhaps, even better, we could simply turn to the word namaste, which in Sanskrit means 'The divine in me bows to the divine in you.' Much nicer.

'THERE ARE NO BAD FEELINGS ONLY FEELINGS' AND 'IT'S OKAY NOT TO BE OKAY'

On first glance these statements also seem reasonable enough but, having worked with many clients over the years, I have become quite worried about their interpretation. Of course, I'm not in the business of arguing that there is such a thing as 'bad feelings'; nor do I think everyone should be 'okay' all the time. However, there is a danger that certain people who subscribe to these statements might end up thinking that being desperately unhappy is a perfectly fine way to live your life.

If you feel bad, even if you don't feel okay, then first things first, it's ultra-important not to beat yourself up about this. All too often I meet clients in my clinic who tend to abuse themselves for not being as happy as they believe they should be. On the other hand, I also meet many clients who appear to be determined to protect themselves from changing their dysfunctional lives – no matter what the cost. And they often hide behind statements such as these.

'YOU WOULDN'T TELL SOMEONE WITH A BROKEN LEG TO GET UP AND WALK!'

Well, no, we wouldn't, but we would help our loved ones to engage in the recovery process and if they refused to do this we would feel understandably disheartened, dejected and disappointed. When a client comes to therapy almost determined not to get better it often reminds me of the old joke about the man who was stuck on his rooftop during a flood.

The man prayed to God for help. A man in a rowing boat came by and he shouted to the man stuck on the roof, 'Jump in, I can save you.' The stranded man shouted back, 'Oh no, everything's okay, I'm praying to God and He will save me.' And so off the rowing boat went. Then a motorboat came by and the fellow in the motorboat shouted, 'Jump in, let me save you.' But the man replied, 'No thanks, I'm praying to God and He will save me.' So off the motorboat went. Then a helicopter came by and the pilot shouted, 'Grab a rope and I will lift you to safety.' To this the stranded man replied, 'No thanks, I'm praying to God and I have faith. He will save me.' So the helicopter flew away. Eventually the water rose above the rooftop and the man drowned. When he went to heaven, he exclaimed to God, 'I had faith in you but you didn't save me, you let me drown. Why didn't you save me?'

God replied, 'I sent you a rowing boat, a motorboat and a helicopter, what more did you expect?'

This joke of course perfectly illustrates the way people need be helped to help themselves. If a person refuses all offers of help there really is very little any of us can do.

CASE STUDY: BRIAN, 39

Brian came to me for counselling as he had been feeling very anxious and suffering from panic attacks for many years. I always record in the first session what other therapy the person has attended, and it emerged that Brian had a long list of therapists behind him. It turned out that Brian seemed to seek a listening ear that enabled him to stay in his unhappy life. He didn't want to change his life – no matter how unhappy it was making him.

Brian had no interest in hearing about personal choice or responsibility – and as soon as we veered dangerously near to autonomy or personal freedom he quickly recited all the reasons why things could never change.

Brian's presenting issue was that he was ill-suited to his job as a teacher. He was shy and introverted with a distinct lack of interest in children or education, but had gone into teaching as a result of his parents' ambitions. He hated his job, it was making him mentally unwell but it was well paid and very secure. Brian was completely resistant to considering a change of employment – at 39 years of age he knew he could take early retirement in about 20 years and he figured that he would suffer on till then, but in the meantime his life was miserable and filled with dread, fear and hopelessness.

Brian gave a comprehensive list of all the different types of psychotherapy he had tried and I suggested that he might benefit from psychoanalytical counselling or else person-centred counselling but he had already been there and tried them both. Brian and I worked together for some time but sadly, I wasn't able to help him. Perhaps my work with him was misshapen by my view that Brian was determined to view me as just another therapist on a long list of therapists who wouldn't be able to help him.

At one session, at a point when I believed Brian might be getting ready to leave our therapy and move on to another therapist, I wondered aloud whether he would ever leave this job that was causing him so much mental pain. Brian answered with spirit, 'Sure you lot are always telling me that there are no bad feelings, only feelings. I've been diagnosed with depression and anxiety – you wouldn't tell a person with a broken leg to stand up and walk!'

In response I reminded Brian about the old joke about God trying to help the drowning man. Brian laughed quietly to himself, acknowledging the humour. After six months of therapy Brian decided to try another route. I hope that someday soon that this lovely, kind, gentle man meets someone who can more effectively provide therapeutic support.

THE NEED FOR INTERVENTION

Ruby Wax highlighted how important it is not to be dismissive of a person's mental pain. She said, 'Mental illness is a physical illness. You wouldn't go up to someone suffering from Alzheimer's and yell, "Come on, get with it, you remember where you left your keys?"' This is perhaps a better analogy than the usual broken leg one as, just for starters, Alzheimer's is a condition in the brain so is closer to what is going on with the mentally ill person.

It also contains the understanding that it can be almost impossible to penetrate the brain of a person with Alzheimer's. We need to work around it, putting the keys on a ribbon around their neck if that works, but equally, when their lives aren't independently manageable, *others need to step in and help*. So if the life of a person with mental illness has become unmanageable it needs to be acknowledged, whether this is a person living with Alzheimer's, alcoholism or anxiety. Continuing to pretend that it is up to the person who is experiencing the mental illness to seek help is sometimes but not always inappropriate. Sometimes an intervention is required when a person who has a mental illness refuses, for whatever reason, to get help. This causes intense pain for loved ones and family members but as the great prayer from Alcoholics Anonymous reminds us:

> *God grant me the serenity to accept the things I cannot change,*
> *the courage to change the things I can change*
> *and the wisdom to know the difference.*

WHERE DO WE GO NOW?

The new openness about mental health has been very helpful in tearing down the stigma about mental illness even if it has, on some level, simplified the important messages. No longer are so many people in fear of their jobs if they mention they have had mental difficulty, nor do people have to keep deadly secrets about their troubles. On the next page, I have added to the following dumbed-down slogans so they make better sense.

Existing slogan	Improved slogan
Talk to someone.	Find someone with whom you can connect and you will feel better if you open up.
It's good to talk.	It's good to talk to the right person at the right time.
Ask for help.	Ask for help, and keep asking until you get the help you need.
Focus on your feelings.	Acknowledge your feelings and always consider the facts as well.
Listen to your gut.	Listen to your gut but also listen to your wise brain for even better counsel.
If it feels wrong, don't do it.	If it feels wrong, consider that we often have to suffer short-term pain for long-term gain.
There are no bad feelings, just feelings.	Bad feelings, when addressed, can change into good feelings.
It's okay not to be okay.	It's okay to try to feel better.
Think positive thoughts.	Think positive thoughts but keep an eye on the realistic thoughts too!
If you look good, you feel good.	If you feel good, you don't care how you look.
You can be anything you want.	You can be anything you want only with a lot of luck, hard work, effort and endurance.
You wouldn't tell someone with a broken leg to get up and walk so don't say such a thing to a person with mental illness.	The person who has mental health difficulties has a difficult road ahead of them and they need all the support they can get if they are to put in enough effort to stay committed and focused on that road.

CHAPTER 6

Anxiety is political: We've never had it so good – so why are we feeling so anxious?

'Nobody has the right not to be offended.'

SALMAN RUSHDIE

I t seems counter-intuitive that we live in a world that has never before been more supportive of the need for a healthy mindset, yet a growing army of anxious people are feeling worse as a direct consequence of all this emphasis on mental health. If we unpack the data, we soon see that untold damage is inadvertently being caused to our collective mental health, not only by our lifestyles, but by guidelines and policies that encourage avoidance strategies.

Political parties are unwittingly promoting and encouraging anxiety by creating a society, through legislature and political 'mental health' policies, where bureaucrats who write mental health policies seem to have misunderstood the correct and appropriate way to handle anxiety. These policies tend to place the focus on helping vulnerable people avoid their distress when it would be far more helpful to provide them with support to learn how to confront and handle the source of their distress. Although these policies might look good, they are not supported by psychological research and they don't really help people. Indeed, they tend to be short-term interventions only interested in helping vulnerable people in the short term – a bit like providing Happy Meals from McDonald's to starving people in developing countries instead of teaching them effective farming practices that will produce food for years to come.

Anxiety can be contagious and a toxic cycle of feeling anxious, overwhelmed and unable to cope is becoming the typical human experience.

The reason why the politicos have become concerned with anxiety is because there are, of course, huge costs involved with this epidemic; it is projected that by 2026 anxiety disorders will cost the English economy more than £14.2bn a year.[93] The problem is that some politicians are more interested in spin and branding and getting the better of the opposition than in implementing boring, long-term effective measures. Some policies that don't help our mental health include:

1. **Trigger warnings** – the most current scientific literature suggests that trigger warnings aren't helpful.
2. **Microaggressions** – it is more empowering to help people to handle microaggressions than to suppress speech.
3. **Inappropriate no-platforming** – it is more helpful to fight inappropriate speech with more speech; to fight suppression with further exploration and deeper analysis.
4. **Emphasis on safe spaces in inappropriate places** – this is adding to a culture of fear and encouraging anxious people to avoid dealing with their anxiety.

THE TROUBLE WITH TRIGGER WARNINGS

A 'trigger warning' is a statement that alerts the viewer or the reader that the material could offend them. However, to date, there is a serious dearth of research on whether there is any psychological benefit to trigger warnings[94] although they can certainly be useful to give viewers a heads-up about the film they are about to see. Despite the general assumption that trigger warnings are helpful to vulnerable people, a review of psychiatric literature shows that there is no evidence to suggest that they are beneficial to mental health outcomes, especially in the context of educational establishments.[95] Given their widespread use, the assumption that there is considerable empirical evidence to support the existence of trigger warnings is dangerously wrong. The truth is, as *Psychology Today* tells us, 'a review of the psychiatric literature shows no studies that link trigger warnings to either short-term or long-term mental health outcomes. As such, trigger warnings are not an evidence-based intervention and are not supported by the scientific literature.'[96]

Richard McNally, a professor of psychology at Harvard, cautioned university faculties against the widespread use of trigger warnings, noting that, 'Trigger warnings are designed to help survivors avoid reminders of their trauma, thereby preventing emotional discomfort. Yet avoidance reinforces PTSD. Conversely, systematic exposure to triggers and the memories they provoke is the most effective means of overcoming the disorder.'[97] Indeed, many scientists and experts in the area of anxiety and PTSD suggest that trigger warnings may actually be counterproductive as they can actually increase the symptoms of anxiety and increase the likelihood of a person developing a disabling level of PTSD in the long term.[98]

Researchers at Harvard asked participants in a study about the impact of trigger warnings to read passages from texts such as *Moby*

Dick and *Crime and Punishment*. Half the participants received this warning: 'TRIGGER WARNING: The passage you are about to read contains disturbing content and may trigger an anxiety response, especially in those who have a history of trauma', while the other half were left to read the passages without any warning. The researchers found that, although trigger warnings led to no self-reported differences in anxiety, the participants who were exposed to the trigger warning rated both themselves and others as more vulnerable to developing PTSD. Also, trigger warnings – not the actual material but the warning itself – actually increased anxiety among participants who held the belief that 'words cause harm'.[99]

An insidiously dangerous aspect that is associated with the rise of trigger warnings is that some reckless film-makers choose to ignore the well-established and effective guidelines on serious subjects such as suicide and self-harm and instead place an emotionally compelling trigger warning before the film. This is a very dark use of trigger warnings as either the film is showing these subjects in an appropriate manner or it isn't, and if it is, then there shouldn't really be a need for anything beyond, perhaps, an advisory notice about the content.

The main people who trigger warnings help are people who wish to score political points and groups that are engaged in virtue signalling. People who suffer from PTSD can't be completely sure of what exactly will trigger their anxiety and it doesn't help their progress if they are led to believe that they won't be triggered when they can be triggered by the most random event. Trigger warnings create a culture of avoidance and weaken resilience, which in turn creates distress, constrains our behaviour and prevents personal growth. If a person feels they need trigger warnings this suggests that they need psychological treatment. If people are sufficiently empowered then they won't feel scared by minor events or by so-called trigger words.

ENCOURAGING SNOWFLAKERY BY WORRYING ABOUT MICROAGGRESSIONS

The psychologist Derald Wing Sue defined microaggressions as 'brief, everyday exchanges that send denigrating messages to certain individuals because of their group membership'. The individuals making the comments can be otherwise well-intentioned.[100] Academics in the field have criticised the concept of microaggressions for its lack of a scientific basis, its over-reliance on subjective evidence, and its elevation of victimhood.[101] Many critics also argue that microaggressions promote avoidance and psychological fragility and the connotations of the word suggest a violence that doesn't exist.[102] There is an argument put forward by sociologists that this culture of serial offence-spotters and microaggression-accusers is encouraging hurt and leading to the creation of a culture of victimhood. Many academics believe that society would be better served if we placed more emphasis on personal responsibility and honour.[103]

The term 'snowflake' to label a person was originally used in the movie *Fight Club* when Chuck Palahniuk said, 'You are not a beautiful or unique snowflake. You are the same decaying organic matter as everything else.' It's now become one of those go-to words that some people use to give themselves permission to insult and denigrate other people. On the other hand, this stuff is complicated and some people do cling to their snowflakery as a way of feeling special – they tend to spot offence everywhere they go. Of course, this isn't therapeutic for anyone.

Microaggression theory holds that whether your action or comment is meant to be aggressive is irrelevant – any and every minor instance of microracism, microsexism, micro-whatever-you're-having-yourself-ism can be labelled as bigoted and offensive. I have no doubt that in some cases, a sustained period of microaggressive behaviour is very difficult to tackle and the target might need both therapeutic support and perhaps legal support to deal with it so they aren't dismissed as drama queens. However, condoning people who are constantly on the lookout for microaggressions is an inducement to victimhood that doesn't help anyone.

Microaggressions have fuzzy boundaries as they are entirely in the eye of the beholder, so a certain phrase can simultaneously be and not be a microaggression depending on who is interpreting the action. For instance, asking a person 'Where were you born?' or commenting that they have 'good English' can be considered a microaggression, depending on the context. Spotting microaggressions can so quickly become utterly joyless and nerve-wracking that this policy of vigilance creates more anxiety than it prevents. It teaches vulnerable people to further explore and nurture their hurt and any offence they may feel, instead of taking the more therapeutic approach and learning to handle people who annoy them. It also rejects the more empowering approach that would lead people to learn not to allow other people's words to cause them distress. The problem is that calling out microaggressions may not be helping our society. People are losing their livelihoods because someone, somewhere took offence at something they said, but perhaps it is time to fight back and reclaim our freedom to cause inadvertent offence? So long as the offence wasn't meant, should we instead promote education, tolerance and understanding of the issues? Surely with all the devastation and distress there is in the world we have bigger fish to fry than arguing that statements such as 'You are so articulate' or 'I love your shoes' are microaggressions because they are deemed patronising.[104] Many of us don't need to censor microaggressions because the truth is that most of us are well able to cope with uneducated people revealing their ignorance, and if we continue to be overly concerned with microaggressions then we will create – if we haven't done this already – a culture of victimhood.

In my book *Cotton Wool Kids,* I write about the current trend to medicalise childhood by diagnosing natural and normal characteristics such as shyness, anger and introversion. This tendency to over-diagnose might lead to very helpful support and interventions at school but it also risks encouraging children to perceive themselves as ill, or special, and we might be in danger of turning childhood into a mental illness if we're not careful.

The first generation of cotton wool kids are growing up and, sadly, many of them are over-identified with their diagnoses. Online forums where users proudly list their mental health issues highlight what the author Angela Nagle named 'the cult of suffering, weakness and vulnerability'.[105] This dangerous new trend that sanctifies ill health to the point that people feel more special because they have been diagnosed with a disorder has created a culture where we are encouraged to act as if we are weak, helpless and aggrieved.

When diagnosed with anxiety or a panic disorder, some people feel a sense of absolution – a deep sense of relief that it isn't their fault that their brain is playing tricks on them. Psychiatric diagnosis, although initially scary and intimidating, has many benefits – it contextualises thoughts, increases understanding and is helpful when sourcing the appropriate treatment. But if a diagnosis becomes an integral part of a person's identity they can begin to fall into a culture of helplessness which can impede recovery. Promoting a culture of victimhood pretends to help people but really it causes untold damage. Abdicating responsibility and blaming other people's behaviour on your distress is a sure-fire way to sabotage happiness. This is why it could be argued that when certain vulnerable groups such as the transgender population begin to insist that the rest of the world needs to learn their range of preferred pronouns, it is more therapeutic to resist any demands or restrictions on our freedom of speech. Although it would be *nice* to remember to use a person's preferred pronoun, it cannot be presumed to suggest respect or disrespect of this person. Pronouns are simply a system of referral and it is obfuscating the truth to give them any more power than that.

All this talk in the media about snowflakes and the lack of resilience among millennials can be mindless and infuriating. However, it is not only people who are in their twenties and thirties who feel like snowflakes – many adults in their forties, fifties and beyond are eaten up by feelings of fragility, anxiety and self-absorption. The difference is that these days the political world, the media and the economy collude in indulging the most fearful and paranoid person so if you're under 30, you're more likely to believe that it is appropriate to behave like a snowflake and to choose not to face dealing with anyone who causes you discomfort. Mental health professionals often say that 'We teach people how to treat us' and many people are teaching their peers some very dysfunctional and unhelpful lessons.

THE DYING ART OF DISAGREEMENT

On 23 September 2017, the Pulitzer Prize-winning journalist Bret Stephens delivered the keynote speech at the Lowry Institute Media Award dinner in Sydney, Australia. Known for his right-wing opposition to Donald Trump and his contrarian views on climate change, there had been some controversy about whether Stephens should be given a platform to speak and this is why Stephens began by thanking the powers that be for the opportunity to speak.[106] In the end, Stephens's celebrated speech on 'The dying art of disagreement' was widely reported as a comprehensive challenge to the new trend to censor and stifle people with whom we disagree.

In his speech Stephens alluded to the fact that he had been lucky to have been given the opportunity to speak when he described the illustrious list of people who have recently been 'no-platformed' – denied a platform to speak – in world-famous prestigious universities:

> This has become the depressing trend on American university campuses, where the roster of disinvited speakers and forced cancellations includes former Secretaries of State Henry Kissinger and Condoleezza Rice, former Harvard University President Larry Summers, actor Alec Baldwin, human-rights activist Ayaan Hirsi Ali, DNA co-discoverer James Watson, Indian Prime Minister Narendra Modi, filmmaker Michael Moore, conservative Pulitzer Prize-winning columnist George Will and liberal Pulitzer Prize-winning columnist Anna Quindlen, to name just a few.[107]

But this isn't just confined to the US – more than 90 per cent of British universities also restrict free speech and almost two-thirds – 63.5 per cent – were described as 'severely restrictive' of free speech.[108] Stephens went on to point out in his speech that, as anyone with a liberal education knows, it is right and proper to have disagreement; indeed, this is often how concepts and ideas are further developed: 'Socrates quarrels with Homer. Aristotle quarrels with Plato. Locke quarrels with Hobbes and Rousseau quarrels with them both. Nietzsche quarrels with everyone. Wittgenstein quarrels with himself.' But, crucially, such disagreements are not regarded as offensive or insulting; indeed disagreements among intellectuals should be high-minded and appreciative of their adversaries. In intellectual discourse, placards need not be waved around and people need not be booed off stage or no-platformed; on the contrary, as Stephens pointed out:

These quarrels are never personal. Nor are they particularly political, at least in the ordinary sense of politics. Sometimes they take place over the distance of decades, even centuries ... to disagree well you must first understand well. You have to read deeply, listen carefully, watch closely. You need to grant your adversary moral respect; give him the intellectual benefit of doubt; have sympathy for his motives and participate empathically with his line of reasoning. And you need to allow for the possibility that you might yet be persuaded of what he has to say.

But this classically liberal mindset is changing and a new more narrow-minded and dogmatic attitude is taking hold. Sadly this isn't making for better, more robust mental health but instead it is weakening our psyches and creating a sense of fragility and fear. When Malia Bouattia, president of Britain's National Union of Students, defended this policy of censorship by saying that 'No-platform and safe space policies create an environment where students and staff are free from harassment and fear', she implied that being exposed to other people's opinions is inherently damaging. It isn't, though — indeed the most up-to-date research suggests that we would all be better off if we were exposed to other people's ideas and views.

HOW DO YOU HANDLE DISAGREEMENT?

- ❖ Do you suppress it and thereby become anxious because you know it could easily rise again at any time?
- ❖ Do you cause yourself inner tension by ignoring it?
- ❖ Do you avoid it by subjugating yourself?
- ❖ Do you compete and try to 'win' the fight?
- ❖ Do you compromise and find some agreement somewhere?

❖ Do you try to collaborate and if that's not possible agree to disagree?

❖ Do you engage and try to put out the fire?

If you find that you avoid disagreement at all costs you are probably *exacerbating* an underlying anxiety within yourself. Martin Luther King Jr told us that 'True peace is not the absence of tension: it is the presence of justice.' Avoiding or suppressing disagreement tends to exacerbate underlying tension without acting to address or resolve it. Equally, if you seek to 'win' by summarily 'beating' the opposition or 'lose' by subjugating yourself immediately, you are again missing the opportunity for psychological growth – it is more psychologically helpful if we can view disagreement as opportunities to learn and, even if you know you're right, you can still learn something about the person with whom you are disagreeing.

If you can learn the art of disagreement then you will be much more powerful and resilient in yourself. If you can learn to make eye contact with the people with whom you disagree; if you can learn to speak your truth clearly without obfuscation; and if you can try to seek the truth without turning to underhand tactics or silencing behaviour, not only will you be a stronger individual, but the world will be a better place, psychologically speaking. Learning the art of handling conflict is one of the most beneficial lessons any of us can learn: as Aristotle tells us, 'Anybody can become angry – that is easy, but to be angry with the right person and to the right degree and at the right time and for the right purpose, and in the right way – that is not within everybody's power and is not easy.' Although it might not be easy, it is certainly worth learning as history shows us again and again that engaging, explaining, listening, sometimes compromising, sometimes collaborating are the tools we need to sustain a progressive society.

No-platforming

Based on earlier strategies used by communists and Jewish activists, left-wing Trotskyist groups in the 1970s such as the International Marxist Group were the first to use the term 'no-platform' when they argued that there should be physical resistance to the next generation of fascists. However, from the very beginning, there were criticisms of the policy of no-platforming and *The Guardian* viewed it as a denial of free speech with the warning that, 'Students should perhaps remember that frustration which leads to a denial of the right of one section of society is not something new. It is a classic pattern of Fascism.'[109]

The policy of no-platforming successfully prevented the National Front and its successor the British National Party from gaining a foothold in the UK, so it can be effective, but in recent times no-platforming has moved from being an exceptionally unusual tactic to be used only when faced with violent extremists to being a valid option to prevent feminists, academics and politicians from speaking. When the likes of feminists such as Meghan Murphy and Julie Bindel, neither of whom has even been involved in physical violence, are no-platformed it is time for society to consider whether we are allowing some groups of distressed people to bully and censor others in a bid for power. The phrase 'hurt people, hurt people' has never been so apt as we see when people who are in serious psychological despair choose to misdirect their energy towards censoring people with whom they disagree instead of focusing on helping themselves.

Dame Jenni Murray, the veteran BBC broadcaster and *Woman's Hour* presenter, pulled out of a talk at Oxford University following claims from LGBTQ+ students that she was 'transphobic'. Murray had been invited to speak at an Oxford History Society event, as part of a series of events called 'Powerful British Women in History', but three student groups joined together to urge their peers to no-platform Murray because she had argued that trans women who have lived as men 'with all the privilege that entails' do not have the experience of growing up female. Considering Murray has spent a large part of her working life speaking about women, gender and politics, it comes as no surprise that she, as a passionate feminist, had views on male privilege, but this comment was hardly transphobic. Indeed, Murray had previously stated very clearly that she 'fully support[s] the right of trans women to be accorded the respect and protection I would demand for any human being, regardless of sex or gender'.[110] The University of Hull is currently reviewing its decision to honour her by naming a lecture theatre after her. However, perhaps reason will prevail as at the time of writing both the staff and the student body have called on the university to reverse this decision.[111]

An article written by the activist Esther Betts gives some insight into the minds of people who seek to no-platform others. Betts had turned up with other trans activists at an event in Bristol that proposed to discuss changes to the Gender Recognition Act in the UK. She had entered the building and, along with her fellow activists, blocked the stairwell to prevent attendees from coming in. The activists wore masks and planned to force entry to the hall where the event was taking place and let off a smoke bomb. In the end, the police were called and their plans were scuppered. I was at this event as I was involved in a Channel 4 documentary called *Trans Kids: It's time to talk*, and it was shocking to see these young activists attempting to intimidate middle-aged feminists. However, I could also see how distressed these young trans activists were. They compared the feminists to Nazis and truly seemed to believe that their own opinions and feelings were more important than everyone else's.

Betts later related in *The Guardian* newspaper that she regretted her actions. Although she no longer agrees with the tactics of no-platforming, she provides some insight into how some people believe that their most productive behaviour is to attack others: 'People asked me at the time, "Why don't you just go into such events and ask critical questions?" My response was that engaging in the event, even in an oppositional fashion, was to inadvertently validate views I considered hate speech.'[112]

Betts, a trans woman, later got a shock when she saw the film footage and realised how intimidating she had been.

> What I didn't realise at the time was that I was engaging in the event anyway. By attending it and blocking the stairwell I was engaging in the event. I was still acknowledging the views of the speakers just in an entirely different, completely non-productive way. I hate to admit it, but we achieved absolutely nothing, which is likely less than had we gone to the event and raised hell intellectually in the Q&A period.

Betts seemed horrified by her behaviour and realised that her attempts at protest had actually made matters worse. 'A better show of solidarity with the trans community would have been to go to the event and make damn well sure that our voices were heard in the form of difficult, intelligent questions.' Betts is right, of course; a more progressive approach is to try to build on previous generations' knowledge by listening to all sides of the argument – even to those with whom you vehemently disagree.

From a therapeutic standpoint, no-platforming creates a sense of fragility and vulnerability when a more helpful and therapeutic approach would be to learn how to confront and challenge people and ideas that seem reprehensible to us. The actor and comedian Rowan Atkinson was insightful when he declared that 'The strongest weapon against hateful speech is more speech.' Atkinson's position was clear; 'All jokes about religion cause offence, so it's pointless apologising for them' and he argued that we should really only apologise for bad jokes. Although Atkinson had some support, many others instantly denounced him as being out of touch with the new world that believes that the strongest weapon against hate speech is blanket censorship.

But maybe Atkinson has the right idea? He is certainly not the only comedian who has become increasingly concerned about the tendency to suppress comedy because of the risk of causing offence; Jerry Seinfeld, John Cleese, Chris Rock, Ricky Gervais and many others have all rowed into this debate with a staunch defence of their right to offend everybody. We need comedy; we need a certain light touch and some irreverence if we are to remain cheerful and good-humoured. Not only that, there are better ways to handle offensive people than blanket censorship – which, let's face it, serves only to drive issues into a toxic underground.

The small German town of Wunsiedel in Bavaria came up with a hilarious and effective way to deal with offensive people and show the world that there is always more than one way to solve a problem. The Nazi leader Rudolf Hess was born in Wunsiedel and every year right-wing extremists arrived into the town to commemorate his birthday. Counter-marches against the neo-Nazis didn't work, so in 2014 a bunch of sponsors agreed to start donating money towards anti-racist causes for every step the neo-Nazis took on their commemorative march. The neo-Nazis were further diminished when the sponsors erected banners along the route for the 'Nazis against Nazis walkathon' and cheered the fascists with banners that said 'Thank you for marching for racial justice' and updating them on how much the marches had raised so far for their good cause. When the neo-Nazis finished their march, they were handed certificates informing them how much money they had raised for their anti-Nazi charity.

Now, *that* is the way to handle offensive behaviour.[113]

WHY NO-PLATFORMING IS BAD FOR EVERYONE'S MENTAL HEALTH

* ❖ It can enable avoidance, which leads to long-term pain.
* ❖ It fosters the idea that words and ideas can hurt us.
* ❖ It discourages people from learning how to be mentally robust.
* ❖ It disempowers people because it colludes with the notion that words are violent.
* ❖ It creates feelings of emotional weakness and vulnerability.
* ❖ It drives toxic ideas underground.
* ❖ It can lead to physical violence as, without words and argument, violence can seem like the only option.

'VIOLENT' WORDS

Words are not physically violent. However, it has become commonplace for people who feel deeply offended by other people's speech to use the words 'violence' and 'assault' to describe the impact of certain words. Saying that words are 'literal violence' implies a physical force, and it is a misuse of the English language to say they are – words can be deeply hurtful but suggesting they can physically harm a person is just confusing for everyone.

Likewise, there has recently emerged a tendency to describe certain facts as racist or fascist or hate speech but it is important that we don't enable facts to be read as anything other than facts. *Facts are facts*; they are objective and they have no agenda. It is *what we do* with the facts that opens up an agenda.

We can't fix everything and if we try to, our mental health will suffer. If you feel devastated by other people's words or the facts they speak, then you need to get some more support from your therapist. On the other hand, if someone's words make you distressed to the point of violence you need help in learning how to handle these strong emotions within you.

Or you could just learn to handle the idea that many people hold misguided views:

> *'In life, it's important to know when to stop arguing with people*
> *and simply let them be wrong.'*
> Mindfulness adage

Answer the following questions to find out how you are handling other people's words and opinions. Do you …

- ❖ Seek offence whether or not it is deliberate?
- ❖ Get involved in feuds on social media?
- ❖ Get blocked by people on social media?
- ❖ Believe that others just don't understand the depth of your feelings?
- ❖ Become enraged by strangers' comments on social media?
- ❖ Become disturbed for days by comments that disagree with your views?
- ❖ Follow social media campaigns because you crave the heightened emotion?
- ❖ Become involved in campaigns that turn violent?

If you identify with any of these then you might be treating your anxiety with the wrong approach.

SAFE SPACES

There are many benefits to the 'safe space' in the counselling context. In a 'safe space' the client can safely rage and rail against others; they can unleash the darkest side of their psyche and in so doing calm the madness in their mind. Often, when working with a client, I will encourage them to view my office as a safe space where they can say what they want to say, without fear of being judged or cynically misunderstood. This is right and proper so that the client can, with some therapeutic guidance, explore their deepest fears, their darkest shadows, and then hopefully move from the unknown depths of their unconscious mind into the more knowable conscious mind. From this, within the counselling context, astonishing gains can be made.

There is a problem, though, and that is that the entire notion of the 'safe space' has been taken out of the therapeutic context and misguidedly moved to the birthplace of free thought and free speech: our educational institutions. In the context of universities, the seats of learning, where ideas and free thought are the most important aspect of the learning, the notion of a 'safe space' is infantilising, intolerant and dangerous. It teaches students to stifle people's dark side without giving anyone the opportunity to explore how and why people might have dark thoughts. More destructively, it teaches young people the insidious and regressive notion that ideas can hurt them.

Universities and academic institutions that should be in the business of expanding our minds are instead encouraging students to shy away from disagreement. The current attempt to change the world into a cotton wool universe where we all nod along and agree with each other is not only impossible and dysfunctional, it has cultivated heightened emotion and serial offence-spotting and it has driven dissension and conflict underground into a toxic underworld.

As Salman Rushdie said, 'College should be a safe space for thought, not a safe space from thought.' Universities used to be where pioneering and innovative ideas were explored but now 55 per cent of UK universities actively censor speech, 39 per cent stifle speech with increasingly strict regulations and just six per cent promote free, uncensored communication.[114]

A 'safe space' keeps people safe from challenge, safe from protest and safe from disagreement. But this doesn't help their mental health or their educational progress, instead it merely conforms to the paradoxical idea that although they are not strong enough to withstand disagreement, they *are* strong enough to stifle speech.

It is not only universities that have misguided policies around the notion of 'safe spaces'; schools are at it too. Avoidance-based measures such as special educational plans that enable students to leave class whenever they wish, or provide special entrances and exits to anxious students might be short-term solutions, but in the long term they send the message to kids that they are too fragile to cope with daily life.

The fallout of this notion is that young people end up operating under the belief that the sky will fall down if they are faced with disagreement. But it won't. Perhaps we should reclaim the old adage, 'sticks and stones may break my bones but words will never hurt me'? Although bullying is a serious issue, it is essential that we retain the knowledge that although words can be horrible they are *always* preferable to physical violence.

From a therapeutic point of view, it is not progress to promote mental fragility by sending the message that reasoned debate is frightening. This is the age of anxiety, where belligerently sensitive people are encouraged to feel anxious and offended and this feeling of offence pretends to bestow power on people. Sadly, the false sense of power that is foisted upon the person who feels offended denies this person the opportunity to harness their true strength that could have emerged from engaging with their fears, from being open to disagreement and learning to tap into their inner power.

CASE STUDY: SADIE, 20

Sadie came to me for counselling when she was 20 years old. A gentle soul, Sadie spoke sadly about how her college experience was dismantling her stability and how she had to drop out of her current course. This seemed a shame as she had already dropped out of her first college course and so, after establishing a good therapeutic alliance with her, I asked her to outline the cost-benefit analysis of the situation.

It turned out that Sadie had left her first course for the very same reason she was going to leave her second course – the college administration were at best flippant, at worst cruelly dismissive, of her need to establish vegan-friendly spaces within the campus. The vegan options in the cafeterias weren't enough for Sadie as the mere sight or smell of meat or dairy products made her feel nauseous. She couldn't stomach seeing people eat meat. 'The way their mouths chew on these big hunks of animal, it's just disgusting!' she shuddered. 'I can't face being around it.'

This was a problem. The world is not a vegan-friendly place and Sadie's extreme reaction to being around meat or animal products would be sure to cause her great distress when she began her adult working life.

It took some time for Sadie to begin to see the bigger picture. Initially the only path she could see ahead of her was to retreat to her bedroom where she could socialise with the vegan community online and she didn't have to face the meat-eaters. As we worked together, it was my role to ensure that Sadie explored all the options open to her. As she was a thoughtful person, Sadie began to worry about whether she was having any positive impact on the world – if she really wished to help the animals, she reflected, then she needed to gain the qualifications necessary to contribute effectively. Reddit campaigns weren't enough.

Sadie joined the vegan society in college and chose to set up an eating area within this space. It was awkward as they didn't actually meet near any cafeteria and yet Sadie could see that by choosing to join in and make a difference she was learning to confront forthcoming challenges in an adult manner instead of running away and hiding in her bedroom. Sadie was studying law and began to look forward to using her future qualifications to bring down the meat-eaters. It certainly seemed a more proactive way to approach life than hiding out in her bedroom. Sadie finished therapy with renewed vigour and hope for her future.

STUDENTS STIFLING ACADEMICS

When Erika Christakis, a child development expert at Yale University, sent a group email analysing whether Hallowe'en costume could be deemed to be offensive, it drew a line in the sand where mental health professionals around the world confirmed that ill-advised policies and misinterpretations of mental health slogans were actually *creating and nurturing* dysfunctional behaviour among young people.

It all began when the dean of Yale University had written about 'inappropriate' Hallowe'en costumes and lecturer Erika Christakis decided to email her students her considered response to this. In her email, Christakis argued that Hallowe'en was an inherently subversive celebration when children and young people should be allowed to dress however they wish – without fear of giving offence or of cultural misappropriation. Christakis also warned about how the adults' need for control could have an inappropriate impact on important stages of children's and young adults' psychological development. Christakis was reflective and considered in this email but also tried to challenge her students to think more deeply about the subject. But the students were outraged by her email, particularly a few lines that she attributed to her husband, a professor of medicine and sociology, 'Nicholas says, if you don't like a costume someone is wearing, look away or tell them you are offended. Talk to each other. Free speech and the ability to tolerate offence are the hallmarks of a free and open society.' Although *The Atlantic* magazine later pointed out that Erika Christakis' message was 'a model of relevant, thoughtful, civil engagement',[115] the students argued that her words had created an 'unsafe space' at the college and so had ruined their 'home'. The students met with Erika's husband, and demanded that he apologise on his wife's behalf. He wouldn't.

Students declared that they couldn't bear to live in the college any more. Hundreds of Yale students, alumni, faculty and staff signed an open letter criticising the Christakises. One month later, Erika decided not to teach at Yale any longer and a year afterwards, she communicated her feelings about the incident when she said that a 'culture of protection may ultimately harm those it purports to protect.'[116]

A small group of faculty members later tried to point out what had been lost: 'In the case of the Christakises, their work has been more directly oriented towards the social justice than the work of many other members of the Yale faculty,' they wrote. 'For example, Nicholas Christakis worked for many years as a hospice doctor, making house visits to underserved populations in Chicago. Progressive values and social justice are not advanced by scapegoating those who share those values.'[117]

But the larger point was perhaps what concerned many mental health professionals – it wasn't right or appropriate to encourage students to believe they were 'unsafe' if they disagreed with the Christakises; better progress is made if anxious people are helped to confront their irrational anxiety. Indeed, if the students truly felt unsafe within their university because of this email, the more therapeutically helpful response would have been to employ some college counsellors to support them. These frightened students had resorted to using dysfunctional coping mechanisms to make themselves feel better.

When Nicholas Christakis rejected the notion that it was his role to create a 'home' for students, one student unleashed a torrent of abuse: 'Then why the fuck did you accept the position?!' she screamed. 'Who the fuck hired you?! You should step down! If that is what you think about being a master you should step down! It is not about creating an intellectual space! It is not! Do you understand that? It's about creating a home here. You are not doing that!'[118]

Allowing a mob to rule and to bully decent people out of their professional role is not a helpful approach for any of us. Colluding with the students and allowing them to believe that an 'unsafe space' was created by Erika Christakis' email is enabling troubled students to wield their power in a dysfunctional way. Sadly, the Christakises are not alone and now it is a regular event to see professionals ousted from their positions because they wish to hold intellectual discourse about some controversial opinions.

THE TRAP OF VICTIMHOOD

A weird result of the current tendency to look for microaggressions, trigger warnings and safe spaces is to bestow more importance upon anyone who can claim hurt or victimhood. The negative impact of this means that is has become beneficial for a person to make whatever suffering they have experienced a front-and-centre element of their personality. This is easily evident on the popular TV shows *The X Factor* or *Britain's Got Talent* as we see that a person's singing ability is no match for their rival's sad back story. The sad fact about this dynamic is that, although focusing on your victim status might bring extra attention (and bonus points on TV shows), it is actually very negative for your mental wellbeing.

With so many people shrinking from honest debate and too scared to voice their opinions, not only is the opportunity to create a progressive society being lost, but fear and anxiety about saying (or even thinking) the wrong thing is spreading like wildfire.

Ordinary, reasonable people on Facebook are increasingly afraid to give voice to their moderate opinions as they know they will be fiercely shot down. Twitter is only for the brave and the cantankerous. So all that is left is to post pretty pictures on Instagram. The problem with this is that research shows us that Instagram has been identified as the social media site most likely to damage your mental health as all this comparison with everyone else's great (fake) lives creates distress.[119] We can't win; no matter what we do our mental wellbeing is being assaulted and so maybe we should gather our resources and learn to stand strong in the face of disapproval and unpopularity.

The junk media makes matters even worse, led by online hysteria, it seeks to polarise every debate with an aversion to detail and 'boring' reasoning. Becoming a slave to Google hits or Facebook likes means that the media is reducing every argument to the barest of essentials, with aggressive and partisan commentary; four legs good, two legs bad becomes the order of the day. Although this is having far-reaching ramifications for our political world, it is also having a lasting and worrying impact on our mental health, our psyche and our inner emotions.

The current trend that seeks to highlight offence and encourage outrage is making us feel that it is necessary to protect ourselves by avoiding everything that disagrees with our viewpoint. This over-the-top reaction is encouraged by media as it sells more content. Feeling distressed by other people's opinions now succeeds in closing the debate and adds points for your side of the argument; it also makes for entertaining reading on social media and so we get more 'likes' if we feel offended or hurt and less traction if we choose not to appeal to others' emotional brains and instead rely on reason and logic.

ARE YOU FALLING INTO A VICTIM MENTALITY?

To identify whether you are inclined towards victim status answer 'Yes' or 'No' to the following characteristics:

- Are you always on the lookout for who's doing you wrong?
- Do you often feel put upon?
- Do you feel more hard done by than most other people?
- Do you believe that you are inordinately unlucky?
- Do you think the reason for your problems lies with your bad luck or other people's bad behaviour?
- Do people feel burnt out by your neediness?
- Do you tend to monopolise conversations with the latest stories of your woe?
- Do you suspect that people screen your calls or say they're busy in order to dodge speaking with you?
- Do your friends and family find you negative?
- Have you a couple of unsolvable gripes that you often turn to when you're feeling down?

Give each 'Yes' response one point and count your score. If your score is four or more then you are probably sliding towards a victim mentality.

WHEN VICTIM OPPORTUNISTS CASH IN

Perhaps the most outrageous – yet – example of opportunistic victim misappropriation is the story of Rachel Dolezal, or Nkechi Amare Diallo, as she now prefers to be called, as she is trans-racial and changed her name by deed poll in 2016.[120] Dolezal began her life as a freckle-faced blonde Caucasian girl, but in 2004, when she was in her mid-twenties, Dolezal began to adapt her appearance so that she looked black.

Dolezal used a mixture of sunbeds and cosmetic techniques to make her skin darker and her straight hair frizzy. She applied to Howard University, a primarily African-American university, and the administration assumed she was black because she looked black, she sounded black, her artwork focused upon the suffering of black people and she ticked the 'African-American' box whenever she filled in any forms.

Dolezal was evidently highly competent and was elected president of a Washington chapter of the National Association for the Advancement of Coloured People. Dolezal also taught courses such as 'The Black Woman's Struggle', 'African and African-American Art History', 'African History' and 'African-American Culture', at Eastern Washington University.[121]

When it emerged that Dolezal was born white, she was dismissed by Eastern Washington University, but she remains unabashed; she was the subject of a Netflix documentary and has released a book about racial identification: *In Full Color: Finding my Place in a Black and White World*. In this book Dolezal defends her claims and compares her own experiences to slavery and explains how she identifies as trans-racial (using startlingly similar language and concepts as transgender activists). Belligerently sensitive to criticism, despite the entreaties of her bi-racial children, Dolezal insists on proclaiming that she 'remains unapologetically black.'

Being hurt or victimised is not a mark of virtue. Experiencing suffering can certainly make you more sensitive to other people's suffering but it still doesn't give you 'better' rights than someone else who didn't experience such suffering. However, in our brave new world, victim opportunism abounds as misery memoirs are now prominent in the bestselling charts and the number of people who describe their suffering in great detail as an easy method to achieve attention and recognition is increasing all the time.

In 2008, Riverhead Books published *Love and Consequences,* an account of a girl who was part white and part Native American, growing up as a foster child in Los Angeles in a world of drug dealers and gang members. Margaret Seltzer's (pseudonym Margaret B. Jones) supposed memoir was praised as 'humane and deeply affecting' by the *New York Times* until it was exposed as total fiction.[122]

The Australian blogger Belle Gibson was more dangerous in her claims as she released a fraudulent book and smartphone app, *The Whole Pantry,* about how she had had brain cancer and had been cured by her own dietary methods. Gibson fooled Apple as they lined up *The Whole Pantry* as a default application for the Apple Watch. The app was launched in 2013 and there were 300,000 downloads in the first month. Attributing one of her claimed cancers to the Gardasil vaccine, Gibson appears to have been extraordinarily immoral in her bid to achieve success through her identity as a victim.

I don't doubt for one second that these victim opportunists suffered troubled childhoods and yet, in psychology, it is well established that victims of terrible suffering can emerge from the experience stronger, weaker or much the same – all depending on how the recovery is managed. Once we become adults, we can attend to our grief from our broken childhood and with some counselling support, we can become stronger individuals. There comes a time in life for most people – some when they reach adulthood, others as late as 40 years old and beyond – when many people can begin the process of recovering fully from their childhood and from then on take responsibility for the rest of their lives. There will always be exceptions to the rule and a certain number of people who suffered immeasurably during their formative years may never recover from their childhood: for the rest of us, the choice is ours.

We ally ourselves with different groups because we benefit from the feeling of connection that it provides. This is well and good and important and yet if there is to be some therapeutic value for this alignment, the group needs to have an eye for a better life in the future. John, 41, was a member of a group that was founded to help address injustices suffered by men. As John later remarked, 'At first it felt great to be part of a group who knew where I was coming from, who didn't doubt my ability to care for my kids or love my kids. But then, after a while, it got a bit weird. Most of these guys had been victims of terrible injustices perpetrated by their ex-partners; really shocking stuff like unfounded accusations of child sexual abuse. I began to feel a bit uncomfortable with my silly stories about how awkward and petty my ex-wife could be. In the end I took a break from the group because, although they were exactly what I needed when I was still raw from the break-up, as time went on, I didn't want to have my rage stoked up against my ex-wife who was also the mother of my kids. These things are complex.'

If people who feel distressed by their past can take ownership of this distress without needing to *remain* feeling put-upon or oppressed, then they are more likely to find true meaning and relief from their suffering. People who feel oppressed need to harness their justified rage if the oppression remains present in their lives, but if the oppression is in the past then identification within the group can be more hazardous. All too often the suffering was real, as were your feelings of oppression, but identification with a group on the grounds of past oppression is sometimes, in the wrong context, therapeutically difficult. And it is these complexities that can lead to a conflicted and false sense of self.

TAPPING INTO YOUR INNER STRENGTH

Although the political world and the media may have led the charge, the extraordinary rise of hysterical social media, social justice warriors and victim opportunists have also had a hand to play in creating a society where we feel we must mentally check ourselves before we say anything even slightly controversial. Yet making mistakes is an integral part of being human and language is often clumsy as we try to find our truth.

It is not helpful for anyone if we enable dysfunctional, avoidant behaviour – it is much more empowering to equip people with the strength to cope with the reality of life's challenges. In fact, learning to view ourselves as mentally fragile and to view disagreements as threatening to our mental health instead of as ideas that can be argued, discussed and dismantled if necessary, is actually *damaging* to our mental health. If society judges each of us to be too fragile to hear little more than an echo chamber of our own thoughts, then we will soon become even more fragile and more easily hurt. Both from a therapeutic and societal viewpoint, we need to banish the anxiety around confronting and handling ideas and people that make us feel uncomfortable. It's not easy but once you have an inkling of how this feels, the empowerment and strength you can garner from it will make you want to fight for more of it.

We need to be allowed to say what we think; we need to be able to challenge people without attacking them; and we need to defend the right to offend. As the controversial commentator Brendan O'Neill pointed out in the equally controversial internet magazine *Spiked-online*:

> Freedom of speech is the most important freedom there is. It is the freedom upon which all other freedoms are based, upon which democracy becomes possible, through which the individual becomes autonomous, a full and morally responsible adult. Because unless we can speak for ourselves and think for ourselves and judge for ourselves, we are not truly free, and instead we become the child-like charges of those who Know Better.[123]

KEY WAYS TO GROW YOUR INNER STRENGTH

❖ Teach people how to treat you: It won't serve you well if you teach people to treat you as weak and fragile. If you can instead tap into your inner power and learn to stand strong you will more easily move to a better place.

❖ Use your body language and tone of voice to evoke respect: Using your body language to stand up straight and proud will help you to harness your inner strength so that you can learn to stand your ground instead of bowing to perceived and imagined threats. This is a much more productive and helpful route to follow than to act put-upon and abused. When you are upset, make a conscious decision to slow down your speech and go a tone deeper so that you don't come across as high-pitched, shrill and weak. Your strength is in your belly and in your heart — use it.

- Earn respect through your actions: Nobody has a right to demand respect; just like love and affection, respect can be desired but it doesn't work if it's forced. It is much more helpful to ensure you are respected as a person through your deeds and through your speech instead of relying upon a victim identity.

- Engage with everyone, as much as possible: Feeling powerless and helpless, hurt people often prefer the passing pleasure of feeling in control by silencing an offender rather than seeking the long-term satisfaction gained by finding the strength to engage with even the most irritating and irrational foe. Sulking is usually the behaviour of a person who hasn't the ability to communicate their hurt. If you begin to sulk, it is helpful if you can find someone who cares about you to listen as you try to articulate your hurt.

- Try to learn something: Rather than taking exaggerated and histrionic offence whenever we can, we could begin to size up and listen to whoever is causing us personal conflict. The social entrepreneur, philanthropist and author Auliq-Ice remarked, 'It's taken years, but part of my own personal growth has involved deciding that I can learn something from even the most annoying person.'

- Pick up your suffering: Life is difficult. We need to acknowledge this. We are all oppressed in our different ways, but the good news is that the world is getting better and you too can become part of this movement to improve the world.[124] As the controversial and much-maligned psychologist Jordan Peterson advises us, 'Pick up your damn suffering and bear it, and try to be a good person so you don't make it worse.'

PART 3

THE RECOVERY: LEAVING ANXIETY BEHIND

CHAPTER 7

Are you getting better or worse?

'I am the master of my fate, I am the captain of my soul.'

WILLIAM ERNEST HENLEY

In my work as a counsellor and psychotherapist, I often find it valuable to ask clients if they are getting better or worse. This question is almost always effective in bringing self-awareness about whether what they are currently doing is helpful or unhelpful. Pausing for a moment to consider the questions below will give you a good indication of whether you are living in a way that is helping you. It will examine the effectiveness of your current approach and further develop your self-awareness.

So, if you consider your feelings of anxiety from the long perspective, are you more or less anxious than ten years ago? Five years ago? Last year? Often life events are markers for when you might have plunged deeper into difficulties and so it might be very easy for you to pinpoint why you became more anxious at certain points in your life; nevertheless, it is important to ascertain whether your day-to-day actions are making you feel better or worse. This list can also be helpful to figure out whether you are more behaviourally driven or cognitively driven and this information could give you some insight into how you should approach your recovery.

BEHAVIOUR: COMPARED TO THIS TIME LAST YEAR

- ❖ Shortness of breath, breathlessness
  Better/worse
- ❖ Heart palpitations, skipping a beat, accelerated heartbeat
  Better/worse
- ❖ Dry mouth
  Better/worse
- ❖ Sweaty or cold, clammy hands
  Better/worse
- ❖ Muscle tension, aching muscles
  Better/worse
- ❖ Diarrhoea, constipation, digestive problems
  Better/worse
- ❖ Difficulty swallowing or lump in the throat
  Better/worse
- ❖ Headaches, neck pain, grinding teeth
  Better/worse
- ❖ Frequently emptying bladder
  Better/worse
- ❖ Hot and/or cold flushes or feeling itchy
  Better/worse
- ❖ Twitchy, trembling or shaky
  Better/worse
- ❖ Numbness or tingling in the hands and/or feet
  Better/worse

COGNITIVE: COMPARED TO THIS TIME LAST YEAR

- ❖ Trouble falling or staying asleep; nightmares
  Better/worse
- ❖ Ruminating; obsessive thoughts
  Better/worse
- ❖ Difficulty concentrating
  Better/worse
- ❖ Feeling fearful or filled with dread
  Better/worse
- ❖ Intolerant, irritable or tetchy
  Better/worse
- ❖ Over-reacting or over-sensitive
  Better/worse
- ❖ Focusing on the negative
  Better/worse
- ❖ Easily alarmed, frightened, or surprised
  Better/worse
- ❖ Avoiding busy traffic, the dark, being left alone, crowds, etc.
  Better/worse
- ❖ Feeling impatient, as if you have no time
  Better/worse
- ❖ Forgetful, distracted
  Better/worse

WHY IS YOUR ANXIETY NOT DIMINISHING?

Anxiety is a condition that is particularly blighted by common fallacies and mistakes; mostly because anxiety itself can lead you to make decisions that are counterproductive to curing the anxiety in the long run. Anxiety impacts your thought processes so it leads you to make inappropriate decisions.

A chief reason why it is hard to get rid of anxiety is because it is so self-sustaining. When you experience anxiety, your brain automatically dives for the nearest avoidance strategy that will act almost like a drug to calm your mind. If you yield to this, you create a vicious circle that will not reduce the anxiety until you are willing to give up the short-term avoidance drugs and commit yourself to the longer-term approach – living without avoidance drugs and learning to handle your anxiety.

Self-awareness is key to the process because the more you know about your avoidance strategies, the more you can avoid the common pitfalls of the anxious brain. Although the following is not comprehensive, it could still be helpful to consider which of these pitfalls are applicable to your anxiety.

RUMINATING OR OVER-THINKING

The worst thing you can do when you feel anxious is to passively obsess about how you feel. And the most common way to exacerbate the anxiety is to believe that over-thinking, worrying and ruminating are necessary to help you calm down. People with anxiety all too often fall into the mistake of believing that they can *think* their way out of their anxiety – that ruminating obsessively will put a solvable framework on any given situation. It won't though. Anxiety tires you out, it drains the body – and ruminating and over-thinking make it worse.

The strategy

Inaction often comes about after a heavy bout of over-thinking and so, although it might feel impossible, getting out and meeting others and, as much as possible, focusing on other people is a key strategy to release you from the churning thoughts and thus relieve your anxiety.

INACTION/NEGLECTING YOUR EXERCISE

Compulsive thinking and anxious behaviour can be mentally exhausting and lead individuals to feel so wretched that they can barely move their head from the pillow. If we aren't careful our brains can become like a whirlwind, driven by a mass of random and scary uncontrolled thoughts and lacking any rationality or perspective. Many anxious people report experiencing 'paralysis by analysis' where they analyse something so much that they feel absolutely paralysed by the weight of it. It is because anxiety makes you feel exhausted that so many people resist exercise as a way to reduce anxiety. But it really works. This is only one of the many reasons why pretty much every therapist in the world seems to recommend exercise for people with challenges to their mental health.

The strategy

If you find your anxiety is worsening, then make sure you bring some exercise into your process of recovery – even a short brisk walk every day will make a small difference. Exercise reduces compulsive thinking and over-reacting because it physically brings your tension down a notch or two. No matter how much you loathe the idea of exercise, you really should consider if there is some way that you can bring some exercise into your life. Exercise is also a helpful method to drain the body of excess energy that can be unhelpfully misdirected into over-thinking. It can also help improve hormone function and neurotransmitter production.

YIELDING TO PANIC

In a weird way, yielding to the panicky thoughts that threaten to overcome a person can bring a strangely satisfying hit as it suddenly feels like 'game on' in the brain – all the waiting around is over and the panic has truly arrived. Well, the panic may have arrived but the true danger has not: although the brain might think it's game on, it's not *really* game on, it's a false sense that something is happening because your brain has yielded to panic.

I was once in the middle of a terribly difficult night when everything was getting on top of me. I started rocking back and forth, ranting to my friend, 'I'm losing it, I'm losing it.' My friend at the time said in a strong voice, 'Don't lose it, Stella. Just don't. You can't lose it.' Something about the impassioned and concerned way he spoke penetrated my brain and I didn't lose it.

When you are anxious your emotional brain starts coming up with all sorts of outlandish, highly unrealistic ideas that are unlikely to occur. For example, before you go on a blind date, your thoughts might go something like, 'Oh my God, I can't do this. I just can't do this!' These thoughts will only heighten your already anxious state. Instead, you need to challenge your thoughts, remind yourself that this isn't a catastrophe, and in reality, no one has ever died from going on a blind date. Yes, you may be anxious, yes, it might be awful and yes, you may come across as nervous, but the worst thing that will happen is that you won't have a good date.

The strategy
Ask yourself the following questions to help you challenge your thoughts:

- ☆ Is this worry realistic?
- ☆ Is this likely to happen?
- ☆ If the worst-case scenario happens, how bad would it be and could I handle it?
- ☆ What could I do instead?

☆ If something bad happens, what does that mean about me?

☆ Is this really true or does it just seem to be true?

☆ What could I do to prepare for whatever might happen?

WITHDRAWING INSTEAD OF REACHING OUT

We know it doesn't work. We know from experience that isolating ourselves can be dangerous and yet so many of us fall into this pitfall again and again.

The thing about withdrawing is that, just like all these common pitfalls, it can work in the short term. Indeed, sometimes the very best thing a person can do is to withdraw from the madding crowd, take some time alone and remember to breathe.

If you are in the middle of extreme anxiety it is perfectly acceptable to withdraw from people and yet, as soon as you can, it is usually more beneficial to put yourself out there and try to enrich your life with people and pursuits. It can be worthwhile to give yourself permission to withdraw for a time because you need to recharge, with the proviso that you will do something from time to time to check if you are ready yet to come out of hibernation. Just as a little hedgehog might poke their head out to see if the sunshine is warm yet, the person who needs to recharge can make themselves go for a very short evening walk to see if they can face the world yet.

The problem with withdrawing is when it moves from a time-out into a much more hazardous hide-out. Anxiety can chemically control your brain and can change your thoughts from bad to worse. Anxious thoughts are often wildly inaccurate and being alone with negative emotions can create a storm of madness with little grip on reality. One of the secrets to reducing anxiety is keeping active and focusing on other people. The more you reach outwards the more likely your anxious thoughts will diminish in the long run.

The strategy

If you can train yourself to reach out to different people in times of trouble, not only will you benefit from the very act of engaging with the world, but you will also deepen some of your relationships. A sad side-effect of this is that it may also reveal the superficiality of some relationships but, on a brighter note, it often reveals hidden depths in other relationships.

ALLOWING NEGATIVITY TO SEEP IN

We humans are social animals and tend to pick up on other people's behaviour. This is why it is so destructive to your psyche if you allow yourself to spend too much time with negative people who bring stress and tension with them. It is much more helpful if you can identify more positive people as this is one of the easiest ways to improve your mental health.

It is not only negative people we must be wary of but negative media and negative self-talk too. Anxiety can create a lot of brain chatter and the timbre of this chatter is often mindlessly nasty towards both yourself and others. You might find it helpful to learn some positive mantras to repeat every time you catch yourself falling into the hole of negative self-talk (see Chapter 8). Tension-inducing media is everywhere – whether you are simply watching TV, scrolling through Facebook or even mindlessly checking out Twitter, you are endlessly confronted with images of war-torn countries, of unbearably sad stories of children with cancer and of the latest corruption from the politicians. It is frightening, it contributes to negative self-talk and it makes anxious people feel inappropriately overwhelmed. It is inappropriate because all the good news stories are not given even a fraction of the coverage that the bad news gets. Hans Rosling's book *Factfulness* gives a comprehensive account of how and why the world is getting better every day. The numbers of people experiencing poverty, hunger and disease are significantly reducing and the child mortality rate has fallen in every single country on the globe. Sadly, our emotional and dramatic brains and the media's dictum 'if it bleeds, it leads' has interfered with our understanding of the world and now many of us assume the world is getting worse when, in truth, it is improving year on year.

The media can be pretty relentless and so we need to become more vigilant about how it is impacting our moods. 'Negative media' is a wide-ranging phrase as it isn't just haunting news stories of disasters that depresses us; it's the endless pictures on our newsfeed of fabulous lives being lived so close yet so far away. These stories of unrealistic perfect lives can quickly make us tense, anxious and chronically disappointed with our lives.[125]

The strategy

Most of us need more vigilance about our tech usage – if you drink too much you will make more of an effort to stay out of pubs; if you feel depressed after media, then you need to stay away from certain online sites. Give your sense of wellbeing a score out of ten before you check your media and afterwards. If you feel better after checking in, that's fine, but if you feel a bit tense and overwhelmed then that's a sign that you need to reduce your tech usage.

FOCUSING ON THE FUTURE INSTEAD OF ENJOYING THE PRESENT

Goal-setting is a known strategy to help reduce anxiety – it is a very structured method that helps a person focus on what they need in life. Goal-setting is a long way from vaguely worrying about future events in a negative, unfocused way as this is an entirely different pursuit and is very destructive to the psyche.

You will find that your anxiety reduces if you can learn to turn your focus to right now; if you can learn to automatically pause and take a break whenever you feel a bit stressed. Even if you are faced with a serious situation, focusing on the future will not make it any easier to manage. Positive mantras, such as 'this is a problem for the future me, this isn't a problem for today' can reduce unfocused worries about the future.

The strategy

Some people find that writing down their vague worries as and when they come to you can be effective as, once you have recorded the worry, you can make a date with yourself to analyse these worries later on and then you are free to refocus on the present that is unfolding right before you. During your scheduled 'worry time' you can tick off each worry into a section marked either 'pointless worry' or 'valid worry' and this can illuminate the wasted time spent on needlessly worrying and, in the long term, this self-awareness can bring about positive changes.

TAKING EXTERNAL SOLUTIONS INSTEAD OF INTERNAL SOLUTIONS

Drinking alcohol or coffee or smoking is a clear example of the way that certain 'solutions' can provide short-term relief but ultimately make the anxiety worse and impede the brain's ability to cope with stress. Alcohol numbs your anxiety but it also reduces your ability to cope with stress. Many people feel considerably calmer after a drink or two but alcohol only numbs your brain to the anxiety *in the moment*; it doesn't provide any real long-term cure. Getting used to alcohol or other substances making you feel better temporarily can provide you with the false idea that this temporary crutch is necessary. Then, after you've consumed the temporary crutch, the chemical impact of alcohol – dehydration, sleeplessness, poor decision-making and 'the fear' – tend to exacerbate anxiety, thus making the whole process false and creating more anxiety than it solves.

Coffee or tea can also be very helpful in the moment but, just like alcohol and other external, short-term solutions, they can easily be misused and so should be used with care and consideration. For some people, coffee can cause a faster heartbeat and this can be a trigger for panic attacks. For others, coffee leads to dehydration, which can cause feelings of stress and tension in the body. Still others find that coffee keeps them awake at night over-thinking pointlessly. Caffeine in itself can be a problem and I have often heard reports of anxiety and panic attacks significantly reducing for people who gave up drinking coffee, Diet Coke and other caffeine-based drinks. It is key to build personal awareness so you can recognise how caffeine might contribute to your anxiety symptoms.

Smoking also feeds the insidious idea that anxiety can only be quelled from outside sources. Nicotine provides an immediate – and temporary – sense of relaxation and so, not only is the smoker seeking external solutions to internal problems, they are also kidding themselves that the nicotine is making them calmer when it is just a fleeting sensation that makes little difference to the person's long-term wellbeing.

The strategy

A tool such as a 'worry stone' (a rock that you rub when stressed) or a worry bracelet can provide a healthier short-term solution than drugs – and sometimes that is exactly what we need – but ultimately the real solution needs to come from inside yourself. For as long as you assume the calming solution is outside yourself you are giving your power away. The key to this is that, with the right support, you learn to give up your dependency on your short-term solutions while building up awareness of the solutions you can find within yourself. This might be slow breathing, mindfulness, yoga or any of the approaches listed in the next chapter.

TAKING MEDICATION OR SIMILAR SHORT–TERM COPING STRATEGIES WITHOUT THERAPY

Medication is especially alluring for anxious people because it is an external substance that offers a short-term, immediate solution – for the anxious person, this is the perfect scenario and it is why many anxious people become either physically or emotionally dependent on their medication. Xanax abuse is a growing problem as it is addictive, it is 20 times stronger than Valium and it is available on the black market. Fifty per cent of the world's sales of Xanax come from the US and 22 per cent come from the UK and, with children as young as 11 years old being treated for Xanax abuse, it is no longer only stressed housewives who turn to tranquillisers to take the edge off their emotions.[126]

Although prescribed medication is often essential for many people, it is equally essential that the medication is combined with some talk therapy. If you are taking medication without attending counselling, you are cutting off your nose to spite your face; you will eventually need higher doses and you are denying yourself the opportunity to learn some long-term coping strategies.

The problem with unhealthy coping behaviours, whether smoking, taking Xanax or dodging engagements, is that these coping behaviours are like a crutch for your brain – they essentially stop the brain from trying to help you cope with stress in another, healthier way, and instead let the crutch handle it. So using a crutch such as Xanax might help you get through the day but it also reduces your ability to cope.

The strategy

Crutches that help you get through the day must be partnered with some real-life strategies such as therapy, self-awareness and self-compassion to help you begin to face your demons. If you're anxious, you need to connect with a therapist; if you don't feel connected with your first therapist, look for another, and another, and another, until you do finally connect because it is only then you will see the extraordinary benefits of good talk therapy.

BEING AIMLESS INSTEAD OF FINDING MEANING

The writer Andrew Solomon wisely advises us that instead of asking 'What does it mean?' we should instead ask 'What does it mean for me?' If you can focus on meaningful, goal-directed activities you will feel less anxious than if you spend time on aimless, meaningless activities. Aimless, meaningless activities tend to provide passing pleasures without nourishing our souls – for some people this can mean scrolling through social media while for others it might mean shopping. Meaningful, goal-directed activities tend to feel good for the soul, leaving you with the knowledge that the activity was good for you on some level. This might mean a lunch with some old friends for some, while for others it could entail going on a retreat with like-minded people.

The strategy

You need, as far as possible, to do what needs to get done in your day-to-day life and if you can find meaning in everyday activity while you can get on with the business of life, then you will find that your anxiety automatically reduces. When you go to work, seek meaning in the work – if the work is inherently meaningless to you, seek meaning in the work relationships or in what you can do with your salary.

If you feel at a loss trying to figure out what gives you meaning, then pull out a page and start answering these questions:

- ❖ What would you do if you weren't afraid?
- ❖ What is your ideal future?
- ❖ What would you like to learn more about?
- ❖ What habits or tendencies do you have that you'd like to change?

If you write a couple of paragraphs on each of those questions you will soon realise what gives your life meaning and what makes you feel empty.

GIVING UP TOO SOON INSTEAD OF FINDING SUPPORT WHEN YOU FEEL FRAGILE

Recovering from anxiety can take a long time and it almost always involves difficult emotions and experiences that are really hard to handle. This is why many people find the recovery just too difficult and so they give up on it. Just like the alcoholic who grabs the glass of wine at the wedding, high-voltage events can tip a person in recovery into an episode of heightened anxiety. Relapses often lead to self-loathing, despair and recrimination where people feel that nothing really works and all the effort is pointless. But often, with a bit of self-compassion and some perspective, the accurate analysis would show that, in truth, they had made significant improvements and one relapse shouldn't take the wheels off the wagon.

The strategy

If you are in danger of giving up before you have fully recovered, I strongly urge you to make an appointment with a therapist who will hopefully provide you with the support you need to continue on a better, healthier road.

BAD TECH MANAGEMENT INSTEAD OF GOOD TECH MANAGEMENT

There is absolutely no doubt that the injection of all this tech and social media into our lives has massively accelerated our stress levels. The average person checks their phone 1,500 times a week and cyber-psychologist Dr Mary Aiken tells us that 'The number of hours people spend on their mobile phones is escalating rapidly each year, jumping an average of 65 per cent in a two-year period.'[127] In her book *The Cyber Effect,* Aiken discusses the *time-distortion effect* of being online. If you turn off your clock display the next time you log on and test yourself on how long you have spent online you will realise that our ability to keep track of time is significantly reduced when we are online. Not only that, but being online is like stepping into a different environment – you are actually travelling somewhere in your mind, and it can take a moment or two to get your sea-legs. Most of us deny this fact and so mindlessly check in and out of cyberspace all day, every day, underestimating or dismissing the dizzying impact this is having on our psyches.

Whether or not we deny it, the impact is familiar to all of us: anxiety, stress, tension, depression and tech rage are all common features related to online behaviour. This is why we need to learn how to manage our tech instead of it managing us.

The strategy

Learn how to turn your phone off once a day – even for 15 minutes – just so you can reacquaint yourself with the concept of being 'uncontactable' for a few minutes. Declare certain rooms 'tech-free' – the kitchen and the bedrooms are good contenders – where the highest form of tech allowed is the radio. You could also declare certain times of the day 'tech-free'– so the phones aren't allowed get turned on until 8.30 a.m. every morning and they must go off every evening at 10 p.m.

TRYING TO SUPPRESS THOUGHTS INSTEAD OF ACKNOWLEDGING THEM

The problem with thought suppression is that it brings about a psychological phenomenon like the 'pendulum effect' in Chapter 3: when you try to avoid thinking a certain thought, you actually have the thought more often than if you had never bothered trying to avoid it at all. This means that the harder you try not to worry, the more you worry. Killing yourself trying not to worry can often be a big waste of time; sometimes simply distracting yourself from your thoughts is far less effortful and much more effective.

An interesting study divided a number of people into two groups; both groups were told to click a button every time they thought about a pink rabbit. Group A were told to think about a pink rabbit whenever they wished and Group B were told not to think about a pink rabbit. The results showed that Group B clicked the button more than Group A. Group A (who were allowed to think about it as they wished) didn't feel compelled to keep thinking about the pink rabbit. This study shows us what we already know instinctively – trying to stop your thoughts is counterproductive to your ability to reduce your anxiety.

The strategy

If you can remind yourself that anxiety is a feeling, just like any other feeling, then you can begin to accept it. Acceptance of your anxiety is critical because when you try to eliminate your anxiety you will often worsen it and you will also perpetuate the idea that your anxiety is intolerable. The reality is that although anxiety is deeply uncomfortable, it is not intolerable.

VALIDATING INSTEAD OF QUESTIONING YOUR FEARS

Although it can be helpful to accept your anxiety this does not, on any level, mean that you should validate your fears. If you validate your fears you are, figuratively, taking your heroin. If you have social anxiety and you avoid a function because you have convinced yourself that you will have a panic attack if you go, you are validating your fears; likewise, if you have health anxiety and you Google your latest physical symptoms, then you are also validating your fears. You may try to convince yourself that this is a case of the boy who cried 'wolf', and this time you really do have a rare and little-known disease but, then, you would think that, wouldn't you? It is far more difficult to resist Dr Google. We shy away from the cognitive dissonance (see later in this chapter) as we don't like to feel as though our thoughts are irrational and so we research the subject and we convince our friends and everybody else that this time it's for real. Most of all, we look for reasons to believe that our minds are rational and our fears are perfectly understandable. But this is seldom the case with chronically anxious people – it is much more likely to be validating fears.

Your brain plays tricks on you when you feel highly anxious so when you have a panic attack you honestly believe that you are having a heart attack. The psychiatrist Dr Kelli Hyland described how she became panicked as a medical student when she saw a person who was having a panic attack. 'I had seen people having heart attacks and look this ill on the medical floors for medical reasons and it looked exactly the same. A wise, kind and experienced psychiatrist came over to [the patient] and gently, calmly reminded him that he is not dying, that it will pass and his brain is playing tricks on him. It calmed me too and we both just stayed with him until [the panic attack] was over.'[128]

The strategy

The endless ability of our brain to deceive us is both impressive and devastating and we should always treat our 'certain knowledge' with a certain level of healthy scepticism and awareness of the extraordinary power of our emotional brain.

AVOIDING ANXIETY TRIGGERS INSTEAD OF FACING TRIGGERS WITH APPROPRIATE SUPPORT

As discussed endlessly in this book, the presumption is that stimuli that trigger your anxiety should be avoided, but this presumption is wrong. Humans often work on the behavioural principle of negative reinforcement; for example, when you avoid leaving the house because of your panic attacks, your brain receives the message that your anxiety was calmed as a result of your avoidance strategy and so thinks you must do more of that in the future (see Chapter 1). Even worse, the idea that the outside world is something you need to fear can then become reinforced in your brain.

The strategy

Research shows us again and again that, with the right support, facing your fears, allowing yourself to be afraid, finding the right support and building yourself up so that you're strong enough to go to a place that makes you feel anxious has a much more positive effect on your mental health than avoiding certain stimuli.

HYPERVENTILATING INSTEAD OF SLOW BREATHING

Breathing exercises can be extremely helpful to quell anxiety. However, like many strategies, these techniques can create more anxiety if they are used in the wrong way. Hyperventilation translates as 'over breathing': it is the process that happens when your body breathes too quickly, takes in too much oxygen and expels too much carbon dioxide. You can then feel you need to breathe even faster or more deeply to compensate for the excess of oxygen and the lack of carbon dioxide. But this only serves to exacerbate the symptoms. Our bodies need carbon dioxide and the body can react negatively to hyperventilation with chest pains, rapid heartbeat, shortness of breath and light-headedness. This can then lead to panic attacks for some people.

The strategy

The solution to this hot mess is to dramatically slow down your breathing. There is no desperate need to breathe deeply – indeed the urge to breathe deeply can sometimes cause further problems for some people. Breathing exercises are covered in the next chapter. These will help your body go from the fight-or-flight response from your amygdala (see Chapter 1) to the more relaxed response of a less frantic part of your brain.

VISUALISING HORROR MOVIES INSTEAD OF CALMING THOUGHTS

When emotions are heightened we often have the wrong types of visualisation, indulging in worst-case scenarios and conjuring up horrible visions. Positive visualisation techniques work very well for some people while other, less visual, people find them very difficult. You will need to practise these visualisations when you are feeling calm before they will work when your emotions are heightened.

The visualisation described in the next chapter (see page 244) could be effective as a tool to use when you find your mind unravelling.

The strategies

If you tend to visualise horrific scenarios in your head then you are probably quite a visual person, so you could commit to learning and practising calming visualisations. There are a range of calming visualisations widely available online for anyone to use. Find a couple that suit you and keep them like pieces of gold in your pocket, to be rubbed anytime you feel the need.

CASE STUDY: LOUISE, 40

Louise was highly anxious when she first arrived in my clinic. A good-looking woman, Louise was feeling overwhelmed by the demands of raising three boys under the age of eight. Her husband, Eoin, worked very hard as an engineer on oil rigs and often had to work far away from home. The upshot was that most of the time Louise felt like a single parent.

Louise used a cognitive distortion known as projection to avoid thinking about her true worries – deep down Louise was worried about her marriage and finances and about whether her boys would cope if she got a divorce. But instead of worrying about these issues, she projected her anxiety by fantasising about outlandishly unlikely and dreadful scenarios that could befall her children.

When her eldest went on a school kayaking trip, Louise spent the whole day imagining gory images of her child drowning. Finally, when she could bear it no longer, she rang the school and asked how the children were. The receptionist was nonplussed and reassured her that had there been any accidents, they would be the first to know. She then rang the outdoor pursuits centre who were rudely dismissive. The extreme anxiety that Louise felt that day eventually convinced her to ring me and make her first appointment. 'I just thought it wasn't natural that I was a gibbering wreck for the whole time Seán was away on his school tour. I started to feel that maybe I was disconnected with myself? But then again, maybe I'm wrong, maybe everyone feels nervous when their first child goes on their school tour?'

Although Louise wanted me to reassure her about this, I was hesitant about readily providing her with the external validation that she had been seeking about the school tour. Instead I explained to Louise all about cognitive distortions and how control fallacies, catastrophising and internal belief systems could ruin her life. The joylessness that characterised Louise's day-to-day existence was saddening to watch. She was gripped with fear and dread and even a visit to the playground usually ended up with some major calamity taking place in her mind. It was unsustainable. Louise's mind had made life hellish for her; worry, dread and terror were constantly at her shoulder, as she dreamed up new ways to ruin any sense of wellbeing she might try to find in her day.

We needed to get to work.

At first we tried mindfulness and Louise found that this helped with her sleeping but didn't manage to calm her waking nightmares. Certain slow breathing exercises helped Louise to bring her anxiety levels down a bit. But more than that, Louise's decision to go to therapy lifted the lid on her anxiety. Knowing that we would discuss her every fear brought some perspective to Louise as she now had an objective sounding board to test out whether her worries were genuine or needless. Louise remained more amenable to analysis of a worry after the event than before but we were still able to make good progress in building awareness of her thought and behaviour patterns.

Over time Louise began to discuss how lonely she felt in her marriage and how distressed she was about the pile of bills that were kept in a drawer in the kitchen. Louise and Eoin had taken out a big mortgage to live in a house that was quite far away from her family and friends. Louise knew she didn't belong in her new community and she didn't have time to reconnect with her old friends. Eoin wasn't there enough to provide emotional support and Louise was bored, lonely and fretful.

Therapy really began to work for Louise when she started to build some emotional awareness about what was really bothering her. After some months Louise had made some serious adjustments to her life and no longer felt the need for further therapy. At Louise's insistence, Eoin had left his job on the oil rigs and taken a job closer to home. Louise began to make some regular trips back to meet her old friends and joined some groups in her new community where she met new friends. Nevertheless, Louise still books a catch-up session every so often when she feels life is getting on top of her: 'I know I'll always be more anxious than most people, and that's alright. It's only when my anxiety is beginning to suck the joy out of life that I need to attend to it.'

IS COGNITIVE DISSONANCE IMPEDING YOUR RECOVERY?

Cognitive dissonance is the uncomfortable feeling that arises when we lie to ourselves in a bid to make sense of information that contradicts previously held beliefs, ideas or values. One way or another, humans are deeply motivated to create internal psychological consistency in order to function in the world, so if we hold two apparently contradictory notions we can feel internally out of harmony.[129] If your beliefs or values don't square with you, then your psyche feels uncomfortable and you are motivated to reduce this cognitive dissonance by either lying to yourself or making changes to ensure that you can square the circle.

In order to relieve our cognitive dissonance and to allow our minds to make sense of information that contradicts our deeply held beliefs, we tend to do some of the following:

- Ignore the new information that conflicts with our beliefs.
- Commit even further to our beliefs in a bid to convince ourselves.
- Avoid any exposure to further contradictory behaviour.
- Project our overwhelming feelings upon others.
- Heed the contradictory information and change our previously held beliefs.
- Learn to live with the two contradictory beliefs.

When the psychologist Leon Festinger read a story in September 1954 in the local newspaper with the bizarre headline 'Prophecy from planet Clarion call to city: flee that flood' he was immediately intrigued.[130] Festinger and his colleagues were interested in this as they suspected the cult this headline originated from would confirm their growing theories of cognitive dissonance, so they organised a team of observers, two men and two women, to become 'covert participant observers' in the cult. By infiltrating the cult, called the 'Seekers', and reporting on their findings, Festinger and his colleagues would be able to study closely how cognitive dissonance would take effect among the group.[131]

Dorothy Martin, a Chicago housewife, was the leader of the Seekers and Martin and the other cult members thought that the earth was soon going to be destroyed by a flood but that the members of their cult would be saved by a flying saucer that would arrive from the planet Clarion.

The 'covert participant observers' joined the cult and from November 1954 until January 1955 they secretly took notes of their observations, while Festinger himself was situated half a mile away from Martin's house in a makeshift office in a hotel.

Festinger's prediction was that the more committed the cult members were, the less likely they were to change their beliefs, no matter how disappointed they became. Martin, the leader of the cult, apparently received her messages through automatic writing from spacemen from the planet Clarion. Some members of the cult were very committed and had given away their money and left their jobs and families, all to prepare for the arrival of the flying saucer that Martin had predicted would arrive just before the world ended on 21 December, 1954.

Prior to the night of December 21, when the alien from outer space was due to arrive, the cult had shunned all publicity. Festinger and his colleagues predicted that when the visitor didn't actually arrive and when the predicted flood didn't wash away all the non-believers, the cult would no longer shun publicity and instead seek to win new members over to their way of thinking as a method to reduce their inner mental pain and cognitive dissonance about the non-event. Events unfolded just as he predicted, and after the shock of no visitor from space arriving at the given time, the group began to actively seek publicity about the non-event.

The sequence of events was as follows:

- Before 20 December 1954: Publicity is shunned by the group and access to Dorothy Martin's house is only provided to those who can convince the group that they are 'true believers'. The 'covert participant observers' find it relatively difficult to enter the cult.
- 20 December: The group awaits a visitor from the planet Clarion in outer space to call at midnight and bring them to a nearby spacecraft. As per instructions from Martin's 'automatic writing', the group removes and discards all metallic objects such as zips and bra straps.

- 12.05 a.m. 21 December: No visitor arrives. A member of the group notices that another clock in the room shows 11.55 and so the group agrees that it is not yet midnight.

- 12.10 a.m.: The second clock strikes midnight but still no visitor arrives. There is a stunned silence among the group.

- 4.00 a.m.: There are some vague attempts to find explanations about the non-arrival of their saviour from the flood. Martin begins to cry.

- 4.45 a.m. Martin is sent another message via automatic writing. It states that the cataclysm has been called off. Apparently, 'The little group, sitting all night long, had spread so much light that God had saved the world from destruction.'

- Afternoon, 21 December. Publicity is actively sought; newspapers are called and an urgent campaign to spread the message begins in earnest.

It is notable that when the predicted events didn't happen the less committed members were inclined to admit that the whole idea was false and give up but the more committed members, those who had given up their homes and families to work for the cult, became even more sure that they were right and that the only reason the earth wasn't destroyed by a flood was because of their thoughts and prayers. Their cognitive dissonance about the event drove them to act as if a huge cataclysmic event had been dodged only through the strenuous efforts of the Seekers.

Mad as it may seem, there is a direct parallel between the Seekers and the effects of anxiety. When we are anxious we often behave in a manner that avoids what we have perceived as a huge threat, and then expend bucketloads of energy convincing ourselves and everyone around us that a huge disaster has been avoided as a result of our extreme safety measures.

ARE YOUR CORE BELIEFS IMPEDING YOUR RECOVERY?

Cognitive dissonance often comes about when our internal core beliefs and values don't correspond with our deeper emotional needs. Our core beliefs are usually shaped by the values in our families, friends and the wider environment. Simple but emotionally destructive beliefs such as 'boys don't cry' or 'good girls don't cause trouble' are easily accepted by many young children and can really define a person's core beliefs and values.

For most humans, our self-image tends to be based upon the core beliefs that have been shaped by our earlier experiences. On the other hand, our behaviour is often driven by more short-term pleasures and emotional needs. So one of my core beliefs might dictate that we should all live and let live; that I should be tolerant, relaxed and even-tempered and that I should never allow stress to create tension in my relationships. But a conflict can arise within myself where I might tell myself, 'I should be an easy-going person' and then, when I lose my mind and over-react wildly to the slightest trigger, I quickly tell myself that this is an extraordinary occurrence. The opportunity for growth is the growing discomfort – the cognitive dissonance – I feel when I make too many excuses for myself.

When loved ones begin to comment on how highly strung I seem to be, I might tell myself that they are misreading the situation – it is not that I am highly strung but that I am under a lot of stress. Again, it is cognitive dissonance that makes me desperately try to come up with credible reasons why everything seems to be telling me that I'm not even a tiny bit easy-going. Finally, when I have a silent tantrum at the supermarket because they have run out of my favourite yoghurt I can no longer deny the reality of my behaviour and I might finally begin to accept myself as a highly strung, anxious individual who needs to begin to gain some self-acceptance and make the necessary changes to adjust my life accordingly. Of course, another option would be to keep on rolling with the cognitive dissonance and tell myself that everyone else is creating all this stress – that the supermarket is run by blithering idiots who can't even stock yoghurt properly – and that life will calm down soon.

CASE STUDY: LUKE 35

Luke came to me for counselling because he had been experiencing panic attacks since the break-up of his relationship with his girlfriend. Luke and Martina had been saving for a deposit on a house for four years and in the previous 18 months had finally saved enough to be able to buy a house for about €300k. The problem was that every house they were interested in was going for well above the asking price.

Martina was anxious that house prices were steadily rising and she wanted to search for a house that they could afford instead of bidding on houses that were clearly beyond their reach. Despite this, Luke refused to view cheaper houses and continued to view only houses with an asking price of €300k. The market continued to rise and Martina became very angry. Luke refused to accept the evidence of the rising market, of houses going for €90k and €100k beyond the asking price, and instead kept on telling Martina that he would find them a bargain. He didn't.

Then one day, Martina saw that a house they had previously viewed as far, far beneath them had sold for €50k above their budget. Devastated, Martina declared that she was buying an apartment on her own and Luke could buy whatever he wanted in the future.

And she did.

Luke found it difficult to make sense of what had happened. He still thought he could have found a bargain but he had ceased following the property market since Martina bought her apartment. He felt she had ruined their plan and he didn't believe that he might have had a part to play in the break-up. I explained to Luke about cognitive dissonance and how sometimes, despite all the evidence to the contrary, we cling to certain beliefs.

At first we used some CBT techniques that helped reduce the intensity and length of time of the panic attacks that Luke was experiencing. Luke learned some slow breathing exercises so that he could learn to breathe slowly when he felt the slightest bit overwhelmed and he also developed a mantra, 'Every breath I take calms me a little more', that he repeated when his panic attacks flared up. Luke also took to journalling so that he could analyse the patterns of his panic attacks.

It took some time for Luke to admit that he was feeling overwhelmed by losing his soulmate and the chance of buying a home because of his irrational belief that he would find a bargain despite all evidence to the contrary. A deep depression threatened to overwhelm Luke completely. So we continued with therapy and explored Luke's core beliefs, handed to him from his parents, that he should be the great provider and that he should shoulder the responsibility of buying a house when, in reality, this was shared between himself and Martina. Luke realised that he needed to feel powerful in his life and that the office politics in his job in a large American firm made him feel small and worthless. He needed to feel his work was worthwhile so he moved to a smaller company where they had a much better appreciation of Luke's abilities. These changes and Luke's growing self-awareness led Luke to feel much better in himself.

Luke eventually ended therapy as a much more connected and self-compassionate young man. He had lost a relationship but he had gained a deeper understanding of himself and he knew that he would be a much easier man to deal with if he ever met another woman as good as Martina.

HOW COGNITIVE DISSONANCE LEADS TO CONFIRMATION BIAS

'Confirmation bias' is a step on from cognitive dissonance. It refers to a tendency to seek information that confirms our thoughts and feelings and to disregard information that contradicts it. For example, Luke would scour the papers looking for evidence of bargains bought and sold, all the while ignoring the fact that they weren't happening in the areas where he wanted to buy. Likewise, I might cling to my diet despite all the evidence that suggests I'm gaining weight and I might seek evidence to prove that I'm right, by avidly reading and sharing random articles that proclaim the wonderful results of this diet among my friends and loved ones.

THE GOLDEN TEACHABLE MOMENT

The important thing about cognitive dissonance is that there are often opportunities for personal growth, should we be brave enough to acknowledge them: when I stand on the scales, I am served with a golden teachable moment where I could admit the truth of my failing diet and realise that I need to do something else if I am to lose weight. But this moment of truth and clarity can be quite fleeting – for some it might only last a few moments; for example, when the flying saucer didn't arrive for the Seekers there was some time when the truth could have dawned, but after that moment many members were swept along on another wave of heightened emotion. This is why anyone who suffers from anxiety needs to be ready to commit to the harsh truth if they are to recover from anxiety in any meaningful way. And, although it can be annoying, it is really helpful to have a trusted friend who can provide that brutal honesty that will shake us out of our confirmation bias and lead us to a more truthful and meaningful place, where obfuscation and denial are banished and empowering truth is king.

CHAPTER 8

Self-care: Learning to honour yourself

I draw the curtains as the sky goes black
And set a match to candles sheathed in glass
Against the keyhole draught, the insistent whine
Of weather through the unsealed aperture.
This is our sole defence against the season;
These are the things we have learned to do
Who live in troubled regions.

ADRIENNE RICH

I n her poem 'Storm Warnings', the poet Adrienne Rich describes the tender watchfulness that many people who have suffered through mental illness learn. In this poem the speaker is aware that the storm is coming, and she must prepare for the turmoil: 'These are the things we have learned to do who live in troubled times.'

This is how we need to view our anxiety and stress. If we know the storm of emotion is coming we must gently prepare ourselves, do what we need to do to make things easier on us and then be prepared to wait out the storm until it passes. The good news is that once we learn to notice the weather warnings and when we accept that just as the storm will inevitably arrive, so it will inevitably leave, then we will act more therapeutically and our anxiety, as a result, will significantly reduce. The table below shows key anxiety behaviours with their self-care antidotes.

Giving your power away	Learning to care for yourself
Avoiding situations	Facing your challenges, gently, tenderly, with commitment and with the right support
Asking your family or friends to keep you calm	Striving to keep calm by using self-care and self-compassion when you feel low
Feeling like your emotions drive you	Focusing on rationality and facts while including your feelings
Feeling helpless in the face of your challenges	Starting small, but with determination and tenderness, making your own decisions and taking control of your life
Feeling out of control	Seeking feelings of competency in the face of difficulties
Depending on external sources to keep you calm, e.g. alcohol, cigarettes, drugs, food	Being ready to use external sources to use as a sticking plaster if needed but being watchful over their long-term impact

Many people find the open-ended conclusions involved in the psychology of the mind frustratingly nebulous and can become impatient with the tendency of mental health professionals like myself to firmly declare, 'Your anxiety could be resolved by confronting your challenges head-on … however, it could also be resolved by taking it slowly and sideways.' As a result, you might prefer to dismiss all the 'waffle' and instead head for the latest, most up-to-date techniques and strategies as a 'quick fix' for your anxiety. While this is understandable, these techniques or strategies on their own will seldom bestow you with the gift of calmness and strength in the face of anxiety. Because the latest technique or strategy is very like the latest diet or eating plan – fine for a short period of time but not a miracle cure.

Although many people speak of a 'eureka moment', these moments usually come after a lot of thought, effort and discussion and then even more thought, effort and discussion. This so-called 'eureka moment' is akin to a band being called an 'overnight sensation' after gigging for ten years straight. Thankfully, this means that no time in recovery is wasted, you are adding to your self-knowledge and, with the right support, you will one day emerge like a butterfly from a chrysalis.

All that being said, the latest strategies and techniques can be very useful as *part* of your toolbox of recovery and so they are listed in this chapter as a handy reference. These strategies should be used as a go-to whenever you feel a bit weaker in yourself: whenever you feel that a storm is coming. When you know yourself well enough to know that you are below par and need some tender, loving self-care you can refer to this chapter and take what you need. As with all things in life, this is not a one-size-fits-all situation and self-care involves figuring out what you need in life and learning to calmly disregard what isn't for you. If you have any physical or mental ailments that could be impacted by these exercises, please make sure to consult your doctor before embarking on them.

HONOURING YOURSELF

What's lovely about honouring yourself is that it's about learning to treat yourself as you would treat someone you love very much: with compassion, understanding and kindness. If you can learn to honour yourself you will find that your anxiety reduces as you provide yourself with enough self-care to quell your nerves. You can learn to honour your body with adequate sleep, exercise, sex, physical contact and nourishment. If you dishonour your body by regularly eating junk or neglecting your sleep or drinking too much alcohol, you will inevitably feel the impact either physically or psychologically as you cannot feel well in the long term if you neglect or dishonour your body. In a similar way, you also need to honour your feelings, values and sense of self. This means learning to speak up appropriately when you have been dishonoured; it means learning never to smile when you feel hurt; it means learning to say 'no' when you need to. It also means living in a way that is congruent with your thoughts, values and beliefs.

When our dog, Daniel, was wounded in a fight, he sat by the fire and licked his wounds with tenderness and total self-absorption. The animal takes this time to heal without fanfare and without needing to apologise for their need for self-care. Equally, if we can acknowledge when we are suffering, if we can honour our mental pain without becoming harsh or self-critical, then when the storms hit, we can usually withstand even the harshest winds.

ALL ROADS LEAD TO CONNECTION

Feeling empowered immediately reduces feelings of anxiety because the confidence that empowerment provides obliterates the disempowerment that anxiety brings. The key is to find the specific ways that make you feel empowered and harness the energy that is required to go after them.

Although there are many ways for a person to feel empowered – and many of them are listed in this chapter – human beings are social animals and no matter how much psychology I study I find that all roads lead back to connection. If you feel connected you will feel empowered. This is good news because forging authentic connections is free and can be started upon right now. If you can find your tribe, the people that you understand and appreciate, and they you, and if you can connect with them regularly, you will immediately feel less anxious and more empowered. Many people find that their most effective stress relief comes from speaking with friends who support and understand them. The friends who always have your best interests at heart give perspective and point you in a less stressful, more self-caring direction. A good indicator of whether a person is good for you or not is to notice how you feel after you've met them – does spending an hour in this person's company drain you or invigorate you? Do you feel better or worse? Because that's all you need to know.

MEETING YOUR EMOTIONAL NEEDS

Humans have all kinds of needs, including emotional ones. Our physical needs such as food, water, sleep and sex are fairly straightforward but our emotional needs can be harder to pinpoint. Just as we weaken when we are deprived of our physical needs, equally we weaken mentally when we don't satisfy our emotional needs. If these needs aren't met in our day-to-day lives for a sustained period of time then there will be a kickback; this might emerge in the form of anxiety or panic or it could expose itself through chronic tension, irritability or feeling stressed all the time. Self-awareness holds the keys to the kingdom because if a person is self-aware about what they need then they can gradually, over time, begin to learn to make sure they meet their emotional needs in a sustainable and enriching manner.

WILLIAM GLASSER'S FIVE EMOTIONAL NEEDS

Almost all approaches to psychology agree that people have certain basic needs, and although there isn't consensus about what those needs are. The American psychiatrist William Glasser, who developed reality therapy and choice theory, identified five emotional needs that we all have:[132]

1. The need for love, belonging and connection
2. The need to feel secure and safe
3. The need to feel competent, significant and powerful
4. The need for freedom and autonomy
5. The need to have fun and feel challenged

Like many other psychologists, Glasser believes that connection – a feeling of love and belonging – is the most important need of all. One of the core principles of Glasser's reality therapy is that, whether we are aware of it or not, we are always acting to meet our emotional needs, but don't necessarily act effectively or helpfully. It's in how we meet these needs that we run into trouble.

1. Love and belonging

If you have a high need for love and belonging then you need to find a place where you feel you fully belong. This can be within your family, friends, the community or the greater population. It could be in a local club (sports clubs are often packed with people who have a high need for love and belonging, e.g. intense football fans are meeting this need by following their team). Depending on your personality, it could even be just your partner or your family.

Negative ways of meeting this need

This could involve choosing to remain with a partner or friend simply because you 'belong' with them. You might also become unhealthily obsessed with your team or your friends, neglecting other more challenging aspects of your life.

2. The need for survival and security

If you have a high need for survival and security you probably desire a reliable job with a well-regulated structure so you 'know where you are' in life. This emotional need can also include nourishment, shelter and sex. It suggests physical security, but it also includes our emotions with aspects of our life such as financial and job security. Some people may be primarily focused on physical security, for example, keenly conscious of locks and safety, or good nourishment and healthy living; while others may be concerned with financial security so they focus on pensions. Or perhaps both physical and financial safety is important to you?

Negative ways of meeting this need

If you are healthily meeting these needs you will have registered that you are willing to forgo certain spontaneous events and happenings because you would rather feel safe and secure – and you will have made your peace with that. However, you might remain in a job or in any situation you dislike because it offers security, to the detriment of your wellbeing, which could make you anxious and stressed in the long term.

3. Power, status, recognition or validation

This includes achievement and feeling worthwhile as well as feeling successful in life (however you may view success). We all, to a greater or lesser extent, want to be recognised as successful in certain fields and as achieving goals. For example, for some this might mean being a good mother; for others it could be being perceived as highly efficient, intelligent or a good provider. If you have a high need for power, and validation from others is important for your wellbeing, you will probably seek to have some status in the world; if you don't feel validated then you will soon feel emotionally distressed and this could manifest in anxiety.

Negative ways of meeting this need

If this need is channelled destructively you might become anxiously obsessed in your determination to achieve success and you could find that you abuse your power by throwing it around or by behaving in a bullying manner.

4. Freedom and autonomy

This includes feeling independent, autonomous and being self-governing; the ability to do what you want and to have free choice is important for the person who has a high need for this. People with this need tend to seek fair play more than others do. They may feel hassled by lots of rules and regulations, and need to live life by their own rules. They might feel stressed and overwhelmed in the face of authority – these people rarely thrive in school or in large organisations, as the reliance on rules and systems makes them feel tense, alienated and oppressed.

Negative ways of meeting this need

If this need is met in a negative manner, you might tend to leave jobs, places and people without really fully meaning to or you may needlessly rebel against authority. If you have a high need for freedom then you need to live a life that is low on rules and high on spontaneity. 'Don't fence me in' is your mantra and you should try to avoid people who wish to suppress your freedom-loving nature.

5. Fun and challenge

Pleasure, enjoyment and learning are included in this need. Some people need lots of challenges and tend to feel the need to seek out thrills. If you have a high need for fun and need more stimulation in your environment, it could be fulfilled by socialising with friends, or by doing courses or improving yourself by reading, art or music. You could also take up an interesting sport – anything that seems fun and challenging should be a fulfilling way for you to relieve any inner turmoil.

Negative ways of meeting this need

If this need is met negatively you could find yourself always looking for the next party, dependent on drink or drugs for your fun. You might also find that you charge on to the next project without ever completing the previous one.

HOW DO YOU MEET YOUR EMOTIONAL NEEDS?

The following table can be worthwhile for a person to fill in both for themselves and with their partner. Sometimes, by filling in this chart, a couple can realise that the source of their fights isn't the fact that your partner is 'naive' to be so free and easy with his passwords but that he has a low need for security and it will simply never be a priority in his life; or that your partner isn't actually obsessed with social media but that she has a high need for love and belonging. Far better to become aware of our own high and low needs so that we can be sure to meet them appropriately without presuming everyone else feels as we do.

Tick the appropriate box for each need, then identify how you might satisfy it.

	Me:	My partner:
Emotional needs	High ☐ Medium ☐ Low ☐ How do I achieve it?	High ☐ Medium ☐ Low ☐ How do they achieve it?
Survival and security	High ☐ Medium ☐ Low ☐ How do I achieve it?	High ☐ Medium ☐ Low ☐ How do they achieve it?
Love and belonging	High ☐ Medium ☐ Low ☐ How do I achieve it?	High ☐ Medium ☐ Low ☐ How do they achieve it?
Power and recognition	High ☐ Medium ☐ Low ☐ How do I achieve it?	High ☐ Medium ☐ Low ☐ How do they achieve it?
Freedom	High ☐ Medium ☐ Low ☐ How do I achieve it?	High ☐ Medium ☐ Low ☐ How do they achieve it?
Fun	High ☐ Medium ☐ Low ☐ How do I achieve it?	High ☐ Medium ☐ Low ☐ How do they achieve it?

CATCH YOURSELF BEFORE YOU FALL

There is little you can do when you're in the middle of an episode of anxiety, because by this point your emotional brain has been triggered (see Chapter 1) and you are in the fight-or-flight zone. However, before you actually reach this point there is a golden opportunity to intervene in your thoughts and redirect yourself to a calmer place. This is a crucial lesson whereby you learn to see the pattern of behaviour and intervene *before* you lose it. It'll take some time for you to learn this but if you can learn it, you'll have it with you for life.

First of all you need to think of the tiniest beginning of your anxiety as a snowflake at the top of the mountain, a little flutter of nerves, say, when your boss asks you to file some documents that you know nothing about. If this continues unchecked the snowflake might turn into a snowball – this could be when your boss asks you to make a series of phone calls when you have a deep-seated aversion to doing this. The snowball of anxiety solidifies and starts to roll down the mountain when you valiantly try to make the phone calls but you can't bring yourself to and so you text instead. If you then lie to your boss and pretend to have spoken to the clients, you might, by this stage, have triggered your anxiety and reached the point of no return. All that you can do at this point is damage limitation – the snowball has gathered momentum and turned into an avalanche of cascading emotion that is completely overwhelming. However, there was a point, somewhere between when your boss asked you to file the documents and when she asked you to make the phone calls, where you could have become aware of your anxiety and made some better decisions. There was another point when, instead of lying, you somehow stuttered out to your boss that you had texted the clients instead of ringing them. Had you been self-aware enough and self-compassionate enough to acknowledge that your anxiety was growing and threatening to overwhelm, then you might have taken some self-care measures. This self-care might have entailed some slow breathing exercises or repeating an appropriate mantra or it might have meant that you honoured yourself and admitted to your boss that you had messaged the clients instead of ringing them. The most important aspect of all this is that you spot the nerves and you act upon them before they completely take over.

Ask yourself these questions when you feel the early stirrings of anxiety:

1. Are you hungry or thirsty? Can you fix this? Have you eaten or drunk in the last three hours? Can you chew gum? It could raise your mood levels.[133]
2. Could you stretch your body? Can you go for a short, brisk walk around the block?
3. Could you put on some good music? Can you watch some good comedy?
4. Have you cuddled a living thing? Could you?
5. Are you dressed? Could you put on some nice, comfortable clothes?
6. Have you over-exerted yourself, physically, emotionally, intellectually or socially, in the last few days? Do you need time to recover?
7. Have you spoken to a person who cheers you up?
8. Could you have a shower?
9. How will you feel about this in three hours, three days, three months and three years?
10. Have you changed your medication recently? Do you need to see your doctor?
11. Can you make an appointment with your therapist?

12. Could you begin with something easy? The easiest way to get over procrastination or avoidance is to begin badly. Could you begin badly?

ZAP YOUR NEGATIVE RUMINATIONS

Becoming swept up with negative emotion is one of the most dangerous tendencies anxious people have. When your emotion is in full flight, your 'inner chimp' (see Chapter 1) is squawking and you can't stop your brain mindlessly churning out negativity. When this happens, hear it out and then say to yourself, 'Roger all that, anxiety, thanks for sharing.' This gives you room to acknowledge the thought without becoming swept up in negative chatter.

Ruminating when you're in a low mood impairs your ability to problem-solve. Many people fall into the trap of believing that over-thinking will lead to insight but the clue is in the word 'over'. If you over-think then you have automatically taken a retrograde step.

Thinking solves problems; over-thinking creates problems.

Stand back and try to calm your emotional brain so that you can rationally ascertain whether you are the source of the stress or if the stress is caused by an external situation. If the stress is caused by an external situation then you will need to square your shoulders and seek the boundaries that will quell this stress. You might need to use your 'strong voice' – this is a deeper, slower voice that comes from your deeper reaches – so that you can assertively speak up. However, if you are the source of the stress because you have created dramas in your head then you will need to use your compassionate self-talk to bring some calm to your harried mind.

CREATING A COMPASSIONATE INNER VOICE

1. First of all, notice the tone of your inner voice. Is it spiteful? Angry? Cold? Vindictive? Bitchy? Try to be as accurate as possible about this voice. Note the actual verbatim speech, notice the words and phrases you use over and over again. Does the voice remind you of anyone in your past or in your family of origin? Get a clear sense of how you talk to yourself.

2. Make an active effort to soften the tone of your inner voice. Do this with compassion and tolerance, saying something like, 'I know you're feeling stressed and worried about the pain in your gut but you are causing me unnecessary pain. Could you let my compassionate voice speak for a few moments?' Try to speak to your inner voice as you would to a good friend who is feeling very emotional.

3. Gently stroke your own arm or hold your face tenderly in your hands (if you're alone) as this will tap into your caregiving system by releasing oxytocin that will help change your biochemistry. Speak to yourself with a term of endearment such as 'darling' or 'honey' and speak with understanding and tenderness. Reframe whatever your harsh inner voice said in a more understanding and tender way. You could, for instance, say, 'I know, sweetheart, that you're feeling really anxious about your physical pain but you've been here before and it has always ended up being digestive trouble and not cancer. It's probably a digestive ailment.'

4. Don't expect this to work magic in a day – this exercise should be done over several weeks and eventually, with time and repetition, your inner voice will move from being harsh and judgemental to being accepting and compassionate.

PRACTISE FLEXIBILITY

Flexibility is a known hallmark of a healthy functioning mind and is probably the most important defence we have against anxiety, so it is worth committing to becoming more flexible as you begin to recover from anxiety's clutches.[134] When you're feeling anxious, you might find that you're rigidly hyper-focused on the source of your anxiety. This is when you begin to fall into destructive patterns and become obsessed with certain thoughts. Bruce Lee evidently understood the power of flexibility when he famously advised us to be like water:

> Empty your mind. Be formless, shapeless, like water. If you put water into a cup, it becomes the cup. You put water into a bottle, it becomes the bottle. You put it in a teapot, it becomes the teapot. Water can flow or it can crash. Be water my friend.

Rigid thinking makes for a more distressed mind. If we get caught up in it, we become brittle and easily cracked, but if we can learn to roll with the punches we are pretty much ready for the next wave that is already, far out in the sea, making its way towards us. If we can be like water, we will be ready to seep into every corner of any given situation, we will find the weak spot and we will penetrate. Water isn't rigid, water is powerful but always flexible.

The more you can face challenges with a flexible approach, the more likely you will succeed. When worry washes over you, however, the first thing to go is often your flexibility – your mental dexterity. You can encourage a more flexible mindset by asking yourself the following questions:

1. Is this really a threat? Yes, you are worried that your doctor has missed your cancer and yes, this might be part of a worrying pattern, but if you can allow the practical nature of this question to ground you for a second you might realise that your overactive mind has moved this situation from bad to brutal.

2. Have I done everything I can to prepare for this? If you truly believe that you might have cancer than you need to make another appointment with your doctor. But to fully prepare, you also need to do some of the self-care techniques (in this chapter) that will ease your mind.

3. Is my emotional brain hijacking my wise brain? We all know the crazed, desperate helplessness of an amygdala-triggered mind. But over-thinking won't cure it and focusing on worst-case scenarios won't cure it either. Self-compassion will help. Mindfulness and slow breathing will also help. When you are in a dark place, you need to choose your poison – choose whatever will get you through the night and then, when the sun comes out again, step up your commitment to recovery and make preparations so that the next time isn't so bad.

MANAGE YOUR CHOICES AND YOUR EXPECTATIONS

This is a key aspect of learning how to free yourself from anxiety. As we saw in Chapter 4, life has sped up more than we can ever comprehend and it's not surprising that we are all feeling more stressed and anxious than ever before. Although choice has improved our lives, too much choice has led to stress, anxiety and feelings of alienation.

Eliminating being too busy means taking back control of your life. Factoring in some do-nothing time means that you have time to breathe, slow down and spend time doing what makes you happy:

being with friends, painting your nails, reading the papers – whatever takes your fancy. Rather than responding to life, you can make your life happen. You can only do this if you eliminate being busy.

In an interesting article in *The Guardian*, Oliver Burkeman tells us that there is only one viable time management approach left:

> Step one: identify what seem to be, right now, the most meaningful ways to spend your life.
> Step two: schedule time for those things.
> There is no step three.
> Everything else just has to fit around them – or not. Approach life like this and a lot of unimportant things won't get done, but, crucially, a lot of important things won't get done either. Certain friendships will be neglected; certain amazing experiences won't be had; you won't eat or exercise as well as you theoretically could. In an era of extreme busyness, the only conceivable way to live a meaningful life is to not do thousands of meaningful things.[135]

LEARN WHEN TO SAY 'YES' AND WHEN TO SAY 'NO'

Learning to say 'yes' and 'no' when you need to is, for some, the trickiest challenge of them all. Pure gold-dust for people who have it and as insurmountable as Everest for those who don't. And yet although many of us say we 'can't say no', we can – because we are well able to say 'no' to ourselves while we are saying 'yes' to everyone else.

It is extraordinary how often anxious people decide to heap on further pressure at the exact times when they should be reducing it. A sign that you should be saying 'no' could be when you say 'yes' automatically. Some anxious people are so used to living on their nerves that they gravitate towards nerve-wracking experiences – they *want* to watch the scary movie, they thrill at the fairground attractions, they seek out exciting experiences and difficult challenges – because their brain is used to feeling heightened stress. But although nervous energy might be familiar, it isn't good for you and it just creates further tension.

Anxiety is cumulative. When you are an anxious person, the more events or thoughts you process or experience – good or bad – the more anxious you feel. Too much is too much – even when it's too much fun. *Only* by doing less will you reduce the anxiety.

The quickest, most efficient way to learn how to combat feeling overwhelmed is similar to the time management solution above. As Elizabeth Gilbert, the author of *Eat, Pray, Love*, said, you need to start 'learning how to say no to things you do want to do'. It might seem counter-intuitive, but we have so much to choose from in this 24-hour culture, so much that we can do, that we need to learn to limit ourselves to do some things instead of trying to do them all. Our only hope is to learn to pick and choose from all this choice – learn to choose the stuff that really matters from the more passing pleasures is an art in itself but it can be the key to learning how to combat feelings of overwhelm. A radical, staunch commitment to learn how to say 'no' to some of the stuff you want and also to the stuff you don't means that you will have enough time and brain space to enjoy the stuff that you have chosen to do. In this way you will 'forge meaning' in the life that you already have (see Chapter 9).

The downside of saying 'no' to things you want is that the sensation of having free time can make you feel uncomfortable, bored and slightly wretched, but when you are recovering from anxiety, boredom and listlessness could be the uncomfortable feelings you need to endure in your bid to get rid of the feelings of being overwhelmed and anxious. Just as you were once taught the correct grip of a pencil or a racquet and it felt wrong and uncomfortable, this might feel uncomfortable at first but with some practice you will soon become used to it and it will be so much better for you in the long term.

LEARN TO SLOW DOWN

Knowing yourself is the first step towards learning to care for yourself and to managing your anxiety. Knowing how you respond in times of stress is often the second step. Many of us tend to go faster when we should be going slower. You might find that, like many people, it's when you feel exhausted that you go into this 'wired' state where you push yourself even harder and take on even more stuff. When you become aware that you are going faster and faster, it is then that you need to watch out for the signals that suggest it's becoming too much – for example, feeling nervy, impatient, irritable and intolerant as you storm through the day – so that you can learn to cut through this false energy and slow down. It's important that you don't wait for the storm to hit before you slow down – if you can slow down before the storm of emotion hits you, you will reduce the impact, the strength and the length of time of any anxiety episode.

When you are feeling fragile try to cut whatever you're doing by 25 per cent – that means you look at your day's schedule and cut out one in four elements so that you can do everything that remains at a slower pace. It doesn't matter whether the day's schedule is cleaning the house, running errands or a full working day. If you ruthlessly clear all the non-essentials from your schedule this will actually improve your productivity in the long run as you won't fall down needless rabbit holes that have been created out of stress and feeling overwhelmed. Changing your pace so that you are moving more slowly will make it easier to breathe more slowly. And if you can slow your breathing you will feel the stress slide off your body.

GOAL-SETTING

There are many benefits to learning the skill of goal-setting, not least that it acts as a fairly immediate and effective stress reliever. Many of us already know the concept of SMART goals – how goals that are specific, measurable, achievable, relevant and time-related are more effective than goals that are vague, irrelevant, impossible or immeasurable. However, if you are going to consider adding goal-setting to your toolbox of recovery, you will also need to consider whether you mean 'micro' goals or 'macro' goals.

Micro goals can often be more helpful than bigger goals – so if you set yourself a macro goal that you want to be more flexible in your communication, you could decide that you need to begin picking up the phone instead of always letting it go to voicemail. A good micro goal to support this would be the goal to ring one person every day. You are much more likely to achieve a micro goal, and begin to build it into your life as a sustainable habit, than you are to achieve bigger, less achievable goals. Ringing one person means that you can go for easier options such as your mother or your best friend when you feel fragile and this still leaves you room to move beyond this to more difficult challenges when you feel more confident.

Macro goals	Micro goals
I will get fit.	I will walk into work every day.
I will limit phone usage.	I will turn off my phone for 15 minutes every day.

GIVE YOURSELF SOME 'WORRY TIME'

Allow yourself a certain amount of time to worry. Worriers mistakenly believe that if they don't worry they will miss something and catastrophe will ensue. But if you allow yourself 30 minutes worrying time a day – in a designated time slot – then you are free to leave your worries behind at other times. This strategy is often difficult for anxious people to wrap their heads around – they know they worry too much but don't feel comfortable allowing themselves to worry. But just like the chronically obese person needs to eat something to keep going, the chronic worrier needs to worry about some things if they are to process their thoughts.

Worrying has some benefit as it highlights any future problems so it can be very proactive to use your phone as a way to confront your worries. For each worry, ask yourself which action you can take right now that could alleviate your anxiety even on a tiny level. Have another file on your phone for worries that are out of your control and note them down too. Take some time at the end of each week to look over your worries and you will find this gives you some added perspective.

The trick is to maintain boundaries around this worrying time. If you allow yourself a 'worry time' slot from 6 p.m. to 6.30 p.m. then, when you worry at other times in the day, you can write this worry down for the agenda at 'worry time'. In this way, you can push away random worries that could otherwise ruin your day. The added bonus of this is that you are learning to discipline your mind and not fall prey to random thoughts when they come out of the blue. It also encourages you to keep a record of your worries and, as awareness grows about how seldom these worries actually happen in real life, it also brings about more perspective.

MEET YOUR PHYSICAL NEEDS: HALT

To stay on an even keel we need our physical needs to be met. This means that we need to have a consistent night's sleep, regular nourishing food, enough exercise and enough liquid. If you aren't consistent with meeting your physical needs you will suffer mood swings – indeed, some people become quite dependent upon their mood swings as they enjoy the weird surge of energy that feeling hungry or wired can provide. But the fallout is intense and the low moods and anxiety are seldom worth the highs. When you are overtired you need some rest, but if you're not careful your tiredness will trigger a stress response in your brain leaving you feeling *more* wired and restless. Indeed, research suggests that feeling tired can actually trigger anxiety as it ramps up the anticipatory anxiety in your brain.[136]

The acronym HALT – hungry, angry, lonely, tired – can be a good way to remind yourself to check when you feel like this and attend to it immediately as this is a danger time for you to fall into your old thought and behavioural patterns. For some people this might be panic attacks, while for others it might be ruminating thoughts; it doesn't matter what your particular Achilles heel is, the point is that when you are hungry, angry, lonely or tired you are much more likely to fall into your old patterns. Attend to it, eat something, deal with your anger, contact a friend or just go for a rest – do something to help yourself when you need to. Become your own therapist.

CULTIVATE GOOD SLEEPING PATTERNS

Sleep hygiene is a crucial aspect of good mental health and it is essential that you take your sleep patterns seriously if you are to reduce your anxiety. Sleep debt makes controlling anxiety much harder, it makes anxious symptoms much worse and it often brings about further anxiety that feeds into further sleeplessness, so it is essential that you build awareness into how you need to sleep.

A full and total commitment to learning good sleep hygiene is often required. Having said that, as a veteran soldier who fought for many years in the trenches of insomnia, I am fully aware of the difficulties that are associated with it. This is like going on a diet and you might need a lot of support to lift you out of entrenched bad sleeping habits. It's no good (in the long term) to suffer long nights of sleeplessness only to catch up with one big bout of sleep – your sleeping patterns need to be measured and regular to impact your mental health in a positive way.

People who suffer from sleeplessness tend to underestimate the powerful impact it has and dislike the neuroticism required to foster a decent night's sleep. But if you can conduct an experiment of rectifying your sleeping patterns and noting your subsequent mood, then you will soon be sold on how crucial a decent night's sleep is to keep you on an even keel.

Answer the following questions now as an audit to your sleep habits.

* Do you need to be in a dark room? Do you need to fix your room by getting blackout curtains or blinds?
* What sort of pillow do you need? How is your duvet? Do you need to attend to this? Should you try weighted blankets?
* What is your ideal sleep routine?
* Where is the tech? Is it turned off?
* Should you sleep alone? Do you need to address this as you fix your sleeping habits?
* What temperature do you need in your bed/bedroom?
* How do you behave when you wake up at night? Does it help?
* How do you behave before bedtime? Does it help?
* How is the noise level? Do you need to attend to it?

YOGA, PILATES AND TAI CHI

'The mind, when housed within a healthful body, possesses a glorious sense of power,' declared Joseph Pilates, the founder of Pilates, in 1939. And he's right, of course. The importance of physical practice to develop our ability to stay in the moment and to connect with our deepest selves cannot be underestimated. Yoga, Pilates, tai chi and many other similar practices develop the body, restore vitality, invigorate the mind and elevate the spirt. The connection between a healthy mind and a healthy body is well established and the more connected our mind and body, the better our relationship with ourselves and with others will become. If you fancy a more solitary pursuit, you can find many online resources that are will help you engage in these activities in the comfort of your own sitting room.

MOVEMENT AND MUSIC

Have you included music in your recovery from anxiety? Could you learn to play an instrument? Emerging data shows that learning to play an instrument helps calm anxiety. Did you know that singing daily for ten minutes reduces stress, clears sinuses, improves your posture and even helps you live longer?[137] No, nor did I, but I did know that it can make us feel more connected with the universe and more grounded in ourselves.

If dancing is your thing, it is important to put in the practical preparation so that you can easily find your music and start dancing without feeling overwhelmed by your inability to get this together when you're already feeling weak. So have the music easily accessible, decide where you would like to dance in your house – have it all set up so it isn't a total brain-ache to help yourself when the time comes for you to need it. Because if it is difficult to do, you won't do it when you are feeling out of sorts.

Whatever takes your fancy – a brisk walk with music, some vigorous dancing or even singing at the top of your voice: if you can get into some physical activity that is also music-oriented before your anxiety sets in, you could successfully avert its approach. Music can be nourishing for the soul and provide a sense of connection for some people and if music is important to you then it should very much be a part of your toolbox of recovery.

ACT ALTRUISTICALLY

The emphasis on the individual over the community has cost us much in terms of our mental health and it needs to be acknowledged more often how much self-absorption is playing a part in our anxiety. As a psychotherapist, I always know that a client is moving into the recovery phase of treatment when they begin to want to 'give back' to society. Altruism is a fundamental aspect of wellbeing and, when you are feeling anxious and fragile, if you can somehow learn to immerse yourself in a pursuit that forces you to think of other people, you will find your anxiety and fragility retreats. Many people find that listening to a friend speaking about their own problems can reduce their anxiety – it gives the brain a break from ruminating and it provides perspective.

REPEAT YOUR POSITIVE MANTRAS

It is well established that anxiety produces a lot of mindless negative chatter; an effective way to combat this is to repeat 'positive coping statements' to drown out the negative overwhelming statements. There are dozens of mantras you can use but it's more effective if you can tailor one to suit your personality. When you've identified a good mantra repeat it three times, three times a day as a matter of necessity. This is like building a muscle of positivity in your mind so that it becomes an automatic go-to when you are feeling stressed.

You can choose from any of the following or make up your own.

- ❖ I accept myself completely and deeply.
- ❖ I can live peacefully and joyfully.
- ❖ I am social and I like meeting people.
- ❖ May I be happy, may I be safe, may I be healthy and may I live my life with ease.
- ❖ Self-care helps me and I feel better after it.
- ❖ I need self-compassion and self-acceptance.
- ❖ All is well in my world and I feel safe.
- ❖ I breathe in calm and I breathe out tension.
- ❖ The only constant in my life is change and I welcome it.
- ❖ I am kind, I am loving and I am fully capable.
- ❖ This is only temporary/This too shall pass.
- ❖ I've made it through before and I'll make it through again.
- ❖ I can take things one step at a time.
- ❖ My mind is like water and I allow it to settle.

SLOW BREATHING TECHNIQUES

The most important part of a breathing technique for an anxious person is learning to slow the breathing. Beyond slowing down your breathing, everything else is your own personal preference. Three-five-seven breathing is a popular technique where you put your hands on your belly and breathe in for a count of three. As you breathe in let your belly expand like a balloon. Hold the breath for a count of five and then exhale slowly for a count of seven. As you exhale, feel your lungs deflate and your belly go in.

Another technique is to breathe in for three, then breathe out slowly for three. Now breathe in slowly to a count of four, hold your breath to a count of four, then slowly exhale to a count of four. Breathe in again for a count of four, see if you can fill your belly first and then your chest – but it's no big deal if you can't – the most important aspect of this is that you slow your breathing down. Hold it for a count of four and then breathe out, slowly, to a count of four. Repeat.

You can try to count slowly but it is enough if you just make sure you exhale longer than you inhale. By doing slow breathing in times of panic you are sending important messages to your brain that it is appropriate to relax at this time. Lengthening our breathing sends signals to the brain that we can leave fight-or-flight mode and instead move into relaxation mode. The focus on counting distracts your mind so that you don't continue to get wrapped up in hysterical thought processes.

MEDITATION

The author Sam Harris tells us that 'Meditation is preparation for the worst day of your life.' If we can sow the seeds in the good times, if we can meditate, think positively and behave in a manner that is helpful to us, then when the hard days hit us we will be better able to cope with them. The hard days are when we need to show ourselves some compassion, be tender to our pain and allow ourselves some slack.

There are meditation classes available in most towns and they are also available online; some people prefer to meditate alone so you will need to figure out which is the best fit for you. Make a commitment for about eight weeks and aim to meditate most days to figure out if meditation is your bag. You can choose how long you wish to meditate for and set a timer for this; 15 minutes per day is a good start. There are umpteen free podcasts that provide guided meditations if you wish. But a good place to start is with some words from Buddhist monk Nhat Hanh: 'Total relaxation is the secret to enjoying sitting meditation. I sit with my spine upright, but not rigid; and I relax all the muscles in my body.'

- ❖ Pay attention to your breathing. This trains your mind to be in the present moment.
- ❖ Sit comfortably, with your hands facing upwards on your lap and your eyes closed.
- ❖ Inhale and exhale as you normally would. Focus on the sensation of air passing into and out of your nostrils or your mouth. Notice how the air is slightly cooler when you inhale and slightly warmer when you exhale.
- ❖ For the first five minutes, after each complete inhale and exhale count silently 'one' and then 'two' for the next one and so on all the way up to ten.
- ❖ Don't be surprised if you lose count or if you go beyond ten, just gently and compassionately invite yourself to return to your breathing and counting.
- ❖ Start again at 'one' every time you lose your way.
- ❖ After five minutes – set a gentle alarm so you know when five minutes has passed – change the count so you count your 'one', etc. before the inhales. This will emphasise the inhale more than the exhale and make the breathing subtly different.
- ❖ Continue like this for another five minutes.
- ❖ After this five minutes stop counting and focus purely on the sensation of your breath going into and out of your nostrils, mouth, throat and lungs.
- ❖ Immerse yourself in your breathing until the last five minutes is over.
- ❖ No matter how you think your meditation session went, take a bow and say to yourself 'well done for trying'. Namaste.

VISUALISATION

If you suffer from anxiety you need two things: a long-term plan that leads you to feeling safer and feeling like you will cope; and a few strategies that can reduce your anxiety in the moment. Visualisation can help you reduce anxiety in the moment by focusing on calmer pictures in your mind. If you haven't tried visualisation before you might find it a bit silly at first but persevere for a while before you give up because, for some people, visualisation is their strongest technique. Read this description of a positive visualisation exercise:

> *Picture yourself in your favourite park, beach or riverside. In your mind's eye, watch leaves pass by on the river or clouds pass by in the sky. Assign your emotions, thoughts and sensations to each cloud or leaf and watch them float by.*

Usually we assign qualities to our emotions, thoughts and sensations, e.g. we decide that 'this is a bad thought and I shouldn't think like that'. This amplifies our anxiety; while if we think 'this is just a thought and thoughts can change', then we can visualise these thoughts as they float away down the river.

If you can practise observing thoughts, emotions and sensations without judgement and with compassion then you might find this exercise works very well for you.

This isn't a strategy that immediately improves your life; you'll need to practise visualisation many times in a relaxed setting until it becomes second nature to you and it is only really then that you will be able to properly benefit from a calming visualisation when you are feeling stressed.

Step 1: Choose your safe place in your imagination; this can be an armchair or a beach, your favourite room or anywhere else you fancy. Once you've found your safe place you might stick with it, so take your time in deciding on this place. Become aware of the sounds, smells and sights that are available in your safe place.

Step 2: Find a comfortable location to practise your visualisation. This can be on your bed, in a chair or wherever else you feel safe. Again, it is important that you stick to this location when you've eventually decided upon it.

Step 3: Close your eyes and immerse yourself in your visualisation. Where are you? What can you smell? How do you feel? Why is it so relaxing? What can you hear? What can you see? What things can you touch? What's around you? Think of every single tiny detail.

Step 4: Consciously relax your body. Slow your breathing.

Step 5: Choose a special object that you imbue with the magic power to take away your stress. This might be a stone on the beach, a box in the park or an ornament in your room. Imagine that your stress is emptied into the object. Imagine a bird coming to pick up the object that contains your stress. Feel how heavy the object is. Allow the bird to strain under the weight and then finally pick up the burden and fly away further and further until it disappears beyond your horizon. Every time your stress comes back, visualise your object and put your stress into it.

Step 6: Practise, practise, practise. If you want to give it a good go, practise visualisation for at least 66 days in a row and then decide whether it works for you.

PROGRESSIVE MUSCLE RELAXATION

Clinical psychologist Dr L. Kevin Chapman noted in *Psychology Today*:'One of the most effective tools that I prescribe in alleviating stress and anxiety is progressive muscle relaxation (PMR). PMR works exceptionally well in combating the somatic symptoms associated with chronic worry and many physiological symptoms (such as gastrointestinal problems) that are endemic to social anxiety. Also very portable.'[138] Although PMR can be tedious to practise at first, it will become easier over time and could become essential for managing anxiety and stress.

1. Find a comfortable place in a quiet room, preferably sitting down because you want to learn how to relax while still awake instead of only when you're asleep. Wear comfortable clothes. Take five slow breaths to begin.

2. Focus on a target group of muscles in a specific part of the body – the hand or the foot, for instance. Take a slow deep breath and squeeze those muscles as hard as you can for five seconds, being careful not to hurt yourself. Really feel the tension in your muscles and only in the group of muscles that you have chosen. Over time it will get easier for you to isolate your chosen group of muscles. After five seconds, release the tension, slowly exhale and remain in this relaxed state for about 15 seconds.

3. Focus on another group of muscles and repeat.

If you're not sure which muscles to target you can use this as a guide:[139]

❖ Foot – curl your toes downward. Release.

❖ Lower leg and foot – tighten your calf muscle by pulling toes towards you. Release.

- ❖ Upper leg – squeeze thigh muscles while doing the above. Repeat on other side of body. Release each time.
- ❖ Hand – clench your fist. Release.
- ❖ Entire right arm – tighten your biceps by drawing your forearm up towards your shoulder and 'make a muscle', while clenching your fist. Repeat on the other side of the body. Release each time.
- ❖ Buttocks – tighten by squeezing your buttocks together. Release.
- ❖ Stomach – suck your stomach in. Release.
- ❖ Chest – tighten by taking a deep breath. Release.
- ❖ Neck and shoulders – raise your shoulders up to touch your ears. Release.
- ❖ Mouth – open your mouth wide enough to stretch the hinges of your jaw. Release.
- ❖ Eyes – clench your eyelids tightly shut. Release.
- ❖ Forehead – raise your eyebrows as far as you can. Release.

THE POWER OF NOW

Eckhart Tolle's seminal book *The Power of Now* explains how all power is available to us in the present moment. Everything you ever want is right here, right now and it is up to you to tap into this power at any given moment. Take a breath and indulge in the power of now. Only the present moment is important and our insistence that we have control over our lives is an illusion that 'only brings pain'. If we can take a moment to remember to slow down, the freedom of life in the present moment can come to us as a gift.

Multi-tasking steals us from the present moment and so Tolle advises us to avoid frantic lifestyles. 'Life is now. There was never a time when your life was not now, nor will there ever be.'[140]

Tolle tells us, 'Wherever you are, be there totally. If you find your here and now intolerable and it makes you unhappy, you have three options: remove yourself from the situation, change it or accept it totally.' We only have the present moment, no more, no less. Fill your cup with the present moment and you will immediately feel better. Notice the sounds in the present moment, the smells, the colours and the shapes of objects in your environment. If you can wallow in the present moment you can help shift your 'hot' thoughts to 'cool' ones and help bring about calmer feelings.

MINDFULNESS

Mindfulness has its origins in ancient meditation practices. Even before the Buddha's birth some 2,500 years ago, Hindus practised mindfulness meditations. The practice can be described as 'paying attention, on purpose, to the present moment, without judgement'. It is an attentive awareness of the reality of things (especially of the present moment); an antidote to delusion, in particular when it is coupled with clear comprehension of whatever is taking place in your mind, your body and your world.

The Buddha advocated that we should establish mindfulness in our day-to-day lives by maintaining a calm awareness of our bodies, our feelings and our minds. But mindfulness isn't inherently Eastern; it is a quality of presence that's innate in all human beings, a natural and beautiful quality of being human that can't be limited to one particular tradition or country.

There are many mindfulness meditation practices like the one below that you can follow but some people prefer to use mindfulness simply as a way of being in the present moment, with compassion and without judgement. If you would like to follow a more specific plan to bring mindfulness into your life then you could learn how to do a body scan, which involves simply focusing on different parts of your body. There are many available for free online or else you can just read through this script and do your own. Just as for a visualisation or meditation, start by sitting comfortably in a quiet room wearing comfortable clothes. Consider committing to this practice for some weeks before you decide whether it is for you or not.

- Start by focusing on your toes, first your big toe on your right foot and then the other foot and so on.
- Then become conscious of your feet. Consider the muscles and bones in your feet. Allow your mind to linger on the make-up of your feet, first one foot and then the other.
- Slowly move your conscious awareness up to your ankles and then your calves.
- Take some time to tune into each part of your body.
- Move on to your knees, your thighs and your bottom sitting on the chair.
- When your mind drifts, gently invite yourself to return to focusing on your body.
- Consider your lower back, then your middle back and your upper back.
- Tune into how your body is supported by your spine and give thanks to the workings of your body if you wish.
- Become aware that it is nice to know that for the next few minutes nobody wants anything from you, nobody expects anything from you, you have nothing to do whatsoever except just relax, just as much as is comfortable for you.
- Soften your belly and breathe into your belly.
- Become conscious of your breathing. Many people find that it's the out breath that relaxes us; maybe you can become more relaxed simply by focusing on the out breath.

- ❖ Become aware of your chest and your shoulders. Relax your shoulders. Roll them if you wish.
- ❖ Tune into your upper arms, your lower arms and then your hands.
- ❖ Focus on your hands. Consider your fingers and your thumbs, one by one.
- ❖ Move your consciousness to your neck and your jaw. Soften your jaw.
- ❖ Soften your facial muscles. Stretch your face if you wish.
- ❖ Pause for a moment to consider your brain. Notice how many thoughts have gone whizzing through your brain on this day. Give thanks to your brain.
- ❖ Take some slow breaths and open your eyes.
- ❖ Well done! Namaste.

POST-TRAUMATIC GROWTH AND BUILDING RESILIENCE

'Post-traumatic growth' is defined when a person experiences positive psychological changes as a direct result of adversities they have experienced, for example a bereavement or a cancer diagnosis. Although post-traumatic growth is not for everyone, nevertheless we can build resilience by the way we learn to handle adversity in our lives.

The notion of post-traumatic growth has been around for a long time and there are references to the potentially transformative power of suffering in ancient Hebrew, Greek and early Christian writings. However, it was only in the 1990s that awareness of this phenomenon resurfaced. Depending on how you manage your tolerance to stress and how you are supported afterwards, you can emerge from adversity more resilient, more aware of your inner resources and more connected with yourself and others. Some people can be profoundly changed by their experiences. This psychological shift, whether it is significant or just a small lesson learned, can lead us to seek renewed appreciation, deeper meaning and more purpose in life.[141] The marker of post-traumatic growth is not only that you have 'come through' the experience but that you are thriving; the marker of resilience is that you have become reacquainted with your inner strength and this imbues you with more confidence to face future strife.

LEARN TO WALK DOWN A DIFFERENT STREET

I first read the following poem by the singer-songwriter Portia Nelson when I was in my mid-twenties and I was very much in the middle of chapter two of life. This poem really moved me at the time as it gave me some perspective to see that life is a long game and, as long as we don't give up, we'll probably come through it okay. It also provided me with some much-needed self-compassion as I realised that a lot of my madness wasn't actually my fault but it was still up to me to haul myself out of it. Mindfulness advises us to be 'a compassionate mess' and this poem gave me the strength to be just that.

Autobiography in Five Short Chapters

BY PORTIA NELSON

I

I walk down the street.
There is a deep hole in the sidewalk
I fall in.
I am lost ... I am helpless.
It isn't my fault.
It takes me forever to find a way out.

II

I walk down the same street.
There is a deep hole in the sidewalk.
I pretend I don't see it.
I fall in again.
I can't believe I am in the same place
but, it isn't my fault.
It still takes a long time to get out.

III

I walk down the same street.
There is a deep hole in the sidewalk.
I see it is there.
I still fall in ... it's a habit.
my eyes are open
I know where I am.
It is my fault.
I get out immediately.

IV

I walk down the same street.
There is a deep hole in the sidewalk.
I walk around it.

V

I walk down another street.

CHAPTER 9

Leaving anxiety behind: Forging meaning and finding purpose

'We cannot bear a pointless torment but we can endure great pain if we believe it is purposeful.' [142]

ANDREW SOLOMON

When the psychiatrist and world-famous psychoanalyst Carl Jung was 12 years old he was pushed to the ground by another child and cracked his head off the pavement. A socially awkward boy, Jung wasn't liked by his schoolmates or his teachers and his first thought the moment he felt the blow was that he didn't have to go to school any more. As Jung lay on the ground longer than he needed to, he decided to capitalise on the attack.

From this point forward, Jung began to experience fainting spells whenever he had to go to school or do his homework. For six months Jung didn't attend school and was sent to various doctors as his parents tried to find out what was wrong with him. During this time Jung nurtured his ailments, which were rooted in avoidance strategies. He was glad not to be at school but wasn't madly satisfied with his new life as an invalid either. 'I frittered away my time with loafing, collecting, reading and playing. But I did not feel any happier for it; I had the obscure feeling that I was fleeing from myself.' As time passed Jung forgot how he first became sick and began to take his status as an invalid for granted. Then one day he overheard his father, Paul Jung, who was an impoverished clergyman, talking worriedly to his friend, and what he said gave his 12-year-old son a shock:

> Then one day a friend called on my father. They were sitting in the garden and I hid behind a shrub, for I was possessed of an insatiable curiosity. I heard the visitor saying to my father, 'And how is your son?' 'Ah, that's a sad business,' my father replied. 'The doctors no longer know what is wrong with him. They think it might be epilepsy. It would be dreadful if he were incurable. I have lost what little I had, and what will become of the boy if he cannot earn his own living?'

Carl Jung was shocked by his father's words.

> I was thunderstruck. This was the collision with reality. 'Why, then, I must get to work!' I thought suddenly.

From that moment onward, Jung became a 'serious child'. He went inside and immediately began working on his Latin grammar.

> After ten minutes of this I had the finest of fainting fits. I almost fell off the chair, but after a few minutes, I felt better and went on working. 'Devil take it, I'm not going to faint,' I told myself, and persisted on purpose. This time it took about 15 minutes before the second attack came. That, too, passed like the first. 'And now you must really get to work!' I stuck it out, and after

an hour came the third attack. Still I did not give up, and worked for another hour, until I had the feeling that I had overcome the attacks. Suddenly I felt better than I had in all the months before. And in fact the attacks did not recur. From that day on I worked over my grammar and other schoolbooks every day. A few weeks later I returned to school, and never suffered another attack, even there. The whole bag of tricks was over and done with! That was when I learned what a neurosis is.[143]

It is only because I have the privilege of hearing people's innermost thoughts when they are in therapy and seeing their steps to recovery that I am aware of how much more common Jung's experience is than many people may think. Jung's experience meant that he figured out at a very early age that if we can extract meaning and purpose from life we are able to bear almost any suffering and, without sufficient meaning or purpose, we can wither. Jung's mental collapse and subsequent recovery also meant that he had good insight into the power of avoidance. He never forgot about the lessons he learned when he was 12 years old and some 25 years later he wrote, 'Life calls us forth to independence, and anyone who does not heed this call because of childhood laziness or timidity is threatened with neurosis. And once this has broken out, it becomes an increasingly valid reason for running away from life and remaining forever in the morally poisonous atmosphere of infancy.'[144]

The data on anxiety, stress and tension and other mental health difficulties continuously suggests that if we can avoid avoidance and find some deeper meaning and purpose in our lives, we will soon move to a better place mentally. This is not easy – not on any level – but it's a better way to handle our inner demons than to allow these demons to ride roughshod over our lives and everybody else's lives.

ANXIETY IS HAVING A MOMENT: SOCIAL CONTAGION

One of the many fascinating things I found out while researching for this book was, in the same way that other trends in human behaviour came in and out of fashion, so certain mental health conditions swept in and out depending on the era. Social contagion is the transmission of an emotional state through contact with another, whether through direct contact or through the media or other sources and it has a very powerful impact on our emotional health. If you are to properly resist a toxic culture you need to educate yourself about this toxic culture and how subtle and insidious social contagion can be for you and your loved ones.

It is important that we retain the perspective of history so we can equip ourselves to view this current epidemic of anxiety with as clear an eye as we would view historical epidemics. We have lived through some extraordinary mental health epidemics in the past – from the mass hysteria during the Salem witch trials in the US to the 'moving statues' in Ireland in the 1980s. Modern doctors are hesitant to positively diagnose historical mental illness without having met the sufferers, yet when we read accounts of certain conditions that have swept through certain communities at different times, it's clear what was going on.

During the Middle Ages there was the 'glass delusion', where people thought they were made of glass, and the 'dancing epidemic' when people felt compelled to dance until they literally dropped from exhaustion. From these accounts it is reasonable to conclude that many mental health conditions get transmitted through social contagion and the more people suffer from them, the more people are susceptible to suffering.

Social contagion was identified as the reason that an eating disorder went from being non-existent to rampant in 12 short years on the island of Fiji. Bulimia was entirely unknown on Fiji in 1995 but then certain TV shows, such as *Melrose Place, Xena: Warrior Princess* and *Beverley Hills 90210*, arrived and the teenagers were presented with accounts of girls suffering from bulimia and anorexia. By 2007, 45 per cent of the girls on the main island were purging.[145]

The twitching teenagers of Le Roy, New York is another example of how social contagion can sweep through a population. In 2012, mass hysteria swept over the town of Le Roy when teenagers from the same high school began twitching uncontrollably. These teenagers were assumed by the townspeople to be suffering from the impact of pollution or vaccines or some other deadly contamination. The kids and their parents were interviewed on TV and all over the media and their behavioural twitches and tics became a huge talking point. Erin Brockovich, the environmental activist played by Julia Roberts in the eponymous film, also weighed in on the phenomenon. Brockovich's team tested the soil and theorised that the school might have been built with contaminated soil. 'We don't have all the answers, but we are suspicious,' Brockovich told *USA Today*. In the end, it turned out that the reason for the twitching teenagers was, yet again, social contagion and mass hysteria at work.

The word 'hysteria' originates from the Greek word for womb. Historically, ungovernable emotional excess was linked to women's wombs and, in today's more politically correct world, we tend to talk about 'mass conversion disorder' or 'mass panic' instead of hysteria. Yet in fairness we females can't complain about this etymology as hysteria is most commonly found among groups of females who spend a lot of time together.[146] This brings to mind the phenomenon of rapid-onset gender dysphoria (ROGD), most common among young females, as described by Lisa Littman in her recent research,[147] as it seems to occur in the context of belonging to a peer group where one or more of the friends have become gender dysphoric and is also associated with an increase in social media or internet use prior to revealing their transgender identity.[148]

Equally, in her book *Hystories: Hysterical Epidemics and Modern Culture* the feminist critic Elaine Showalter details how hysterical epidemics require three ingredients: enthusiastic medics and theorists, unhappy and vulnerable patients and supportive cultural environments.[149] It is for reasons such as these that mental health professionals need to become more politicised so that we can lead the way in ensuring that the cultural environment is healthy – if anxiety is becoming more widespread through social contagion then we need to become more vigilant if we are to protect ourselves from it.

When we examine the startling growth of the number of people suffering from anxiety-related illness, it could be argued that anxiety is the epidemic of *our* day and is being passed on just as other mental health conditions were passed on in other generations. Colman Noctor, a child and adolescent psychotherapist with St Patrick's Mental Health Services in Dublin, is alarmed by the extraordinary increase in the number of young people suffering from anxiety. 'In the last five to ten years, I would say anxiety has become the epidemic of this generation,' he says. 'I have never met more anxious children than I do now. I have never met so many anxious parents as well.'[150]

There have been countless epidemics of mental illness in years gone by and there will be countless more in the future. As with most matters in life, the majority of people tend to stay firmly on the fence, preferring not to get involved and deciding firmly to neither believe nor disbelieve the latest theories of the day. But this isn't strong enough, as those who shout loudest get heard most and, if the loudest among us are feeling neurotic, hysterical and engulfed in anxiety, then everyone becomes more anxious. It is not good enough to sit on the fence; we need to be stronger than that. As Matt Haig pointed out, being calm is now being perceived as a revolutionary act – so at least some of us need to get off the fence and begin to fight against this pervasive and toxic culture.

We need to be protective of our sense of self; we need to learn how to tap into our inner strength so that we don't get carried along in this wave of stress, tension and anxiety and we also need to vigorously call out the psychological toxicity that is found in our environment. If we are to prevent anxiety and stress becoming even more widespread, then we must recognise that avoidance tactics are usually short-term solutions. Building awareness that we need to engage fully with our fear if we are to combat it is essential if we are to promote good mental health in society; we also need to encourage other people to take as much responsibility as they can for their own mental health.

No more can we shake our heads as political policies inadvertently trash our mental wellbeing; no more can we look the other way when asinine mental health slogans cause more harm than good; nor can we mindlessly roll our eyes at our online screen addiction without admitting to ourselves that it is negatively impacting our wellbeing. It is now time to fight back against the extraordinary rise in anxiety among the general population. Because just as other mental health issues have spread around the world in years gone by, today anxiety is spreading at a frightening speed.

FORGING MEANING AND FINDING PURPOSE

The psychologist Viktor Frankl's 1946 global bestseller *Man's Search for Meaning* chronicled his experiences in Auschwitz concentration camp during World War II. Frankl managed to stay sane while enduring incredible hardship by forging meaning for his life despite the senseless brutality he endured. He accomplished this by thinking of his love for his wife, Tilly, and by helping other inmates in the camp. While in Auschwitz, Frankl noticed that the way a person imagined the future affected their longevity. He concluded that a person's psychological reaction to their experiences is the result of not only the current condition of their life but also the freedom of choice that is always available to human beings, even during extreme suffering. Our hope for the future rests upon our ability to forge meaning from each moment.

With meaning and purpose we can do anything and without it we are lost. *Seeking* meaning isn't really the road ahead because this relies on the external and if you've learned anything from this book, it is that the external is not a reliable method of attaining satisfaction. *Seeking* meaning isn't helpful because it suggests that we dash about bouncing from religion to exercise to education looking for 'an answer'. By contrast, *forging* meaning is a much more internal pursuit. Forging meaning entails looking at your life as it is now and finding meaning within that. So you examine what is important in your life, who you love and what sort of impact you wish to make in this life that you already have, and you work with that.

* What does life expect from you?
* What do you need to do in this life?

It is in the answers to these questions that you will find your meaning. If you hate your work but you do it to keep a roof over your head, forge some meaning from this – while at the same time acknowledging that you will need an end date for this as you also need to honour yourself. If you love your friends, then forge meaning from meeting them more often. Some people forge meaning by engaging in a cause greater than themselves, but you don't have to dash off to Africa to help the needy – the needy are seldom further than a few miles away from our day-to-day lives. By engaging in a cause and creating a better world we automatically light a flicker of hope that sustains us in dark times. So if we are going through hell, it is not enough, as Winston Churchill said, 'to keep going', because we need to do better than that, we need to assign some meaning to our current hell and find a purpose to our lives that gives us some hope for the future.

Frankl concluded that:

> What was really needed was a fundamental change in our attitude towards life. We had to learn ourselves and, furthermore, we had to teach the despairing men, that it did not really matter what we expected from life, but rather what life expected from us. We needed to stop asking about the meaning of life, and instead think of ourselves as those who were being questioned by life – daily and hourly. Our question must consist, not in talk and meditation, but in right action and in right conduct. Life ultimately means taking the responsibility to find the right answer to its problems and to fulfil the tasks which it constantly sets for each individual.[151]

The good news is that it is this very responsibility to help others that automatically provides us with the meaning and purpose we need to make sense of our lives and it gives a lot more long-term satisfaction than shallow and vacuous stabs at happiness.

Of course, extraordinary stories of great men like Viktor Frankl surviving the Holocaust can feel alienating and depressing for us lesser mortals and so I include a more relatable story that still holds the same message. The writer Andrew Solomon, in his seminal TED Talk 'How the worst moments in our lives makes us who we are', described how he was bullied unmercifully as a child. Solomon is one of those people who was patently gay from a very young age and the other kids, always alert for any 'difference', bullied him, called him names and isolated him throughout his childhood.

Many years later, at his 50th birthday party, Solomon's four-year-old boy, George, made an unexpected public announcement: he wished his Daddy a happy birthday and appreciated the presence of cake at the party. Then little George finished his unscripted speech with a random declaration when he suddenly said, 'And Daddy, if you were little, I'd be your friend.' At that moment Solomon was filled with emotion and he was 'finally unconditionally grateful for a life I'd once have done anything to change.' All the hurt, rejection and devastation during his childhood had found some meaning and purpose when his little boy George told him that, as a child, George would have willingly chosen Solomon to be his friend.

When we've gone through great trauma and come out the other side, it is only then we can look back at our lives and be grateful for everything – yes, everything – we've gone through. In the middle of it all, or when we're trying to stagger our way up the hill out of the wreckage there is often nothing but bitterness in our hearts, but then, when life gets better and we realise this, we appreciate it all the more because of our unique experiences. It is at this point that many of us tend to be glad for it all; and to be glad for everything that happened. Freud tells us that 'one day, in retrospect, the years of struggle will strike you as the most beautiful.' Because, if we have found the right support and if we have nurtured ourselves to thrive in our lives, then our experiences will have made us find meaning and purpose in life – and without these experiences we wouldn't have this inner depth and we would be in such a different place that we wouldn't even be who we are.

Solomon has some advice for those of us who have come through trauma:

> I survived that childhood through a mix of avoidance and endurance. What I didn't know then and do know now, is that avoidance and endurance can be the entryway to forging meaning. After you've forged meaning, you need to incorporate that meaning into a new identity. You need to take the traumas and make them part of who you've come to be, and you need to fold the worst events of your life into a narrative of triumph, evincing a better self in response to things that hurt.[152]

Most of us survive our traumas through a mix of avoidance and endurance. But surviving isn't enough – the way to *recover* from our trauma is by learning to confront your life, by finding meaning and purpose in your life by getting into the driving seat and becoming the master of your fate, the captain of your soul.

THE HERO'S TASK

Life is difficult and the human condition dictates that we will suffer great pain at some stage of our lives. However, if we can suffer our fate instead of avoiding it, then we can become the writers of our own drama and emerge stronger and more resilient. We need to be able to shine a light into the corners of our hearts so that when we feel unwell, marooned, hopeless and alone we will know how to bring ourselves back to a place where we can once again enjoy the feeling of peace in our soul, standing strong against whatever waves are heading towards us.

In this era of diagnosis, distress and victimhood, there is little talk of heroism and yet, if we are to move beyond our mental distress, we must tap into our inner warrior and slay our inner demons. It is not easy to move emerge from mental distress – in fact it is almost definitely the hardest thing you will ever do – but if you can do it, the sense of freedom and achievement will be so profound that it will give you the strength to feel able to face anything down.

'We each have an appointment with ourselves, though most of us never show up for it. Showing up, and dealing with whatever must be faced in the chasms of fear and self-doubt, that is the hero's task', wrote the Jungian analyst James Hollis.[153] The hero's task is your task and it is my task. If you are to confront your anxiety, your fear and your tension, you will need to set aside your helplessness, your feelings of powerlessness and your feelings of despair and instead tap into your inner hero. If you can do this often, you will get to know your deepest self and you will also discover that you, too, can be heroic.

References

1   James, O. (2014) *How to Develop Emotional Health*. London: Pan MacMillan.

2   Nevid, J. S. (21 May 2016) 'An anxiety checklist: It's more than just nerves'. *Psychology Today*. https://www.psychologytoday.com/intl/blog/the-minute-therapist/201605/anxiety-checklist

3   Bandelow, B. and Michaelis, S. (2015) 'Epidemiology of anxiety disorders in the 21st century'. *Dialogues Clin Neurosci*. 17(3): 327–335

4   Amunts, K. *et al.* (2005) 'Cytoarchitectonic mapping of the human amygdala, hippocampal region and entorhinal cortex: intersubject variability and probability maps'. *Anat Embryol (Berl)*. 210(5–6): 343–52

5   Rosling, H., Rosling, O. and Rosling-Ronnlund, A. (2018) *Factfulness: Ten Reasons We're Wrong about the World – and Why Things are Better than You Think*. New York: Flatiron Books

6   Yu, K. *et al.* (2017) 'The central amygdala controls learning in the lateral amygdala'. *Nature Neuroscience* 20(12): 1680–1685

7   Bailey, R. (28 March 2018) 'The limbic system of the brain: the amygdala, hypothalamus, and thalamus.' *ThoughtCo*. https://www.thoughtco.com/limbic-system-anatomy-373200

8   Kagan, J. (3 February 2000). 'Understanding the effects of temperament, anxiety, and guilt.' *Project on the Decade of the Brain*. http://www.loc.gov/loc/brain/emotion/Kagan.html

9   Kahneman, D. (2011) *Thinking Fast and Slow*. New York: Farrar, Straus and Giroux

10 Peters, S. (2012) *The Chimp Paradox: The Mind Management Programme for Confidence, Success and Happiness*. London: Vermilion

11 Leith, W. (27 May 2018). 'Say "No" and change your life'. *Sunday Independent*.

12 Peters, S. (2012) *The Chimp Paradox: The Mind Management Programme for Confidence, Success and Happiness*. London: Vermilion

13 Siegel, L. (5 June 2012) 'This is the difference between thinking fast and slow.' *Business Insider*. https://www.businessinsider.com/nobel-prize-winner-this-is-the-difference-between-thinking-fast-and-slow-2012-6?IR=T

14   Beck, A. T. (1976) *Cognitive Therapy and the Emotional Disorders*. Oxford: International Universities Press

15   Lickerman, A. (12 November 2009) 'Magical thinking: How to avoid an insidious thought error.' *Psychology Today.* https://www.psychologytoday. com/us/blog/happiness-in-world/200911/magical-thinking

16   Hecht, D. (2013) 'The neural basis of optimism and pessimism'. *Exp Neurobiol.* 22(3): 173–199

17   Tucker, N. (2018) *That Was When People Started to Worry: Windows into Unwell Minds.* London: Icon Books

18   Buchanan, D. (5 January 2018) 'Perfectionism is destroying the mental health of my generation.' *The Guardian.* https://www.theguardian.com/ commentisfree/2018/jan/05/perfectionism-mental-health-millennial-social-media

19   Gardner, H. (2011) *Creating Minds: An Anatomy of Creativity Seen Through the Lives of Freud, Einstein, Picasso, Stravinsky, Eliot, Graham, and Gandhi.* New York: Basic Books

20   Blair, L. (22 June 2016) 'Am I a perfectionist?' *The Guardian* https://www. theguardian.com/commentisfree/2016/jun/22/am-i-a-perfectionist-google

21   Esposito, L. (18 January 2016) 'Is anxiety a choice?' *Wired for Happy.* http:// wiredforhappy.com/is-anxiety-a-choice/

22   Clear, J. (12 July 2018) 'How long does it actually take to form a new habit? (Backed by science).' https://jamesclear.com/new-habit

23   Carlson, N. R., *et al.* (2007) *Psychology: The Science of Behaviour.* Toronto: Pearson Education Canada

24   Marchiano, L. (27 December 2017) 'Collision with reality: What depth psychology can tell us about victimhood culture.' *Quillette.* https:// quillette.com/2017/12/27/collision-reality-depth-psychology-can-tell-us-victimhood-culture

25   Joelson, R. B. (2 August 2017). 'Locus of control: How do we determine our successes and failures?' *Psychology Today.* https://www.psychologytoday. com/ca/blog/moments-matter/201708/locus-control

26   Ibid.

27   Boyes, A. (2015) *The Anxiety Toolkit: Strategies for Fine-Tuning Your Mind and Moving Past Your Stuck Points.* New York: TarcherPerigee; Clifford, N. L. (21 March 2015) 'How most anxiety can be beaten by just one simple method.' *Psychology Today.* https://www.psychologytoday.com/us/blog/think-well/201503/how-most-anxiety-can-be-beaten-just-one-simple-method

28   American Psychiatric Association (2013) *Diagnostic and Statistical Manual of Mental Disorders: DSM-5* (5th edn) Washington: American Psychiatric Association

29   WHO. *International Classification of Diseases*, ICD-10

30   Abramowitz, J. S., Deacon, B. J., Whiteside, S. P. H. (2012) *Exposure Therapy for Anxiety: Principles and Practice.* New York: Guilford Press

31   Carbonell, D. 'Exposure therapy for fears and phobias'. http://www.anxietycoach.com/exposuretherapy.html

32   Kaplan, J. and Tolin, D. (6 September 2011) 'Exposure therapy for anxiety disorders'. *Psychiatric Times.* http://www.psychiatrictimes.com/anxiety/exposure-therapy-anxiety-disorders

33   Abramowitz *et al.* (2012) *Exposure Therapy for Anxiety: Principles and Practice.* New York: Guilford Press; Carbonell, D. 'Exposure therapy for fears and phobias'. http://www.anxietycoach.com/exposuretherapy.html

34   Clifford N. L. 'How most anxiety can be beaten by just one simple method.' *Psychology Today.* https://www.psychologytoday.com/us/blog/think-well/201503/how-most-anxiety-can-be-beaten-just-one-simple-method

35   Preissner, S. (8 October 2017) 'Each uploaded photo fooled my 800 closest friends that I was happy'. *The Journal.* http://www.thejournal.ie/readme/stefanie-preissner-each-uploaded-photo-fooled-my-800-closest-friends-that-i-was-happy-3631216-Oct2017/

36   Roantree, M. (8 June 2018) 'Pass it on'. *Stellar*

37   Richards, T. A. 'What is social anxiety?' https://socialanxietyinstitute.org/what-is-social-anxiety

38   Day, E. (4 June 2016) 'Bryony Gordon on her struggles with drugs, bulimia and OCD: "Cocaine shut up all those voices in my head"'. *The Daily Telegraph.* https://www.telegraph.co.uk/health-fitness/body/bryony-gordon-on-her-struggles-with-drugs-bulimia-and-ocd-cocain/

39   Gough, L. (24 October 2016) 'A mother's journey helping her son recover from OCD'. *The OCD Stories.* https://theocdstories.com/symmetry-ocd/a-mothers-journey-helping-her-son-recover-from-ocd/

40   Koran, L. M. *et al.*, American Psychiatric Association (July 2007). 'Practice guidelines for the treatment of patients with obsessive-compulsive disorder'. *American Journal of Psychiatry.* 164 (7 Suppl): 5–53

41   Abramowitz *et al. Exposure Therapy for Anxiety: Principles and Practice.* New York: Guilford Press

42   Gough, L. 'A mother's journey helping her son recover from OCD.' *The*

OCD Stories. https://theocdstories.com/symmetry-ocd/a-mothers-journey-helping-her-son-recover-from-ocd/

43 Singh, K., Fox, J. R. and Brown, R. J. (2016). 'Health anxiety and internet use: A thematic analysis.' *Cyberpsychology: Journal of Psychosocial Research on Cyberspace*, 10(2), article 4

44 Feinmann, J. (25 May 2003) 'Are you ill informed?' *The Observer.* https://www.theguardian.com/theobserver/2003/may/25/features.magazine67

45 Mneimne, M. 'Avoidance and exposure'. *The Albert Ellis Institute.* http://albertellis.org/avoidance-and-exposure/

46 *Today with Seán O'Rourke* (18 July 2018). RTÉ Radio 1

47 Boyes, A. (5 March 2013) 'Why avoidance coping is the most important factor in anxiety.' *Psychology Today*

48 Tucker, N. (2018) *That Was When People Started to Worry: Windows into Unwell Minds.* London: Icon Books

49 Solomon, A. (2012) *Far from the Tree: Parents, Children, and the Search for Identity.* New York: Scribner

50 Thompson, S. (5 June 2018) 'Health heroes.' *The Irish Times.* https://www.irishtimes.com/life-and-style/health-family/prof-donal-o-shea-the-shocking-fact-is-that-most-ill-health-now-comes-from-our-lifestyle-1.3508252#.WxZQnG-yUD8.twitter

51 St Patrick's Mental Health Services. https://www.stpatricks.ie/mental-health/anxiety; National Alliance on Mental Illness. https://www.nami.org/Learn-More/Mental-Health-By-the-Numbers; National Alliance on Mental Illness. https://www.nami.org/Learn-More/Mental-Health-Conditions/Anxiety-Disorders

52 Mental Health Foundation. https://www.mentalhealth.org.uk/statistics/mental-health-statistics-most-common-mental-health-problems

53 Anxiety and Depression Association of America. https://adaa.org/about-adaa/press-room/facts-statistics

54 Martin-Merino, E. *et al.* (2009). 'Prevalence, incidence, morbidity and treatment patterns in a cohort of patients diagnosed with anxiety in UK primary care'. *Family Practice*, 27(1), 9–16

55 Anxiety and Depression Association of America. https://adaa.org/about-adaa/press-room/facts-statistics

56 O'Keeffe, L. *et al.* (2015). 'Description and outcome evaluation of Jigsaw: An emergent Irish mental health early intervention programme for young people.' *Irish Journal of Psychological Medicine*, 32(1), 71–77

57   Begley, S. (23 July 2012) 'In the age of anxiety are we all mentally unwell?' *Reuters.* https://www.reuters.com/article/us-usa-health-anxiety/in-the-age-of-anxiety-are-we-all-mentally-ill-idUSBRE86C07820120713

58   Ehlers, A. (1997) 'Anxiety disorders: challenging negative thinking.' Quoted in the *Wellcome Trust Reviews*

59   WHO (2002) 'The global burden of disease'.

60   O Regan, E. (30 September 2018) '"We live in an age of anxiety" – Surge in mental health problems in last six years'. *Irish Independent.* https://www.independent.ie/irish-news/health/we-live-in-an-age-of-anxiety-surge-in-mental-health-problems-in-last-six-years-36285433.html

61   Cannon, M. (2013). 'The mental health of young people in Ireland: a report of the psychiatric epidemiology research across the Lifespan (PERL) Group Dublin.' *Royal College of Surgeons in Ireland*

62   Twenge, J. M. *et al.* (2010) 'Birth cohort increases in psychopathology among young Americans, 1938–2007: A cross-temporal meta-analysis of the MMPI', *Clinical Psychology Review* 30, 145–154.

63   Bedell, G. (27 February 2016). 'Teenage mental health crisis: rates of depression have soared in past 25 years.' *The Independent*

64   O'Brien, C. (26 May 2018) 'Record numbers of students seeking counselling for anxiety.' *The Irish Times*

65   Nolan, M. (3 June 2018) 'The Age of Anxiety.' *The Sunday Times*

66   Remes, O. *et al.* (2016) 'A systematic review of reviews on the prevalence of anxiety disorders in adult populations.' *Brain and Behavior* 6(7)

67   Nolan, M. (3 June 2018) 'The Age of Anxiety.' *The Sunday Times*

68   Safi, O. (6 November 2014) 'The disease of being busy'. https://onbeing.org/blog/the-disease-of-being-busy/

69   James, O. (2007) *Affluenza.* London: Vermilion

70   Ibid.

71   Roberts, P. (2014) *The Impulse Society: What's Wrong with Getting What We Want?* London: Bloomsbury

72   Krobath, M. (2 May 2018) 'What did Keynes get right about the modern world?' *Credit Suisse.* https://www.credit-suisse.com/corporate/en/articles/news-and-expertise/what-did-keynes-get-right-about-the-modern-world-201805.html

73   Graeber, D. (2018) *Bullshit Jobs: A Theory.* London: Allen Lane

74   Appleyard, B. (6 May 2018) 'Heigh-Ho, Heigh-Ho, It's off to joke jobs we go'. *The Sunday Times*

75   Jericho, G. (20 February 2017) 'Latest job statistics: full-time work is disappearing for women, but not for men.' *The Guardian*. https://www.theguardian.com/commentisfree/2017/feb/21/latest-job-stats-full-time-work-is-disappearing-for-women-but-not-for-men

76   Thoreau, H. D. (16 November 1857) 'Letter to Harrison Blake'

77   Nield, D. (15 September 2016) 'Here's why you feel busy all the time'. *Science Alert*. https://www.sciencealert.com/these-could-be-the-reasons-everyone-feels-busy-all-of-the-time

78   MacDonald, F. (15 November 2015) 'Science says that technology is speeding up our brains' perception of time'. *Science Alert*. https://www.sciencealert.com/research-suggests-that-technology-is-speeding-up-our-perception-of-time

79   James Cook University (19 November 2015) 'Wired society speeds up brains … and time'. https://www.jcu.edu.au/news/releases/wired-society-speeds-up-brains-and-time

80   'Instagram ranked worst for young people's health'. *RSPH/YHM* https://www.rsph.org.uk/about-us/news/instagram-ranked-worst-for-young-people-s-mental-health.html

81   Tucker, N. (2018) *That Was When People Started to Worry: Windows into Unwell Minds*. London: Icon Books

82   Damour, L. (12 November 2017) 'It's not just hormones.' *The Globe and Mail*. https://www.theglobeandmail.com/life/parenting/drama-queens-whats-really-going-on-in-a-teenage-girls-head/article28549947/

83   Gershon, L. (24 June 2015) 'What makes work meaningful? Ask a zookeeper.' *Daily Jstor*. https://daily.jstor.org/meaningful-work-zookeepers/

84   Mineo, L. (2017) 'Harvard study, almost 80 years old, has proved that embracing community helps us live longer, and be happier'. *The Harvard Gazette;* Ferro, S. (2018) 'Happy relationships are the key to a fulfilling life.' *Mental Floss*

85   Popova, M. (2013) 'Brené Brown on vulnerability, human connection, and the difference between empathy and sympathy, animated.' *Brain Pickings*. https://www.brainpickings.org/2013/12/11/brene-brown-rsa-animated

86   Parkinson, H. J. (30 June 2018) 'It's nothing like a broken leg: why I'm done with the mental health conversation.' *The Guardian*. https://www.theguardian.com/society/2018/jun/30/nothing-like-broken-leg-mental-health-conversation?CMP=share_btn_fb

87   Ibid.

88   Tucker, N. (2015) *The Time In Between: A Memoir of Hunger and Hope.* London: Icon Books

89   Peterson, J. (2018) *Twelve Rules for Life: An Antidote to Chaos.* Toronto: Penguin Random House

90   Ehrenreich, B. (2010) *Smile or Die: How Positive Thinking Fooled America and the World.* London: Granta

91   Ibid.

92   Breslin, N. (2015) *Me and My Mate Jeffrey.* Dublin: Hachette Books

93   Nolan, M. (3 June 2018) 'The Age of Anxiety'. *The Sunday Times.*

94   *The Economist* (12 October 2017) Evaluating the evidence on micro-aggressions and trigger warnings. https://www.economist.com/united-states/2017/10/12/evaluating-the-evidence-on-micro-aggressions-and-trigger-warnings

95   Bellet, B. W., Jones, P. J. and McNally, R. J. (2018) 'Trigger warning: Empirical evidence ahead'. *Journal of Behavior Therapy and Experimental Psychiatry.* 61, 134–141; Dickson, K. S., Ciesla, J. A. and Reilly, L. C. (2012) 'Rumination, worry, cognitive avoidance, and behavioral avoidance: examination of temporal effects.' *Behav Ther.* 43(3): 629–40; McLean, C. P. and Foa, E. B. (2014) 'Prolonged exposure therapy for post-traumatic stress disorder: a review of evidence and dissemination.' *Expert Review of Neurotherapeutics* 11, 1151–1163

96   Whitley, R. (23 March 2017) 'Trigger warnings and mental health: where is the evidence?' *Psychology Today.* https://www.psychologytoday.com/us/blog/talking-about-men/201703/trigger-warnings-and-mental-health-where-is-the-evidence

97   McNally, R. J. (20 May 2014) 'Hazards ahead: the problem with trigger warnings, according to the research'. *Pacific Standard.* https://psmag.com/education/hazards-ahead-problem-trigger-warnings-according-research-81946

98   Lahad, M. and Doron, M. (2010). *Protocol for Treatment of Post Traumatic Stress Disorder: SEE FAR CBT Model: Beyond Cognitive Behavior Therapy.* Amsterdam: IOS Press.

99   Bellet, B. W., Jones, P. J. and McNally, R. J. (2018) 'Trigger warning: Empirical evidence ahead'. *Journal of Behavior Therapy and Experimental Psychiatry* 61, 134–141

100   Paludi, M. A. (2012). *Managing Diversity in Today's Workplace: Strategies for Employees and Employers.* Westport: Praeger

101   Haidt, J. and Lukianoff, G. (September 2015) 'How trigger warnings are hurting mental health on campus'. *The Atlantic*

102   Friedersdorf, C. (14 September 2015). 'Why critics of the "microaggressions" framework are skeptical'. *The Atlantic*

103   Campbell, B. and Manning, J. (2014) *Comparative Sociology* 13(6) 692–726

104   Lilienfeld, S. (23 June 2017) 'The science of micro-aggressions: it's complicated.' *Scientific American*

105   Nagle, A. (2017) *Kill all Normies: Online Culture Wars from 4chan and Tumblr to Trump and the Alt-Right*. London: Zero Books

106   Stephens, B. (24 September 2017) 'The dying art of disagreement'. *The New York Times* https://www.nytimes.com/2017/09/24/opinion/dying-art-of-disagreement.html

107   Ibid.

108   Pells, R. (13 February 2017) 'More than nine in 10 UK universities restrict free speech on campus, report claims.' *The Independent*

109   Smith, E. (23 March 2016) 'A policy widely abused: the origins of the "no platform" policy of the National Union of Students.' *History and Policy*. http://www.historyandpolicy.org/opinion-articles/articles/a-policy-widely-abused

110   Turner, C. (7 November 2018) 'Jenni Murray pulls out of Oxford talk after students try to "no platform" her over "transphobic" comments.' *The Telegraph*. https://www.telegraph.co.uk/education/2018/11/07/jenni-murray-pulls-oxford-talk-students-try-no-platform-transphobic/

111   BBC (4 December 2018) 'Jenni Murray: University of Hull to review theatre name change amid trans row'. www.bbc.com/news/uk-england-humber-46442389

112   Betts, E. (26 November 2018) 'I regret my tactics at a trans rights protest. Here's why.' *The Guardian*. https://www.theguardian.com/commentisfree/2018/nov/26/trans-rights-protest-gender-critical

113   Finnis, A. (2017) 'This German town has come up with a genius way of humiliating neo-Nazis.' *Shortlist*. https://www.shortlist.com/news/german-town-came-up-with-a-genius-way-of-humiliating-neo-nazis/60649

114   O'Neill, B. (5 February 2018) 'Jacob Rees-Mogg and the rise of the new intolerance'. *Spiked-online*. http://www.spiked-online.com/newsite/article/jacob-rees-mogg-and-the-rise-of-the-new-intolerance/21088#.WnhNN6hl9PZ

115   Friedersdorf, C. (9 November 2015) 'The new intolerance of student activism'. *The Atlantic*

116   Christakis, E. (28 October 2016) 'My Halloween email led to a campus firestorm'. *The Washington Post*

117   Friedersdorf, C. (9 November 2015) 'The new intolerance of student activism'. *The Atlantic*

118   Friedersdorf, C. (2015) 'The perils of writing a provocative email at Yale. *The Atlantic*

119   MacMillan, A. (25 May 2017) 'Why Instagram is the worst social media for mental health'. *Time Magazine*. http://time.com/4793331/instagram-social-media-mental-health/

120   Lawson, D. (15 June 2015) 'The truth in black and white: today, victimhood's seen as morally superior.' *Daily Mail*. http://www.dailymail.co.uk/debate/article-3123995/DOMINIC-LAWSON-truth-black-white-today-victimhood-s-seen-morally-superior.html

121   Elgot, J. (12 June 2015) 'Civil rights activist Rachel Dolezal misrepresented herself as black claim parents.' *The Guardian*. https://www.theguardian.com/world/2015/jun/12/civil-rights-activist-rachel-dolezal-misrepresented-herself-as-black-claim-parents

122   Kakutani, M. (26 February 2008) 'Margaret B. Jones – *Love and Consequences: A Memoir of Hope and Survival* Review'. *The New York Times*

123   O'Neill, B. (5 February 2018) 'Jacob Rees-Mogg and the rise of the new intolerance'. *Spiked-online*. http://www.spiked-online.com/newsite/article/jacob-rees-mogg-and-the-rise-of-the-new-intolerance/21088#.WnhNN6hl9PZ

124   Rosling, H., Rosling, O. and Rosling-Ronnlund, A. (2018) *Factfulness: Ten Reasons We're Wrong about the World – and Why Things are Better than You Think*. New York: Flatiron Books

125   MacMillan, A. (25 May 2017) 'Why Instagram is the worst social media for mental health'. *Time Magazine*. http://time.com/4793331/instagram-social-media-mental-health/

126   Nolan, M. (3 June 2018) 'The age of anxiety'. *The Sunday Times.*

127   Aiken, M. (2016) *The Cyber Effect: A Pioneering Cyberpsychologist Explains How Human Behaviour Changes Online*. London: John Murray.

128   Tartakovsky, M. (2018). '9 ways to reduce anxiety right here, right now.' *Psych Central*. https://psychcentral.com/lib/9-ways-to-reduce-anxiety-right-here-right-now/

129   Festinger, L. (1957) *A Theory of Cognitive Dissonance*. California: Stanford University Press

130   Festinger, L., Riecken, H. W. and Schachter, S. (1956). *When Prophecy Fails: A Social and Psychological Study of a Modern Group that Predicted the Destruction of the World*. Minnesota: University of Minnesota Press.

131   Ibid.

132   Glasser, W. (1999) *Choice Theory: A New Psychology of Personal Freedom*. London: HarperCollins.

133   Smith, A. (19 July 2013) 'Effects of chewing gum on cognitive function, mood and physiology in stressed and non-stressed volunteers'. *Neuroscience* 13(1): 7–16

134   Kashdan, T. B. (2018) 'Psychological flexibility as a fundamental aspect of health.' *Clinical Psychology Review* 30(7): 865–878

135   Burkeman, O. (19 April 2014) 'This column will change your life: stop being busy.' *The Guardian*. https://www.theguardian.com/lifeandstyle/2014/apr/19/change-your-life-stop-being-busy

136   Goldstein, A. N. et al. (2013) 'Tired and apprehensive: anxiety amplifies the impact of sleep loss on aversive brain anticipation.' *Journal of Neuroscience* 33(26): 10607

137   *Higher Perspective* (8 September 2018) 'New research says singing daily reduces stress, clears sinuses, and helps you live longer'. https://www.higherperspectives.com/singing-daily-2603018816.html

138   Boyes, A. (28 January 2013) 'Psychology experts share their best stress relief tips: stress relief tips from the experts'. *Psychology Today*. https://www.psychologytoday.com/intl/blog/in-practice/201301/17-psychology-experts-share-their-best-stress-relief-tips

139   *Anxiety BC*. 'How to do progressive relaxation.' https://www.anxietybc.com/sites/default/files/MuscleRelaxation.pdf

140   Staff reporter (21 June 2008) 'Eckhart Tolle: This man could change your life'. *The Independent*.

141   Tedeshi, R. G. and Calhoun, L. G. (2004) *Post-traumatic Growth: Conceptual Foundation and Empirical Evidence*. Philadelphia, PA: Lawrence Erlbaum Associates

142   Solomon, A. (2014) TED Talk: 'How the worst moments in our lives make us who we are.' https://www.ted.com/talks/andrew_solomon_how_the_worst_moments_in_our_lives_make_us_who_we_are/transcript

143   Jung, C. G., and Jaffe, A. (1989) *Memories, Dreams, Reflections*. New York: Vintage Books.

144   Jung, C. G. (1970). *Symbols of Transformation: an Analysis of the Prelude to a Case of Schizophrenia.* Princeton, NJ: Princeton University Press.

145   Kravetz, L. D. (31 July 2017) 'The strange, contagious history of bulimia.' *The   Cut.*   https://www.thecut.com/article/how-bulimia-became-a-medical-diagnosis.html

146   Bartholomew, R. (31 March 2017) 'Why are females prone to mass hysteria?' *Psychology Today.* https://www.psychologytoday.com/us/blog/its-catching/201703/why-are-females-prone-mass-hysteria

147   Littman, L. (2018) 'Rapid-onset gender dysphoria in adolescents and young adults: A study of parental reports'. *PLoS ONE* 13(8)

148   Kaltiala-Heino, R. *et al.* (2015) 'Two years of gender identity service for minors: overrepresentation of natal girls with severe problems in adolescent development'. *Child and Adolescent Psychiatry and Mental Health* 9(9)

149   Showalter, E. (1998) *Hystories: Hysterical Epidemics and Modern Culture.* Colombia: Columbia University Press.

150   O'Brien, C. (26 May 2018) '"I'm petrified. I can't eat." Ireland's teenage anxiety problem.' *The Irish Times*

151   Frankl, V. (2006) *Man's Search for Meaning.* Boston: Beacon Press

152   Solomon, A. 2014. TED Talk: 'How the worst moments in our lives make us who we are.' https://www.ted.com/talks/andrew_solomon_how_the_worst_moments_in_our_lives_make_us_who_we_are/transcript

153   Hollis, J. (2004). *Mythologems: Incarnations of the Invisible World.* Toronto: Inner City Books